ACROSS THE FRONTIERS
Ireland in the 1990s
CULTURAL – POLITICAL – ECONOMIC

Edited by
Richard Kearney

WOLFHOUND PRESS

First published 1988 by
WOLFHOUND PRESS
68 Mountjoy Square,
Dublin 1.

British Library Cataloguing in Publication Data

Across the frontiers: Ireland in the 1990s.
1. Ireland - 1970
I. Kearney, Richard
941.50824

ISBN 0-86327-209-6 HB
ISBN 0-86237-210-X PB

Cover design: Jan de Fouw
Typesetting: Redsetter Ltd., Dublin.
Printed and bound by Billings & Sons Ltd., Worcester.

CONTENTS

Introduction: Thinking Otherwise

RICHARD KEARNEY

Ireland can no longer be contained within the frontiers of an island. Since the signing of the Anglo-Irish Agreement and the Single European Act, we find ourselves committed to a new 'totality of relationships' extending well beyond the limits of the Nation State. Moreover, the massive impact of the communications revolution in television, video and popular culture means that Ireland today is intimately interconnected with a wide variety of cultures – in Great Britain, the Continent, America and elsewhere. In short, our fate as a nation is increasingly influenced by international happenings and accords. And our consciousness of the extended Irish community created by past emigrations (with over 70 million people of Irish descent now living outside of Ireland)[1] is being rekindled by the emigrants of the 1980s. 'Ourselves Alone' is a catch-cry of the past. But how do we decide our future?

Our present state of affairs is, by most accounts, bleak. One third of the population of the Republic live below the poverty line; fifty thousand young people emigrate each year; over a quarter of a million are unemployed, with rates of up to 60 per cent in some of the new urban developments in Dublin; and inequality is growing rather than diminishing, with social welfare insufficient to meet the minimum needs of a large proportion of the people.[2] The continuing bloodshed of the North speaks for itself. These factors combine to produce a state of aimlessness, as observed by a recent commentator: 'This aimlessness is connected with the sense that the nation, the country, does not have a future; it has a shrinking economy with a growing national debt and a soaring budget deficit, getting or keeping jobs is a matter of great anxiety; it seems the violence in the north will never stop and the country never be unified in peace; on all sides people are terrorized by talk of 'concern', problems, and challenges beyond those they already experience'.[3] If where we are

7

is patently not good enough, where do we go from here?

The Forum for a New Ireland, initiated in 1983 and followed by the Anglo-Irish Agreement in November 1985, was a timely effort to rethink some of the preconceptions about who we are and what we want to be. In his opening address, John Hume declared that the Forum was not a 'nationalist revival mission', adding that the failure to resolve the national question has been due, in large part, to our inability to place the project for a new society 'above some of our most cherished assumptions'.[4] The subsequent international accord reached by Ireland and Britain on the governance of the North, effectively implied a partial sharing of sovereignty by both nations. And it is surely not insignificant that the portentous reference to a 'totality of relationships' – contained in the communiqué issued after the Anglo-Irish Summit of December 1980 – has been *positively* invoked by such different party leaders as Charles Haughey, James Molyneux, Margaret Thatcher and John Hume.

Our commitment to European integration, secured in our signing of the Single European Act, entails a further pooling of sovereignty. The movement towards social and economic cohesion in Europe, involving the lifting of frontiers separating the 12 member-states of the Community by the early nineties, represents a watershed in Irish history. Might not 1992 be to the last part of this century what 1916 was to the first – an event which radically transforms our established political institutions? Both dates signal a challenge to our sense of national self-understanding. Both raise the fundamental question: are we to live in a dependent, independent, or interdependent society? A single Europe, in brief, has radical implications for future relations between the Republic, Northern Ireland and Great Britain.

In addition, we are compelled to recognize that new developments in communications technology will by the 1990s have connected Ireland – via satellite and cable systems – not only with European but with global networks. The European Space Agency Satellites are currently equipped to link up information centres throughout the Community; while the launching of European TV stations by the French (SEPT) and the Germans (SAT I) herald a more interconnected audio-visual culture in the years ahead. Such moves by EC member states to champion an advanced and high quality system of European communications is, in large part, a response to the already global influence of American media and popular culture. (These issues are debated by Desmond Bell and Georges Duby below). But what does all this mean for the future of public broadcasting in Ireland? And what impact is it likely to have on our inherited notions of national culture and identity? Should we be trying to counter this growing internationalization of communications as promoted by the televisual project for a 'Europe without frontiers' and the multi-cable system? And even if we should, could we? Are we heading for a bureaucratic Euro-state which will homogenize culture and centralize power *or* for a democratic European federation of decentralized and equal regions? Who decides? Have we any say in the matter?

II

To date, most discussion of Ireland's role in the Europe of the nineties has concentrated on economics.[5] This is understandable when one recalls that the European Community was initially founded as an 'economic market' (beginning with the Coal and Steel Community in 1951); and when one also considers that most of the legislation for the Single Europe of 1992 is concerned with the creation of an 'internal market' based on the suspension of tariff barriers and the harmonization of indirect taxes. But European integration is not only about economics. We cannot live by VAT alone, as Edgar Fauré reminds us below. And that is why this book, while acknowledging the decisive role of finance, seeks to extend the frontiers of investigation to include examination of the political, social and cultural dimensions. Moreover, each of these implies the other, as is evident in the various contributions to this volume. One cannot talk of economics without at the same time talking about politics and culture. Statistics cannot be divorced from ideology.

It is unlikely that Ireland or any other European state in the 1990s will be able to maintain inherited notions of absolute autonomy. The movement towards a more cohesive community of nations now seems irreversible. Indeed, it has been evident for some time now that no individual Nation State can remain unaffected by global market forces – East or West. Wall Street sneezes, as the adage goes, and the rest of the world catches cold. Even Moscow needs a Kleenex. The same holds for oil crises and nuclear accidents – as the Middle East wars and Chernobyl remind us. Nuclear fallout does not recognise borders. A state's ideology is no guarantee of immunity. The erosion of frontiers between Nation States – be they liberal capitalist, communist or mixed socialist – is increasingly inevitable. And Ireland's decision to ratify the Single European Act in 1988 was just another step towards its growing interinvolvement with other nations.

But if the dissolution of national frontiers is an inevitability, it is one that can be responded to in very different ways. And this is where I would insist that we *do* have a say in the shaping of our future. Ireland's relationship to the New Europe could indeed be that of a vassal sub-state to an Imperial Super-State, thus confirming the worst fears of our anti-Europeans. But it could also be the very opposite – a community of self-directing regions relating in a democratic and equal manner to the other regions of a federal Europe. While the former 'malign' scenario finds some vindication on a purely economic front (eg, a *laissez-faire* flow of capital and manpower to the affluent centres of power after 1992), the latter more 'benign' scenario finds support in the reference to Social and Economic Cohesion in Art. 23 of the SEA, but also in a number of proposals already approved by the European Parliament (eg, the Hume Report on Regional Policy in October 1987); the Council's ruling in February 1988 that a 'special effort' be undertaken to ensure an equal division of aggregate wealth and resources to the regions, involving a doubling of funds to the least well-off between 1987-92; and the formal declaration by the EC President, Jacques Delors, in June 1988, on the necessity of a 'social dimension' to counterbalance and redress the inegalitarian tendencies of a purely economic market.

Those who invoke the 'malign' scenario argue that 1992 will see an economic juggernaut riding ruthlessly through the smaller nations. They warn of a centralized super-state mushrooming up in Brussels determined to impose a Euro-identikit on the independent member-states. Ireland, in this view, would fast degenerate into a retirement haven for burnt-out capitalists from the Continent, a celtic disneyland where Europe's employed are quaintly entertained by its unemployed – in short, a nation of glorified 'gillies and grouse-beaters'.[6]

It is my view (not necessarily shared by all my contributors) that there are some good reasons at present to credit a more benign reading. Apart from the positive proposals mentioned above, one could point to the decisive influence of the majority socialist grouping in the European Parliament – a grouping inspired by such pioneering Europeans as Mitterand of France, Papandreou of Greece and Gonzalez of Spain. Taking heed of Mitterand's insistence since 1981 on the necessity for a 'social' redrafting of EC policy, the Commission has recently acknowledged the difficulties facing the smaller nations of Europe in 1992 and has renewed the demand that the Single Market must have a 'social conscience'.[7] While the Cecchini Report to the EC in May 1988, anticipates increased growth for the Community after 1992 (with output up by 7 per cent, the creation of an extra 5 million jobs, decrease in price levels by 6 per cent and improved budget balances overall), there has been legitimate concern that the advantages of the Single Market may lead to unequal growth for different regions of the community. Michael D. Higgins expresses this concern forcefully below. Without the 'social dimension', 1992 will simply mean that the rich countries get richer and the poor countries (like Ireland) poorer.

To prevent such a development, the Commission has promised a doubling of the Social and Regional Funds to the peripheral regions; a radical reformation of the Common Agricultural Policy; the establishment of a commonly agreed system of European labour laws to guarantee worker protection and consultation. All of these measures are crucial to Ireland's future in the 1990s (see Murphy and Matthews below). Aware of this, Delors has insisted that the EC must develop 'a *social* as well as an *economic* dimension . . . aimed at enlarging the resources available for helping the long-term unemployed, youth unemployment and rural development, as well as the backward regions of the Community and those facing major restructuring problems'. In this it must be '*revolutionary*', he adds. And it must be achieved 'both because it is absolutely necessary and because it carries with it the goal of a united and strong Europe'.[8] Finally, one could mention on the credit side, the strenuous efforts made by the Greek presidency of the EC throughout 1988 to advance the radical social implications of regional development and workers' rights (eg, the direct appeal to management and labour that all workers should participate in the shaping of the internal market and in the sharing of its profits). These efforts issued in the Community's approval of a 'Statute' ensuring worker involvement in the decision-making structures of European industry in Luxembourg (14 October 1988).

Whether Ireland after 1992 conforms more to the malign or benign scenarios is in large part a matter for us to decide. A lot will also depend, of course, on who holds the balance of power in the European Community as a whole. But we can't go on forever declaring ourselves a nation apart when anything goes right, and a victim of external influences when anything goes wrong. We do have some significant say in our future: and we are responsible for making our voice heard. Too easily we forget that the European Community has a democratic parliament with representatives elected by *us*. If we don't like the way things are going, we elect somebody else to speak on our behalf.

But there is also much that can be done at a more immediate local level. There are many examples of existing community projects in Ireland which can benefit enormously from European Community funding. The local community at Ros a 'Mhíl in County Galway took the initiative recently to avail of the European Regional Fund to construct a new pier for fishing and sea-transport, thereby radically transforming their future economic prospects. Other notable initiatives taken at local level and subsequently acquiring international funding or support include: the North West Centre for Development in Derry, the North Centre City Action Project in Dublin, the Brookfield Business Co-operative in Belfast, the

Development Scheme in Shannon and the Headstart Project in Bray.

The Shannon Scheme has no doubt been the most spectacular example of how a regional model, drawing from the energies and resources of the neighbouring community, can successfully evolve into a centre for international co-operation. (The existence of an international airport ideally suited for the promotion of East-West trade and exchange has obviously been a decisive factor). But there are less conspicuous instances of such success. The Headstart project, which began as a community arts group in Bray and a social employment scheme financed largely by the European Social Fund, has recently launched itself as an international cultural centre. In October 1988, it hosted an Irish-Soviet Conference in Bray to discuss problems of community. And it was quite fascinating to witness a delegation of 20 Soviets – including historians, artists, philosophers, musicians and social workers from over six ethnic communities in the USSR – engage in dialogue with a member of the local travelling community on the question of minority rights! Finally, I might mention the extraordinary success of Paddy Doherty's North West project in Derry which operates at a grass roots community level and runs an employment programme supported by the international Ireland Fund. At present, it is the second highest employer in Derry after Dupont.

Such projects do not need directives from Nation-State or Super-State bureaucracies to get going. They spring up at community level, encourage a real sense of participatory democracy and then, ideally, interconnect with other community projects in Europe or elsewhere in the world. The phenomenon of the local linking with the international is also explored by Rosemarie Rowley and Ivor Browne below. It epitomizes what Browne calls the 'granular society' that is now emerging globally. Writing recently of community projects in Ireland availing of European Regional funding, Breandán Ó hEithir makes this timely point: 'Ireland is as much in control of its affairs as Greece, Portugal or Denmark and also as much a part of the evolving European Community. Blaming the community for what may well be our own shortcomings, lack of vision and inertia, is no more than a variation on the old Irish theme, "God help us all, but 'twas the drink that brought us down".'⁹ Enabling our local and regional communities to develop a sense of self-confidence and hope in their future is the best contribution we can make to the European Community.

III

Of the twelve national leaders at the Hannover Summit in 1988, it is significant that only Mrs Thatcher proved a reluctant signatory to the movement towards European integration. The reasons for her resistance are revealing. She fears that the lifting of frontiers will threaten the separate and sacrosanct integrity of the British nation. This integrity, as she made plain in her Address to the College of Europe at Bruges in September 1988, is based on the following six principles:

1. an imperial tradition proud of the 'civilizing' impact of its colonial past;

2. the right to preserve checkpoint barriers to prevent the free mobility of EC citizens (ie, the 'wogs begin at Calais' view of Europe) while approving the free mobility of capital implied by a selective economic reading of the Single Market (eg, deregulation of transport and capital movements and opening of markets for banking, insurance and financial services);

3. the rejection of a sharing of sovereignty in further progress towards European political integration;

4. opposition to common European directives on the devolution of power to sub-national regions;

5. disapproval of EC legislative proposals for an agreed set of workers rights and social welfare payments to cover all member states;

6. disapproval of egalitarian structural funding aimed at redistributing wealth to less well off and peripheral regions (such as Ireland, South *and* North).

Consistent throughout these six 'outs' to Europe is the Prime Minister's determination to preserve Britain as the most centralized nation in Europe today (Ireland, alas, being a close second as Barrington reminds us below) and her equal determination to prevent the 'social dimension' of justice, equality and environmental protection being brought into Britain through the European back door. On this latter point indeed, it is highly revealing that the emphasis placed on the Social Programme by Delors and Papandreou, while bitterly opposed by Thatcher, has been welcomed by European, British and Irish Trade Union Congresses as well as by the major parties in Ireland, North and South. The catch-cries of reactionary British nationalism may still work in colonial outposts like Gibraltar or the Falklands – they don't work in Europe.

The question of national identity and sovereignty is, of course, a crucial one. But here again, Europe will be what we make of it. Margaret Thatcher's caricature of an homogeneous identikit Europe is only conceivable if certain extreme Eurocrats were given their head, and the current social and cultural dimensions were deleted from the agenda. That this could happen looks most unlikely. Indeed, from Ireland's point of view, the European horizon would appear to offer some auspicious signs for the resolution of our 'national question'. The North and South of Ireland, for example, are taken together for consideration in the decisive matter of social and regional funding. Civil war wounds and partition mentalities are put aside when our MEPs congregate in Europe. In Strasbourg politicians from the nationalist and unionist communities make common cause and vote together on local interest issues in a manner unthinkable in Belfast, London or Dublin. In short, how is it that John Hume, Ian Paisley and John Taylor can become allies on the plane for Europe?

In this context, it might be recalled that the original project for an integrated Europe, as drafted in 1950 by Jean Monnet and Robert Schuman, was not just for an economic community of 'coal and steel' but for a larger political community capable of transcending 'national rivalries' – and particularly the rivalry between Germany and France which had caused two world wars in the first part of the century. Monnet himself, who lived through both wars, spoke of the ideal of solidarity between European nations as a 'leap in the dark'. Forty years later, it is a reality. If the French and Germans have been able to reach across the frontiers – as symbolized in the famous handclasp between Mitterand and Kohl at Verdun – why not the Irish and the British, the nationalists and the unionists?

At the International Symposium on European Cultural Identity, held in Paris in January 1988, most participants agreed that the 1990s would see a gradual movement beyond the frontiers of the traditional Nation States. The rise of the European Nation States between the 18th and 20th centuries proved to be one of the most dynamic events in world history. Fuelled by the liberationist principles of Renaissance humanism, the Enlightenment and the French Revolution, the European states developed a keen sense of national identity and sovereignty. The final break-up of the Holy Roman Empire had released new energies for the self-determination of the different nations of Europe. And this transition from the old empires of medieval Christendom and monarchy to a modern Europe of diverse Nation States spelt a significant advance for civil, political and religious rights. The declaration of human rights after the French Revolution in June 1793 made this clear in its insistence that 'sovereignty resides in the people' (Art. 25), and that each people has the right to determine its own future and where necessary 'to revolt against a corrupt power which violates its rights' (Art. 35). In so far as this right to national self-determination coincided with the evolution of the modern Nation State, one could argue that nationalism was an indispensable feature of modernity. But the

Europe of competing nationalisms has itself come to grief in our own century. As Edgar Morin observes in *Penser L'Europe*:

'The notion of Europe which emerged in the 18th century corresponded to a common age of national sovereignties, wars, the Right of Peoples and the balance of powers. Europe harboured within her both conflict and the means of regulating conflict. Her wars prevented any attempt at hegemonic unification and upheld polycentrism. But when the national states transformed themselves into Nation-States, when the wars became massively and totally national and when advances in armament made carnage possible on a huge scale, then Europe had reached its peak and began to sink into the abyss.'[10]

As we face into the 1990s, we leave the Europe of competing nationalisms behind us. The various communities within the Community will have to find new ways of relating to each other. What is clear is that the notion of an absolute right to national self-determination will become increasingly questionable if Nation States break up – as I believe they will – in the direction of greater integration on the one hand and greater local and regional democracy on the other. While the movement towards integration is propelled by forces of economic cohesion and communications, the parallel movement towards decentralization is being pioneered by the advocates of the 'social' policies of redistribution and regionalization. The fate of the latter still hangs, of course, in the balance.

Foremost among such advocates is the Northern Irish MEP, John Hume. In his influential *Report on Regional Policy*, drafted in July 1987 and unanimously approved by the EC parliament in October 1987, Hume offers persuasive arguments for a radical regionalization of Ireland. His *Report* opens with five principal observations:

1. that government is highly centralised in Ireland and lacks any regional authorities;

2. that devolution of powers would have the effect of releasing local energies;

3. that such a regionalised structure would enable Ireland to derive the maximum benefit from the Community's structural funds;

4. that the example of the regional bodies which have been established in Ireland, notably the Shannon Free Airport Development Company, demonstrates that such bodies successfully promote their region nationally and internationally and stimulate the fullest use of the region's indigenous resources;

5. that the creation of regional authorities need not be costly if existing local bodies are placed on a more rational basis.

The Hume Report goes on to recommend that regional authorities with executive and planning powers should be created, on the basis of the nine physical regions used for administrative purposes by the IDA. It urges the Irish government to take full advantage of the possibilities offered by EC practice and legislation to undertake a radical programme of 'regionalization and decentralization by devolving powers and, where practicable, transferring Government departments from Dublin'. Such a programme would enhance the indigenous potential of regions and involve local and regional authorities in a genuine practice of participatory democracy. It would also lead to the full development of much neglected 'natural resource' industries such as forestry and aquaculture as well as advancing the technological development of peripheral regions now being bled by unemployment and emigration.

While Hume's proposals met with enthusiastic approval from the European Parliament and many Irish MEPs and commentators (see Barrington *et al* below), it has been largely ignored by the Irish government. Although the European Parliament and Commission have been insisting on the importance of regional participation since 1982, arguing that 'top-down' government does not work and wastes money, the Irish and British governments have refused to take any real initiative. In contrast to decentralizing trends in most other European countries – Denmark, Spain, Italy and France, as well as Switzerland and Yugoslavia – our two sovereign governments have persisted in keeping intact what T. J. Barrington has described as the 'iron fetters of a political and administrative centralisation unique in European democracy'. Is it not ironic that the two governments that have most frequently accused the European Community of wishing to centralize power are the very ones who most resist the Community's directives to decentralize!

V

Having joined Hume, Barrington and others in the debate on a Europe of regions with a series of articles in *The Irish Times* in January 1987, I was struck by the passionate controversy this subject aroused. Apart from the very considerable support the project enjoys here in Ireland, there are also frequent objections raised. These are generally threefold: A Europe of regions, some argue, risks being neo-imperial, neo-tribal and neo-conservative. My answer to the first is this: the New Europe cannot become a New Empire if power is devolved to a wide diversity of equal and largely self-governing regions. Moreover, as the Belgian Prime Minister, Wilfried Martens, reminded Mrs Thatcher after her Bruges speech, 'Empires differ radically from the European Community in that they are not answerable to a democratically elected legislature and parliament'. My answer to the second is: the New Europe cannot be neo-tribal if regions remain interconnected and open to the free mobility of citizens across the European Community. (A further guarantee against the danger of a protectionist tribalism would be to ensure that each region has at least one cosmopolitan urban centre where the local and the international can co-habit; eg, Barcelona in the Catalan region). Finally, my answer to the objection of neo-conservatism would be this: if so, why does Thatcher oppose such a new Europe and Mitterand, Gonzales, Papandreou and Suarez propose it? The major proposals for a Europe of equal regions have consistently come from the majority Socialist grouping in the EC. There is, of course, no guarantee that this radical project of a decentralized, regionalized and equal community will be realized. What *is* certain is that there is far more chance of bringing such a society about *within* Europe than *without* it.

The fact that the British and Irish governments have tended to put their respective 'nationalist' interests above their 'European/regionalist' ones is particularly regrettable in the Northern Ireland context. Is it not probable that a lasting solution to the Ulster conflict is most likely to be found in a New Europe where the borders separating the Nation States of Britain and Ireland would be transcended in favour of a federation of equal and democratic regions? Such a prospect would be abetted at an economic level by the harmonization of VAT and excise tariffs North and South of the border and, at a legal level, by the availability of an internationally recognized Court of Law in Strasbourg (putting an end to divisive and inflammatory cases such as Stalker, Gibraltar, the Birmingham Six, the MacAnespie border shooting, or indeed the dispute over Sellafield).

We need to move beyond the established, and ultimately failed, model of the Nation State towards a society without frontiers. But 'without frontiers' should not mean – in the European or Anglo-Irish contexts – 'without differences'. The New Europe must not herald (to borrow a phrase from Hegel) a 'night in which all cows are black'. On the contrary, the more we transcend national boundaries the greater the need for decentralized regional government. What we are talking about then is not the liquidation of nations but their supercession (*aufhebung*) into a post-nationalist network of communities where national identities may live on where they belong – in languages, sports, arts, customs, memories and myths – while simultaneously fostering the expressioin of minority and regional cultures within each nation.[10a] (In Western Europe there are over twenty minority languages, in addition to immigrant ones, involving over seventy million speakers).

It is in this context of a European federation of equal regions that we might begin to talk genuinely about a reunification of Ireland. An Ireland without frontiers is obviously an Ireland without borders. This does not, however, entail a 'united Ireland' in the traditional sense of this term. For the Nation States of Britain and Ireland, which constitute the very basis for the opposing claims of nationalist and unionist ideologies, would be superseded by a European constellation of regions. An alternative model would have emerged transcending both the nationalist claim to exclusive unity with the Republic and the unionist claim to exclusive union with Britain.

There are already significant movements in this direction: the proposed harmonization of fiscal and social legislation between North and South and the integration of our respective economic institutions in preparation for the Single Market; the fact that both the Republic and Britain are signatories to the European Convention of Human Rights and are therefore liable, through directives from the European Court of Justice if necessary, to harmonize legislation on equal pay, women's rights, minority rights, civil and religious liberties and regulations on environmental pollution and nuclear safety (all of which have in recent years been subjects of dispute between the two jurisdictions). But directives from Strasbourg or Brussels will be of no avail if changes are not also made at ground level. In the recent SDLP position paper to Sinn Féin, John Hume expressed the view that 'solutions to the problems of division in Ireland have been postponed by Nationalist/Republican concentration on the language of ideological rectitude rather than trying to face the political reality'.[11] Perhaps Unionist leaders could apply a similar argument to their own ideology.

How Ireland will fare in the Europe of the 1990s remains open. And as most of the contributors to this volume point out, there are considerable obstacles at a number of levels – *political* (Higgins, Fennell, Bew), *socio-economic* (Murphy, Browne, Barry) and *cultural* (Gibbons, Bell, O'Leary). We have enough professional Panglosses telling us we are heading for the 'best of all possible worlds'; we also need our Cassandras alerting us to the pitfalls. But whether one is looking through bright or dark spectacles, it remains clear that Ireland's future role in an enlarged 'totality of relations' extending to Britain, the Continent and beyond, will depend largely on what we make of it. It will depend on politicians we choose to elect in Ireland and in Europe. It will depend on action we take at local level to decentralize power and bring about real participatory democracy. Then we could have the strength of 'ourselves' without the limitation of 'ourselves alone'. It will depend on whether we lend support to that current in European politics committed to a radical 'social dimension' or that committed to narrow neo-conservatism. It will depend, in short, on whether we take sides with the generous and egalitarian vision of Monnet, Spinelli and Delors or with the reactionary vision of neo-imperial nationalists like Mrs Thatcher. The answers to the questions 'whither Europe?' and 'whither Ireland?' are intimately connected. But taken together or apart, they must never be allowed (as Higgins, Browne and Fennell remind us below) to obscure the most comprehensive of all questions: whither the *world*? The future of both Ireland and Europe will utlimately depend on the creation of a new International Order, based on the UN principle of mutual interdependency.

VI

Two important areas of the debate not yet touched on are the *military* and the *cultural*. I conclude my introduction with a few brief remarks on each.

On military matters, I see no reason why Ireland should not develop a positive policy of neutrality. It could thereby reassert and exploit its internationally recognized role as a peace-broker in world affairs. (A role fittingly rewarded in its receipt, along with other peace-keeping forces in the UN, of the 1988 Nobel Peace Prize). Certainly, European integration must not be allowed to mean a common policy of militarization. If they so wish, other European member-states can remain within NATO (which excludes Ireland) or the Western European Union (which excludes Ireland, Denmark and Greece). Far from necessitating a compromise of our neutral stance, it is arguable that the European Community can actually profit from the existence of such an independent voice in its midst. This not only facilitates its desired role as an honest broker between East and West (keeping a distance from both US and Soviet military policies), but also serves to encourage other neutral countries such as Austria and Sweden who wish to consider membership of the Community *without* military involvement.[12]

The bogeyman of Ireland's forced militarization in Europe must be dispelled. As a small country which has experienced the ravages of colonial and imperial policies, we should be the last to condone the Community degenerating into a new Euro-Empire ambitious to rival the super-powers in geo-political warplay. On the contrary, our neutral history places us in a unique position to militate for a non-aligned Europe committed to world disarmament and strongly opposed to the notion of an Atlantic Alliance (advanced by Thatcher and others) which divides the world into antagonistic blocs. On such matters, our historical bias is, thankfully, an anti-imperialist one. The recent EC-Comecon Agreement, in addition to the explicit commitment of the EC (under the Greek Presidency of 1988) to work for disarmament by initiating 'a systematic dialogue between the 12 and the Soviet Union as well as the other East European countries', augurs well. Ireland should take immediate steps to prevent any attempts to militarize the European Community by adopting the following measures: actively champion the recent EC policy of openness to the 'other Europe' lying to the east of its borders; approve the Irish CND draft declaring Ireland a Nuclear-Free Zone (this would entail such practical safety measures as a ban on nuclear armed aircraft flying over our territory and nuclear ships entering our harbours); initiate constructive disarmament and demilitarizing programmes at both the EC and the UN, thereby reaffirming our merited reputation as original sponsors of the UN Non-Proliferation Treaty[13] and champion of small communities against the domination of large powers.

VII

Having considered some of the economic, social, political and military implications of Ireland's role in the 1990s, there remains the crucial question of *culture*. This is the ultimate horizon of the reflections contained in this volume and might even be said to signal its originality. Even though 'Cultural Perspectives' constitutes a separate section, the questions raised there inform the book as a whole. The society we inhabit in the 1990s and beyond will witness an even greater convergence of politics, economics and culture. And this is especially true of the ever-expanding impact of the communications revolutions. If the industrial modern era was largely governed by factors of production, the post-industrial future (or postmodern era) will be determined by factors of communication.[14]

To date, most discussion of Ireland and 1992 has been confined to the economic consequences of the removal of the tariff barriers and the apportioning of structural funds. While readily acknowledging the centrality of this dimension – and devoting a section of this volume to it – I would repeat that the economic cannot be adequately understood in terms of economics alone. Cultural questions of evaluation, motivation and imagination cannot be precluded from a comprehensive grasp of the facts and figures likely to condition our future. In other words, to the question: *What* are Ireland's financial prospects for the 1990s? we must add the more challenging and penetrating questions: *Why* are they this rather than that? *Who* decides? – and in *whose interests*?

The cultural debate on the future of Ireland is what enables us to critically interrogate both the 'obligatory optimism' of the Euro-admen and the 'dogmatic pessimism' of the whiners and gripers. Since ancient Greece, a guarantee of human culture has been the provision of an 'agora' or open space of discussion where conflicting interpretations can be aired and opposing viewpoints articulated. I would like to think the present volume honours this definition of culture and dialogue – a definition expressed in the very roots of the term itself (*dia-legein* meaning to 'welcome the difference'). The fact that the different contributors to this volume do not conform to a 'single line' is a virtue. For cultural dialogue is as much a matter of critical negation as of utopian affirmation: they are the siamese twins of genuine debate. To juggle with Kant, if critique without affirmation is empty, affirmation without critique is blind.

What are the central issues at stake in the cultural debate? Perhaps the most dominant is the question of identity and difference. What does it mean to be Irish? Is it some unique 'essence' inherited from our ancestors? Is it a characteristic of a specific language (eg, Gaelic) or religion (Catholic/Protestant) or ideology (nationalist/unionist)? Is it a matter of ethnic memory, genetic heritage or geographical residence? One thing is certain: the question of what it means to be Irish – who we are and where we are going to – cannot be limited to the frontiers of our island. The affirmation of a dynamic cultural identity invariably involves an exploratory dialogue with *other* cultures.

This is not just a feature of modern or post-modern cultures; it has always been so. And Ireland is no exception to this model of identity in dialogue with difference. Our cultural history reads like a litany of intellectual migrations which have established extensive associations between Ireland and the wider world. This is especially true of our cultural links with Europe. Those with Britain are so intimate as to require no further mention. The link with the Continent reaches back, in our literary memory, to the famous *navigatio*'s of Irish thinkers and missionaries between the seventh and tenth centuries, as recorded in the *Immram* genre of popular voyage tales and as exemplified by the expeditions abroad of figures like Eriugena, St Cilian, Columbanus, Sedulis Scottus and Clement Maelcomer who travelled throughout the Continent and were renowned for their intellectual achievements. These cultural bonds with Europe were reconfirmed after the seventeenth century when a number of Irish Colleges were established in Paris, Salamanca, Rome and Louvain for the education of Irish Catholics abroad. And this cross-fertiliza-tion of Irish and European minds was also evident in the intellectual itineraries of Irish Protestant thinkers such as Berkeley, Burke, Toland and Tone in the eighteenth century and in many of our great writers – Joyce, Beckett, Yeats, Shaw, Stephens – in our own century.

The current ERASMUS scheme to promote greater exchange between the European Community's educational centres, together with the project to restore and network the Irish Colleges on the Continent, point to real possibilities of re-establishing these histor-ical links with Europe.

On the threshold of the nineties, we recognize that we are enter-ing into a new relationship with Europe which may enable us to overcome the traditional antagonism between Nation States and redefine our cultural identity positively rather than negatively. In certain periods of our history, we found ourselves cut off from Europe and the larger world. Plagued by colonialism, famine and emigration, we became obsessed by the struggle with the 'old enemy' England and settled for a rather insular definition of national identity and culture. But since such dark times in our history, we have begun to re-explore the rich diversity and openness of our intellectual traditions. There are growing signs in our culture today – both popular and artistic – that the *plurality* of our heritage is being recognized anew. And this also augurs well for a more creative relationship with our most immediate neighbour – Great Britain.

Joyce it was who defined culture as a 'bringer of plurabilities'. And it is perhaps salutary to recall this ideal when we observe that Europe itself is not some homogeneous 'essence' but a rich plurality of cultures which over the centuries have commingled and confronted each other in creative dialogue. It is for this reason that Europe needs the specific national cultures which make it up quite as much as these cultures need the universalist horizon of Europe. This is, no doubt, what Joyce had in mind when he journeyed to Paris, Zurich and Triest and creatively conjugated Irish 'particulars' with Greek and Biblical 'universals' in *Ulysses* and *Finnegans Wake*. For Joyce, as for many migrant Irish minds before and after him, Europe was a map without frontiers, a free space of exploration and peregrination, a place where Irish myth and memory could engage in dynamic dialogue with the cultures of other lands.

Current trends would suggest that in the 1990s Irish culture will be more than ever interconnected with international culture. This is certainly the verdict of the Irish artists – Bono, Durcan, Jordan and Ballagh – who contribute to the 'Migrant Minds' debate in this volume. Such a view is based not only on the self-evident fact that an increasing number of artists are forging their vision abroad (following the example of Joyce, Beckett and Le Brocquy) as well as at home, but also on the fact that contemporary Irish culture is largely blended from both national and international idioms. This mixing of the 'foreign with the familiar', to borrow Joyce's phrase, is witnessed in most art forms – in the music of Irish groups such as The Chieftains, Van Morrison, The Pogues or U2; in the films of

Irish directors such as Jordan, Murphy, Quinn, Comerford and O'Connor; the writings of Irish authors such as Heaney, Banville, Durcan, Ní Dhomhnaill and Bolger; and the visual art of an emerging generation which includes Ballagh, Coleman, Elanna O'Kelly and Dorothy Cross. More and more, the arts in Ireland are evolving in terms of media-mixing and central to this process is, of course, the critical influence of the communications revolution – and in particular the pervasive impact of electronic media such as TV, radio and video.

VIII

I return therefore to the crucial phenomenon of communications raised at the outset. We can no longer take 'culture' to refer exclusively or even primarily to the accredited realms of literature, painting and music. No discussion of culture today or tomorrow can exclude discussion of the audio-visual media of television and cinema.

Until recently, the Irish universities and arts councils have given scant official recognition to these popular media. And it is surely a sad reflection on Ireland's unpreparedness to explore the options facing television and video after 1992 that no representative attended the European Television Task Force in Munich in June 1988.[15] There are signs of change. The last few years has seen a number of major studies of TV and cinema in Ireland,[16] the creation of a Media Association and the introduction of comprehensive courses in media studies, particularly in the NIHEs. Indeed, other European nations have also been remiss in this regard as Joe Mulholland, Head of Programmes at RTE, pointed out at the international conference on European Cultural Identity held in Paris in January 1988: 'For an assembly such as this television would appear to be more despised than respected. Despite its faults, however, and we are all conscious of them, television has opened up a window on the world for the masses which they would otherwise never have. Television has contributed enormously to the democratization of knowledge and culture. And we should not forget that here in the West the specified places of Culture are still of limited access for those who live in the slums'.[17] Mulholland goes on to warn Europeans against the danger of an emerging television *à l'americaine* – one which threatens the continued existence of public broadcasting and offers the prospect of future generations of European youth watching the same vacuous video clips. This threat is exacerbated by the current trends towards commercial deregulation (see Bell below). So that the very technology which could be servicing intellectual exchanges between continents is more often being used for the promotion of a uniform global market. Even our unconscious is becoming slowly colonized by an Americanized mass media. The lowest common denominator of soap and kitsch is the staple diet of deregulated TV – a mix between the Eurovision song contest and a Coca-Cola ad. The best weapon against this is the diversity of our images, ideas and languages. But even this will disappear unless rapidly abetted by a rejuvenated public broadcasting policy and further Community support for transnational satellite channels such as SAT I, SEPT or indeed C4 – all of which are committed to high quality programming and the fostering of minority regional cultures. Moreover, the fact that these cultural channels are transnational in scope in no way prevents them from operating on a decentralized basis with co-production input from the most peripheral regions of the Community. There is some existing evidence to suggest that minority cultures actually benefit from transnational television.[18]

There are signs that the warnings are being heeded. Apart from renewed support for publicly financed cultural channels at a European level, the Commission has recently approved a number of innovative measures. These include : (1) the declaration of 1988 as the Year of European Cinema; (2) the promotion of multilateral financial assistance for TV co-productions between member states of the Community; (3) the establishment of a European Network for the Promotion of an Image-Sound Industry; and (4) the MEDEA project launched by the Commission which has already resulted in the creation of a Televisioin Fiction in Europe Fund (the proposal at the Delphi meeting of April 88 was for one and a half million pounds to be spent over the first year on the promotion of original TV scripts).

In short, one of the major cultural challenges of the 1990s will be audio-visual literacy. Or to borrow Joyce's felicitous formula: the culture of the future belongs to Shaun the post-man (the man of communications) as much as to Shem the pen-man (the man of letters). If European nations – and particularly the smaller and peripheral ones like Ireland – are to compete with the communications advances in the US and Japan, concerted action is required from all the community partners.

European integration must not mean European uniformity. This is surely one of the most decisive wagers of our time. As I argued at the Paris conference on European Cultural Identity: 'the task facing those concerned with our cultural future is to ensure that a Europe without frontiers does not mean a Europe without differences. The rich plurality of European culture, historically and today, resides in the fact that it is multi-linguistic, multi-ethnic and multi-confessional. If we talk of a European family, we must do so in the plural'.[19] Concretely, this means ensuring that national and regional cultures are fully fostered within the new Europe. The adoption of the ARSI resolution to positively encourage minority and regional cultures by the Parliament in October 1981, was a significant moment. And as John Hume argues below, the European measures taken in support of 'lesser used languages' (such as Irish, Welsh, Scots Gaelic, Basque and Breton) are far more likely to succeed than most steps taken by national governments to date.[20] If we deplore the threat to a rare species of flora or fauna, how much more we must deplore the threat to one of our languages – an indispensable and irreplaceable reservoir of memory and meaning. The European project of the 1990s challenges us to overcome national and territorial conflicts by entering a more extensive 'totality of relations' where cultural specificities are actively celebrated. This is a far cry from nostalgic calls to recover the pristine unity of the old European Empires. A new Europe can only hope to rediscover its identity in its very diversity.[21] It is not a *fait accompli* – it is an act of faith.

But it is not a credo supported by reasonable grounds. There is much evidence that local culture can be enhanced rather than annihilated by contact with other cultures. As the contributors to our 'Migrant Minds' discussion indicate, it is often by journeying beyond the frontiers of Ireland – either physically or imaginatively – that we find a new desire to return and rediscover what is most valuable in it. Ireland has nothing to fear from exposure to alien cultures. On the contrary, it is often the migrational detour through other intellectual landscapes which enables us to better appreciate our own traditions. Do our writers not show us how indigenous material from Irish myth and history can be successfully conjoined with the most innovative forms of international literature? Do our artists and musicians not show us how we can proclaim Irish origins while transcending national barriers and communicating with the citizens of other European and world cultures? And do not our best film and TV directors exemplify how visual images deriving from a specifically native culture can be appreciated throughout the international capitals of the world? Perhaps it was in anticipation of such feats that Joyce recommended the cultural project of 'hibernicizing Europe and Europeanizing Ireland'.

In the 1990s nothing should be allowed hinder our entitlement to a triple citizenship – of Ireland, Europe and the world.

NOTES
1. The following is an approximate breakdown of the 70 million plus people outside of Ireland claiming Irish descent: US 42 million; UK 13 million; Canada 5 million (including some 50% of the Newfoundland population); Australia almost 5 million (one-third of the population); New Zealand 700,000; Argentina 300,000.
2. See the report by the Economic and Social Research Institute in Dublin entitled

Poverty and the Social Welfare System, commissioned by the Combat Poverty Agency and published in September 1988.

3. Vincent Buckley, *Memory Ireland*, Penguin Australia, 1985, pp. 53-54.

4. *Proceedings of the New Ireland Forum*, Vol. 1, Dublin Castle, 1984.

5. See *The Single European Market*, A supplement to *The Sunday Tribune, 2 October 1988;* Chris O'Malley *'Over in Europe'*: *The Issues facing Ireland in the European Community*, Orchard Press, 1988; Dermot McAlease and Alan Matthews, 'The Single European Act and Ireland: Implications for a small member State' in *Journal of Common Market Studies*, Vol. 24, No. 1, September 1987; Eithne Murphy, 'The Economic Implications of the Single European Act for Ireland' in *Studies*, Vol. 77, No. 305, Spring 1988 (this issue of *Studies* also contained several articles on the 'military' implications of the SEA); and a series of four articles on *1992* in *The Irish Times*, 10-14 May 1988.

6. See remarks by Bishop Murphy of Cork at the Cork Conference on the Single European Market, 25 September 1988 (as reported in *The Irish Times*, 26 September 1988) and by Declan Kiberd in *The Irish Times*, 5 October 1988 and by Matt Merrigan, *The Irish Times*, 18 October 1988. Some of the remarks by Michael D. Higgins, Desmond Bell and Luke Gibbons below also give some support to the 'Malign' scenario.

7. See *L'Europe des Uns, L'Europe des Autres* by Claude Cheysson in *Le Monde*, 5 May 1988.

8. Jacques Delors, President of the Commission of the European Communities, Introduction to the *Cecchini Report: The Benefits of a Single Market*, Brussels 1988.

9. Breandán O hEithir, 'Self-Help and Gravy from Brussels', *The Irish Times*, 6 July 1988.

10. Edgar Morin, *Penser L'Europe*. Gallimard, Paris, 1987, p. 53. Further support for this reading of European nationalisms can be found in Chris O'Malley's *Over in Europe*, pp. 122-126: 'The replacement of Monarchy by nation was graphically represented by the French Revolution and the wars which followed sowed the seeds of nationalist ideas all over Europe. Without nationalism – which put the people as a whole in the commanding role – there could have been no development of democratic systems . . . The areas where Europe has a role to play (today) are basically those where national governments on their own have been losing control. They are primarily the twin areas of giving Europe an effective voice in world affairs and of building a strong economic framework within which we can develop with greater confidence . . . This is what the building of a European Community is all about: strengthening democracy in a world where national governments have been losing control. In the light of this challenge, we have to revise our concept of nationalism. Instead of regarding European unification as a threat to our nationalist ideas, we should see it as a logical continuation of them. The underlying goal is to strengthen the control which the ordinary community has over its own destiny.' – Unfortunately, O'Malley sees the solution lying in greater centralised decision-making in Brussels rather than in regional and local self-government within Europe. There is only one cursory and rather reluctant allusion to the latter in the entire book (p. 126).

10a. Such a post-nationalism as I argued in my articles in *The Irish Times* on 'Postmodern Ireland' (28-31 January 1987) is not to be confused with anti-nationalism. On the contrary, it attempts to critically reinterpret our nationalist traditions retrieving what is enabling and democratic, discarding what is disabling or sectarian. I would have no hesitation in using the term 'New Republicanism' (invoked by John Hume below) to designate this approach.

11. See SDLP position paper exchanged with Sinn Féin, published in *The Irish Times* September 1988.

12. See *The Irish Times* report, 29 September 1988 on Austria's discussion with the

Irish government on the question of neutrality within the European Community. At a meeting held at the UN on 28 September 1988 between the Irish and Austrian Ministers for Foreign Affairs, it was stated that Ireland's neutrality had never become an issue with our EC partners since joining the Community in 1973. The Austrians also expressed interest in the way EC membership had lessened Ireland's excessive economic dependence on Britain for trade and investment. Austria itself has an extremely dependent relationship with the West German economy. See *The Irish Times* 29 September 1988.

13. For Irish CND Policy statement see Carol Fox 'Ireland should resist Militarization of EC' in *The Sunday Tribune*, 11 September 1988.

14. See the chapters on Habermas, Marcuse and Gramsci in my *Modern Movements in European Philosophy*, Manchester University Press, 1986 and Part III of my *The Wake of Imagination*, Hutchinson, 1988.

15. See Colum Kenny, 'European Television Faces up to US Invasion'. *The Irish Times*, 22 June 1988.

16. See *Television and Irish Society* ed. M. McLoone and J. MacMahon, RTE/IFI, Dublin, 1984: 'The Media Issue' of *The Crane Bag*, Vol. 8, No. 2, 1984; 'The Media Issue' of *Studies*, Autumn 1984, ed. by Lelia Doolan; *Cinema and Ireland* by L. Gibbons, Kevin Rochett and John Hill, Croom Hewlm, 1987; *Irish Television Drama* by Helena Sheehan, RTE, Dublin, 1987.

17. Joe Mulholland, 'Propositions Concrètes' in *Europe sans Rivage: De l'Identité Culturelle Européenne*, International Symposium, Paris, January 1988, Albin Michel pp. 318-321.

18. See Siej. 'Help from Europe for Irish Film Makers?' *The Irish Times*, 6 April 1988.

19. For a more developed presentation of these arguments see R. Kearney, 'Pour une Intelligentia Européenne' in *Europe sans Rivage, ibid*, pp. 114-119.

20. Hume's argument and it is one shared by Faure, Morin and Duby below – is that peripheral and repressed cultures are more likely to flourish in a federal Europe of interconnected regions than in a Europe of isolated Nation-States. Nation-States have been notoriously oppressive of minority cultures and languages for the reason that they were obliged, historically, to homogenize their respective populations in order to operate as a single identity and thereby effectively compete with rival Nation-States. Hence the tragic plight of the Breton language in France, Basque in Spain, Scots and Irish Gaelic under the British Empire, Armenian in Turkey, Hungarian in Romania and so on.

See also John Hume, 'The European Parliament and the Future of Lesser Used Languages' in *The Lesser Used Languages of the European Community*, Comhar Teoranta, Dublin, 1981, pp. 5-10 and Seán MacRéamoinn 'Perspectives Historiques' in *Europe Sans Rivage, ibid*, pp. 99-100. It is to be noted, moreover, that the preservation and even revival of lesser used languages such as Gaelic is not necessarily motivated by tribal nostalgia or separatist paranoia, as some argue. On the contrary it is often motivated by a desire for common roots which *overcome* conflict, as John Robb of the New Ireland group recently remarked: 'The present Gaelic language revival in the North of Ireland is to a considerable degree, the child of conflict yet it represents much more. It is also reaction to remote control, an assertion of the right to be different. It represents a search for roots, respect for heritage and a desire to understand better the country in which we live. Northern Protestants, in particular those who are descended from Scottish forbears, should resent any implication that Gaelic/Gallic is alien to them. We should therefore consider much more seriously the obligation on us to complement the work of our Catholic fellow Ulstermen by giving the Northern revival a new momentum so that together we may serve a language which may be in danger of withering elsewhere in Ireland.' *The Irish Times*, 16 September 1988.

21. A Europe of equal regions should ideally be one where we can say *vivre la*

différence and 'we are all in this together' at one and the same time. Indeed, as the contributors to our final section on European Cultural Identity cogently argue, the very idea of a European culture remains properly elusive for the reason that it is not a reduction to some common 'essence' but a 'cauldron of diversities' where the very absence of homogeneity proves to be its greatest strength. As Edgar Morin argues in *Penser L'Europe*: 'Europe is a community of multiple faces which cannot be superimposed on each other without creating a blur . . . Europe's only unity lies in its multiplicity. Its unity is itself plural and contradictory, stitched together from the interactions between peoples, cultures, states and classes. The difficulty of 'thinking Europe' is first of all the difficulty of thinking about this unity in multiplicity – this *unitas multiplex*' (p. 27). All attempts to simplify Europe by way of abstraction, idealization or reduction are mutilating. Europe, as Morin explains, 'is a *complex* (*complexus*: what is woven together) whose proper function is to assemble the largest possible diversity without confounding it, to associate contraries while safeguarding their separateness. And this is why we need not only a just modesty but also a just thinking which may comprehend the gordian knot that makes up Europe with all its political, economic, social, cultural, religious and anti-religious histories intermixing and interconnecting in both conflict and solidarity' (p. 29). Morin goes on to argue, accordingly, that European history can no more be defined by geographical frontiers any more than geographical Europe can be defined by historical ones. This means for Morin that Europe cannot be properly understood in terms of frontiers at all, which are always fluxile and changing, but only in terms of the particular originality which produces and organizes it – and that Morin identifies as its very 'absence of unity' (p. 36). This celebration of Europe as fundamentally polycentric and polylinguistic is a sure safeguard against the opposing view of Europe as a hegemonic empire in its own right – a view not only evident in the chauvinistic 'Europo-centrism' of much colonial policy in the 19th and 20th centuries but also in the barbaric dreams of a 'New Europe' championed by Hitler and Mussolini (see Morin, *op. cit.* pp. 92 and Kearney, 'Pour Une Intelligentsia Européenne', *ibid.* p. 115). The truly pluralist nature of European identity constitutes a basic 'resistance to all forms of political or cultural hegemony'. Europe still retains, as Morin and other contributors to the 'identity debate' below remind us, a rich diversity of transnational cultures (German, Latin, Slav), national cultures with their own languages, and also an extraordinary variety of 'micro-cultures' (made up of the micro-ethnic texture of Europe whose riches have survived thanks to the ultimate failure of the historical projects of 'national unity' – including those of Germany and France). What ultimately distinguishes Europe from the immense cultural spaces of the American or Asiatic worlds is the fact that it continues to constitute 'a universe of little cultural departments at local, regional, provincial or national level', Morin, *op. cit.*, p. 67. California and New England have much more in common, for example, despite the huge geographical distance that separates them, than Brittany or Provence, not to mention Portugal and Sweden, or Italy and Denmark. Whence Morin's salutary conclusion: 'The organizing principle of Europe can only be found in that historical principle which links its identity with perpetual becoming and metamorphosis. It is the vital urgency to save its identity which today calls Europe towards a new metamorphosis' (Morin, *ibid.* p. 67).

I would just add, finally, that any temptation Europe may have to close in on itself, to constitute itself as some self-contained homogenized entity must be resisted by appealing both to its inner dynamic of diversity and to its insatiable hunger for dialogue with other cultures – and not just the 'other Europe' or the New Worlds of America and Austral-Asia which Europe gave birth to, but also and perhaps especially the more heterogenous cultures of the Third World.

— PART I —
POLITICAL PERSPECTIVES

Frontiers of the Mind

T. J. BARRINGTON

I

The visionaries and the politicians have joined in the task of level-ling the frontiers of Europe; but what, so far as we Irish are concerned, about the frontiers of the mind, of our own minds? Almost like the tariffs and quotas we decided to forego when we joined the European Community half a generation ago there exist the internal, the intellectual, linguistic, institutional, emotional frontiers persisting like Green Pounds to impede the free flow of community. The age of self-sufficiency, of those firesides – the forum for the wisdom of serene old-age, of that vision of the future as a return to the 19th century, all are in practical terms dead and gone; yet, in our embedded ideas, institutions and perceptions they are in full control. How can we retain our sanity while living this double life, externally in a practical world of the late 20th century, internally in an emotional world of the late 19th? Our failure to resolve this dilemma helps to explain why we do so poorly in both worlds, why we live in a muddled mediocrity. As the young people once more begin to pour away what chances have we of doing better in the new world opening before us? Better than we did in the polit-ical and economic union with the United Kingdom in 1801? Or the European Common Market, with all its mufflings and derogations, of 1973? George Russell, with his poet's eye, warned us in 1916 that we were setting out on the road to Independence with no intellec-tual baggage. He saw the need 'to create national ideals which will dominate the policy of statesmen, the actions of citizens, the univer-sities, the social organisations, the administration of State depart-ments, and unite in one spirit urban and rural life' (Russell, p. 9). Now that we are well on the way to Interdependence have we yet packed those bags?

This is not the place nor have I the competence to attempt comprehensive answers to those questions; but at a time when great new institutions and freedoms are being created in Europe there is the insistent question about our own ramshackle institutions and the quality of their contribution to freedom, equity and efficiency.

Faced with the impact of the newly built institutions of Europe will our institutions follow the path of our indigenous industry after 1801 and 1973? Will a lick or two of paint be enough to prevent their collapse from dry rot? Or must our institutions, too, launch themselves into a major programme of reconstruction?

The conventional answer is that we seem to be doing reasonably well as we are. We have, like everyone else, a few problems but we are getting them under control. What need is there for new thinking about our society? For change, adaptation, development? Are we not as good as any? Raising questions that hark back to 1916 only gets in the way of practical men who have a practical job to do.

II

The record does not support this complacency which is possibly the most impenetrable of our frontiers. We are, of course, splendid people and we know how to lose with style, a process in which we have had some practice; but, overall, our performance has been pretty poor. We managed to establish and maintain a decent democratic society here; but beyond that, in the light of stated 'national objectives' – language, unity, jobs for all, ending emigration – how well have we done? As Professor Joe Lee has pointed out in relation to economic growth, at Independence we were one of the best off countries of northern Europe but 'we are now perched through our own efforts at the wrong end of virtually every relevant league table' (p. 99). I would suggest that that be written in bold letters in every office of every public institution in the State. But is it true? Alas, yes, as even a cursory look at the evidence will show. Let us take a few quantitative examples – of bumping along the bottom where it would be well to be near the top, and of floating to the top where it would be best to be near the bottom.

A study of economic growth in 24 European countries between 1913 and 1970 shows our growth rate in that period as either the worst or the second worst, vying with Britain for the bottom place. (Bairoch and Lèvy-Leboyer, 1981, p. 10). OECD figures for 1970 to 1984 show Ireland to have picked up a bit, but still to be the fifth poorest of the 19 European members of the organisation, and of the four poorer countries only one had a slower rate of growth over the period 1970 to 1984 (derived from OECD, 1986, p. 110). Not much to boast of there.

If we did not do so well it was not for want of spending both on capital and current account in the period since 1970. In the 1970s there was adopted a policy of spending our way out of our difficulties. We threw away the prudent peasant virtues that saw us through World War II with accumulated budget deficits of sixteen million pounds! (Whitaker, p 82). When we followed a different god we did not do so by halves. Beginning with a deficit in 1972-3 of a mere five million pounds we have since run a deficit every year, reaching a peak of £1,395m. in 1986. The accumulated deficits have now come to just over eleven billion pounds. (Whitaker, p. 106; Budget, 1988 p. 100). We borrowed to meet those deficits and, as home funds began to dry up, the gap was filled by borrowing from abroad. The foreign debt had reached just short of ten billion pounds in 1987, amongst the highest per head of population in the whole world. It is fair to say that most of the members of the OECD responded to the economic disturbances of the later 1970s and early 1980s by running budget deficits but we did so with special flair. So we're up at the top, the wrong end, of that league table.

A budget deficit means that income, that is basically taxation, does not meet expenditure and where the deficits are large and interest rates high a vicious circle soon establishes itself. In 1988 almost one third of the income from taxation was required to meet the service of the public debt (Budget 1988, p. 101) which meant there was less to meet normal expenses. Hence, either cuts or higher taxation, or some mixture of the two. Or major tax reform. For this in 1980 the people in unprecedented numbers took to the streets in peaceful protest. In consequence the Commission on Taxation was set up. In five major reports the Commission have shown the taxation system to be both inefficient and inequitable. They also documented the bureaucratic incompetence and arrogance at the heart of the system (Fifth Report: *Tax Administration*, 1985). They made far-reaching proposals for reform. The result? Paralysis.

On fairly consistent showing, public institutions in Ireland are of themselves not reformable. In consequence the people, in sullen mood, their protests fobbed off, will not permit overt tax increases. Deficits, somewhat reduced, continue at a very high level and unproductive borrowing continues. So, let posterity pay! Rigid with fear before the apparently malevolent gaze of public opinion Irish government has come to a sorry pass in terms of public consensus, near the bottom of another league table.

In relation to our means we continue to be one of the big spenders of the OECD. The figures are not free of ambiguity but we seem to rank fourth or fifth in that league, after Sweden, Denmark, the Netherlands and, possibly, France, all of them very much richer than we are and with much longer traditions of government (eg OECD, 1987b p. 132). We also rank in the big league so far as the size of our public service is concerned, reckoning about 30% of those at work to be employed in it, a formidable mobilisation of human resources in terms of quantity and, in terms of education, training and intelligence qualitatively more formidable still (AYD, 1988; Humphreys; OECD, 1982; Rose). Such bigness in itself may not be an impediment to good government – Sweden, relatively the biggest, is a very well governed country; but bigness allied to centralised complexity is a major problem, as Mr Mikhail Gorbachev has been documenting (*Perestroika*, 1987). Relative bigness with intense centralisation and without the support of very superior organisational skills, such as are clearly lacking in this country, has been disastrous. In relation to Big Government we are up near the top of the league.

Where we are unique is in mobilising great resources of money, men and institutions, on the one hand, and, on the other, returning such poor results in growth, employment and public satisfaction. Is it any wonder that at every one of the six general elections held in the 1970s and 1980s (so far) the electorate sacked the outgoing government? It is clear that there is more to this sustained dissatisfaction than the perceived inefficiencies of individual politicians and of political parties. The experience of almost two decades suggests that the people are clearly saying that during that time the quality of Irish government as a whole was simply not good enough: the decisive, rough and ready judgement of democracy. What is the missing ingredient? It is conceivable that the people are saying, as they have been saying in other parts of Europe: 'Give us more democracy'. It is noteworthy that all of those up with us in the big spending league have been doing this very thing, at varying paces, over the past couple of decades, that their politicians and those in government have been at pains to listen to those perhaps inarticulate grunts, to interpret them and to adapt institutions accordingly.

III

Which brings us back to the point made at the outset – the stock of ideas such as it is, and now largely spent, that we possess for living in a Europe without frontiers, and the consequent bewilderment about democratic development, about citizenship, about institutions, about welfare in the widest sense. What can we learn from our European partners? What thoughts can we work out for ourselves? How is our society evolving and what institutional adaptations are called for by that evolution? Those ideas that constitute the foundations of democracy laid down in the 18th and 19th centuries – constitution, rule of law, suffrage, representation, redress – do they need to be supplemented to meet the needs of the late 20th century? Or is it enough just to dust them down a bit and carry on basically as before?

There is the progression of Greek tragedy from *hubris* to *crisis* to *nemesis*. I believe one can see the same progression in Irish political society and the grave danger of a similar outcome. We have shown a masterly capacity for doctoring the critical to the chronic, thus avoiding the hard decisions that are inherent in crisis. But fudge and evasion, too, meet their nemesis. Palpably we have run into the Crisis of Big Government. We have a Crisis of Bureaucracy. In this context the OECD talk (1981) about the Crisis of the Welfare State, which is also underlined by our own financial difficulties. And these difficulties themselves are but one symptom of our Crisis of Democracy: our continued inability or refusal to pay for what we consume is a major abdication of responsibility.

A crisis is a problem calling for solution, and an idea is a proposal for solution. Are any of the ideas we cobbled together in the early 1920s capable of providing us with the solutions we need? Or are we like Corkery's picture of the men in the barn flailing away long after the grain has been beaten from the corn? Since the State was founded one of those ideas has been intense centralisation, making us probably the most centralised of all European democracies. As Professor Lee has pointed out, the centralisers have had things all their own way – and look at the results! (Lee, p. 96). But are we capable of learning from our mistakes? There's not much evidence that we are.

As I write, Fine Gael have published proposals, *A Better Health Service*, to which the Lord Mayor of Cork and former party spokesman for health, Mr Bernard Allen, has put his name. At the foundation of the State most health services and many welfare services were administered by district bodies, several to a county. In the 1920s in the interests of efficiency and economy these services were for the most part concentrated in county councils. In 1970 health was taken from the counties and concentrated in eight regional health boards – also in the interest of economy! Now, Mr Allen wants the eight regional health boards concentrated into one major bureaucracy and promises in consequence, in the last words of the pamphlet, 'a saving of at least £30m. annually'. This is the language of a generation ago or more. Modern health thinking has moved decisively away from this technocratic mould, this removal of responsibility from the people and its concentration in central bureaucracy. On the contrary, the World Health Organisation, and following them our own Department of Health (eg its consultative statement on health policy, *Health – The Wider Dimension*, 1986), see health policy for the future as a thrust towards the prevention rather than the treatment of illness, towards care rather than cure, towards greater personal and community responsibility. The things that kill us prematurely we tend to bring on ourselves by our lifestyles. If we could be persuaded to take more responsibility for our health the expectation of life of the older ones amongst us in this country would rise to the levels of other European countries and the money available for health care would, at least in part, be better spent.

Part of modern health thinking is to integrate the new personal services at community level, but Mr Allen would split them into five separate services reporting not to any community representatives but to a centralised bureaucracy, a classic illustration of the close connection between concentration at the centre and fragmentation at the periphery. One wonders where Mr Allen has been doing his thinking. He might care to ponder the connection through personal and group responsibility between the health of the citizen and the health of democracy and how to undermine both by forcing them further apart. But this is just another in a long line of ad hoc proposals and decisions to boost bureaucracy at the price of tearing off one more of the tattered remnants of our democratic system.

Not long before this publication the leader of Fine Gael, Mr Alan Dukes, published an interesting manifesto called *The New Politics*. Newness notwithstanding, old ideas, long since emptied of life, continue grimly in orbit.

In this context the present Fianna Fáil government has been wielding some blunt axes. For example, the Minister for the Environment, Mr Padraig Flynn, in his zeal for economy of travelling expenses has abolished the nine Regional Development Organisations, no doubt to impress our European partners as to our commitment to genuinely endogenous regional development.

We have just over 110 directly elected local authorities, only about 40 of which have any significant functions. The Progressive Democrats, through their Deputy Leader, Mr Michael Keating, not to be outdone in narrowing the base of representative democracy, in May 1988 proposed to reduce the 110 plus to 10. For comparison, the lowest tier of local authorities in France, the *communes*, number 36,000; in the Federal Republic of Germany the *gemeinde* number over 8,000. In smaller countries, Sweden has just over 300 local authorities and Denmark, closest to us in size and population, has almost 300; in both countries the local authorities play a very large part in government. They are, of course, all out of step except our Johnny.

One of the striking features of independent Ireland has been the steady slaughter of local authorities, the reducing of their role, and the marginalisation of local representatives. As one can see from the foregoing, the appetite grows by what it feeds on. For the time being at least our *parliamentary* democracy may be just neglected but is not under serious threat; but the other side of the democratic coin, our *local* democracy, is being steadily destroyed. Policy? Or carelessness?

IV

No thought seems to be given to the price to be paid for the neglect of the comprehensive care and development of our democracy, to

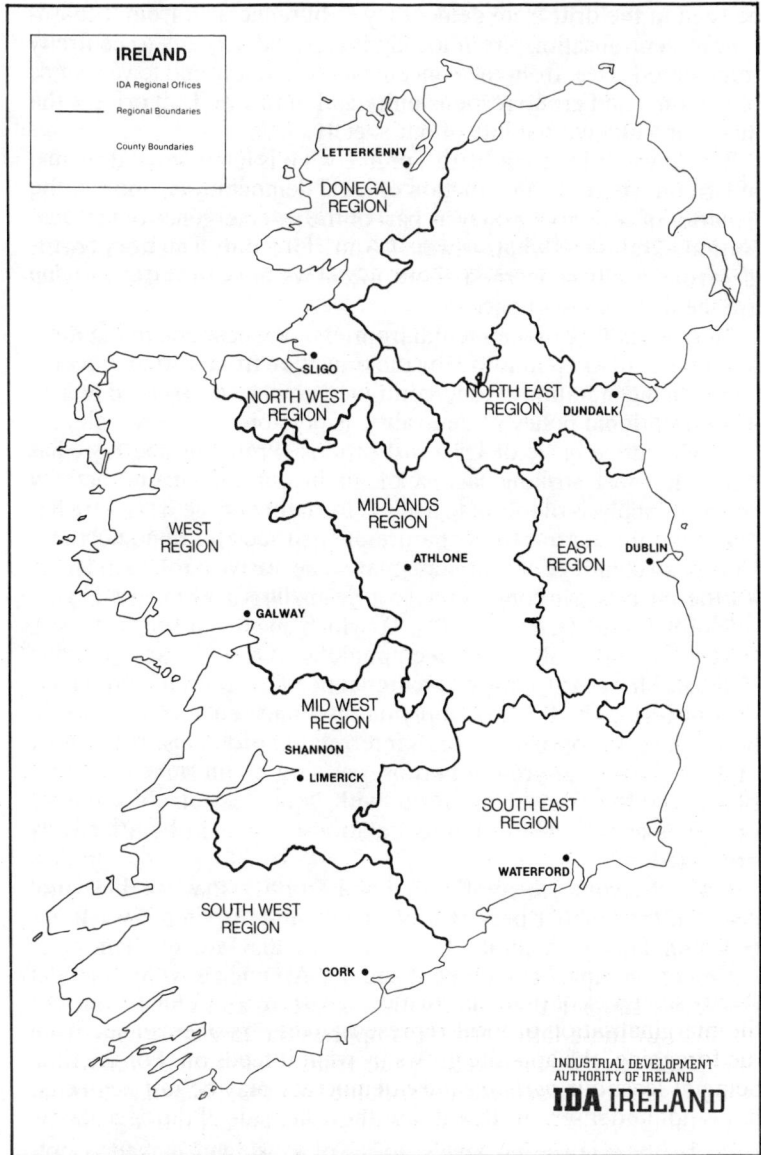

See page 34. Ireland's nine development regions. (Map courtesy of IDA).

be seen in the drift from democracy to bureaucracy, from localisation to centralisation, from locally integrated services to centrally fragmented ones, from the concentration in fewer and fewer hands of personal and group responsibility and initiative.That price is the increasing ungovernability of our society.

The key word there is 'drift', unlike what is happening, it seems, in Britain where the destruction of local democracy is, apparently, a matter of conscious policy as part of the re-emergence of the Two Nations. But is this what *we* want? And, if it is only a matter of drift, is anyone really concerned about *where* we are drifting to or *what* are the likely consequences?

Here is another of our mental frontiers – the easy and thoughtless acceptance of drift, followed by the transition from drift to practice, and then the mutation of long-continued practice into settled policy. 'Our traditional policy of neutrality' is possibly a fair example. As that perceptive critic of Irish institutions, Professor Joe Lee, has said 'the most striking lacuna of all in our intellectual activity concerns analysis of the state itself. The nature of the Irish state has become quite central to the nature of Irish society. In no northern European country does the state play so pervasive a role. And in no northern European country has so little analysis been devoted to the role of the state' (*loc. cit.* p. 92). To which one might add that much of such limited analysis has been muddled. Or, to borrow a saying of Hugh Munro's, we have 'a national need to see things crooked'. Part of this is the habit of applying disconnected *a priori* slogans, however inappropriate, to real, interrelated problems. If we think of the state for our present purposes as a set of interrelated institutions, we find ourselves faced with some extremely complex problems as to how those inter-relationships might be effectively organised.

Here we come to another mental frontier that we have not crossed, the frontier between the simple and the simplified. It is a common fallacy to think that structures that are in themselves extremely complex can be kept simple. An engine without a gear change is simpler than one with a gearbox and clutch, but the addition of these latter greatly simplifies the task of driving from one place to another, because the transmission of power to the wheels can be more closely related to the changing terrain. Something similar is true of single organisations. A rational hierarchy of sub-systems and levels does not look, and indeed is not, simple but it greatly *simplifies* the delivery of services and the supervision of staff as well as, in particular, management, co-ordination, planning and command. On the other hand a 'flat' organisation is clearly simple but remains limited to simple tasks, and an unsystematic simplicity of such bodies is a recipe for chaos. This is the elementary case for careful organisation which makes possible the move from the simple through the complex to the simplified.

If one scrutinises most Irish public organisations severally and collectively one finds ample evidence that this transition from the complex to the simplified – which is the heart of good administration – has not been made. Attempts to achieve this on an ad hoc and piecemeal basis merely compound the confusion. To attempt to simplify a single service without adequate regard for the effects on related services can increase, not reduce, complexity. It is now widely recognised – though the news has apparently not yet reached this country – that to concentrate at the centre the management of a widespread service makes for fragmentation and disorder at the periphery; somehow a moving balance has to be struck appropriate to the several levels involved.

It is a big part of good management so to organise as to get as many decisions taken within broad rules as low in the organisation as possible. Hence, a hierarchy of decisions being siphoned off at various levels of the organisation, ranging from the delivery of straightforward services 'on the ground', through middle levels for intermediate decisions, to major decisions about finance and legislation 'in the heights'.

But decisions are by no means uniform within the hierarchical levels of different organisations. They vary in the way problems present themselves, in who is immediately affected, and how, in the intensity of their impacts, in the skills they require. That is to say that decision-making organisations although hierarchically organised may require totally different decision-making structures depending on the nature of the decisions to be taken in each. The Fine Gael health document, already cited, gives a neat example of how to confuse this point. In its third page it says the single Bord Sláinte it proposes would function 'in a similar manner to Telecom Éireann and An Post'. Fair enough in relation to the parent government department; but in relation to 'customers', to whom it would present 'a streamlined and integrated organisation on a country-wide basis', the difference in front-line decision-making could hardly be greater. Decisions by a telephone maintenance man or a sub-postmistress differ in kind from those of a doctor: there what may be at stake may be suffering or death, the difference between impersonal technology and intensely personal services. Similar considerations apply to welfare services of various kinds. This point, that effective social services require intensive personal consideration and extensive co-ordination through local discretion, decision-making and accountability given the issues at stake, was one determinant of the massive Danish structural reform referred to below. This is almost certainly the headline for the impending major transition of modern democracy, from Welfare State to Welfare Society.

Where there are extensive services there is not only this hierarchy of decision-making and service but also a hierarchy of territory where the operations take place, usually a relatively small area where the services are thick on the ground and, as the services become more rarified, the area of service aggregating an increasing number of such areas. In this way the hierarchy of decision-making can be matched to the hierarchy of territory. There will be a place for everything and everything will be in place.

Most public institutions impinge on one another, either for co-operation or frustration or a bit of both. As we have seen, very large resources of men and money are bound up in these institutions and there is a clear need to get better returns from these resources. A significant contributor to this is the right use of territory to marry the decisions and services to the place and match their respective hierarchies: this facilitates communication between the various bodies at each level and thus joint or co-operative decision making. It has been said that the crucial contribution to telecommunications was not so much the invention of the telephone as the telephone exchange, an insight that has not penetrated the organisation of Irish government. Effective 'exchanges', or cross-over points and centres of decision, are needed at the various levels of the organisational and territorial hierarchies, and at each of those, provision for democratic representation and participation, so that the integrating forces for genuine co-operative thinking and action will be strengthened and there will evolve appropriate levels of genuinely representative mini-government, growing at each level from the local community up, and culminating in the European one. As a matter of history and of empirical fact there are about four of these territorial units in use within this country ranging from the sub-county district, through the county, the region and the State as a whole. But when we look at how the various public bodies use those territories we find virtually nothing in common – kinds of services, degrees of managerial discretion, local accountability and, above all, areas of operation – all contributing to *dis*organisation.

Under the driving force of the late Dr Tom Walsh we tried, in *Towards a New Democracy?* (pp. 65-79), to define institutional roles at each of these levels and to link each level with democratic representation. Briefly, one can think of the sub-county district as the area for the delivery of the personal and community services; of the county for the delivery of those services requiring an intermediate level of technology; of the region for hi-tech delivery and for co-ordination, planning and development; and the State for nation-wide services such as central taxation, defence, foreign affairs.

In a nutshell, this is a scheme for mobilising our resources, applying them to best effect, and for rehabilitating our democracy.

V

Consciously or not, we are engaged in the total reversal of the current that flows in the successful countries of Europe, from bureaucracy to democracy, from centralisation to localisation, from central fragmentation to local integration, from the building up of personal and group responsibility and initiative, to increasing governability.

These are big claims and there is no space here to document them in full or even adequately. But let three examples try to illustrate the points made. The comparison is with the response of Danish government as compared to that of Irish government to three almost identical challenges. Why Denmark? Because of all our European partners its major differences from Ireland are fewer. Of course, it is economically a much more successful society and it is an advanced social democracy; but the scale of operations is not so different from our own and there is much to learn there in relation to economic, social and, I believe, political development that would help us to tackle our own problems. The population is somewhat bigger (5.1m as against 3.6m) but the area is smaller (43,000 sq. km as against 70,000). The gross domestic product per head in 1986 was $13,033 as against $6,899, making it about the best off of the European Community countries as against Ireland's ranking of ninth. There are a large number of parties in the Danish parliament and the government is normally a coalition, sometimes leaning to the Left, sometimes to the Right.

The Danes had a tax revolt in the late 1960s, a surprising out break of public irresponsibility in so well developed a social democracy. The remedy adopted was not to treat the public as naughty children whose foibles had to be fobbed off nor, as we have been considering, an excuse for a further tightening of the centralising screw; quite the contrary. The policy adopted was to treat the public as fully grown adults entitled to respect and shared responsibility. Hence, during the 1970s, there was undertaken a massive redistribution of responsibilities from central government to nearly 300 reformed local authorities exercising a wide range of functions and a wide degree of discretion (Mikkelsen). Startlingly wide by our standards. The system adopted was a two-tier one. Each of the 275 authorities in the lower tier was based on a town and its hinterland, having a typical population of some 15,000. The higher tier consists of 14 counties. In addition there are the two major municipalities of Copenhagen and Fredriksberg. To these authorities was steadily transferred over the ten years 1970 to 1980 about 70% of the total business of Danish government. This move to genuine public participation on the one hand and, on the other, the corresponding slimming down of central government (Bogason, pp. 136-7) concentrated the central energies on overall problems. The major transfer of responsibilities, as events showed, heightened the public sense of democratic responsibility and, with it, of consensus. So, when a financial crisis struck in the early 1980s there was provided that essential room for manoeuvre by central government that in Ireland was apparently absent.

The second example illustrates this. In the late 1970s and early 1980s most of the members of the OECD responded to world economic disturbances by running budgetary deficits. According to the OECD Danish survey (1987a, p. 54) not many of them tackled the resulting problems as effectively as did Denmark. Certainly Ireland did not as the following figures show:

BUDGETARY DEFICITS AS % OF GDP (DENMARK), GNP (IRELAND) 1981-1988

	1981	1982	1983	1984	1985	1986	1987	1988 (est.)
Denmark	−7.2	−9.1	−7.0	−4.1	−1.8	+3.1	+0.2	−1.2
Ireland	−7.4	−7.9	−7.1	−7.1	−8.4	−8.6	−6.8	−6.3

Sources: Denmark: OECD, 1984, p. 9; 1987a, p. 9; Danish Embassy, Dublin.
   Ireland: *Budget, 1988*, p. 100.

The figures are not strictly comparable but the trends are clear enough. They show the difference in decisiveness between a government conscious of the support of responsible public opinion and a government slowly and tentatively discovering since 1987 that a consensus for responsibility may possibly be there for the evoking. The point here is not whether, on *economic* grounds, either government was correct in hastening quickly or slowly in correcting its deficit but that on *political* grounds the Danish government enjoyed the freedom to take decisive action.

The moral of this would seem to be that not only is it the logic of a democratic society that in major matters at least the people are to be trusted but also that, perhaps incoherently, they are seeking means of expressing their capacity for responsibility. These may be commonplace thoughts in many democracies, but not in Ireland.

The third example relates to the adoption of the Single European Act which provides for a European Community-wide market by 1992. This was the product of long gestation and of a difficult birth. The Danish government, in the conduct of Community negotiations, is subject to the firm supervision of a parliamentary committee. The Committee, in the negotiations on what was to become the Single European Act, laid down conditions that Denmark's 11 European partners, including Ireland, were not prepared to accept and the Danish government, faced with the choice of 'sign or – '

appealed to the Danish people by referendum against the parliamentary restriction on their freedom to sign. The referendum was held in February, 1986, and endorsed the proposals for the Single European Act. In consequence, the Danish parliament was the first of the Twelve to ratify the treaty in May, 1986. The Treaty was to take effect from 1 January 1987.

The Irish government, on the other hand, had no such restrictions placed on it, in the negotiations or in the signing, Ireland, unlike Denmark, being such a committed European! Everything seemed so simple that, notwithstanding some indication that the ratification of the Treaty might be challenged in the Courts on constitutional grounds, the proposal to ratify the Treaty was not put to the Dáil until close to the end of 1986, and was submitted for the President's signature between 23 and 25 December, that is, about one week before the Single European Act was due to come into effect. A tight squeeze; but the Bill was at once challenged in the Courts by Mr Raymond Crotty and the starting date planned for the Treaty came and went (Crotty, ch. 5). In April 1987 the Supreme Court ruled that the ratification *was* unconstitutional. This meant that the Constitution had to be amended and the amendment confirmed by referendum. This process was not completed until May, 1987 and Ireland, last of the Twelve and the only one not to make the 31 December 1986 deadline, finally ratified the Treaty. As a consequence the coming into force of the Treaty was delayed six months to 1 July 1987.

This shows, yet again, the difference in style between the two governments and the decisiveness and speed with which problems are tackled and settled in Denmark. Whereas, in Ireland, government action is so often deferred usually in the hope that the problems will go away and that decisions and action will be unnecessary. Something rotten in the state of *Denmark*?

Here we see the malaise of government overloaded beyond the capacities of those, politicians and officials, who engage in it. And that malaise itself comes from the indiscriminate catchall nature of Irish government, the iron grip of centralisation on the minds of those engaged in it and the failure, in consequence, to realise the importance of divining the real nature of actual and impending problems and of effective solutions, of defining appropriate roles and degrees of discretion for the individuals and organisations involved.

VI

Because Ireland is small and relatively poor it has not been grasped that Big Government is a major feature of Irish life, not Big Government in any absolute sense but big in comparison to the resources of the country, human and material. We are still trying to run vast modern operations with the management style and authoritarian paternalism of the small, one-man business common two generations ago when the State was set up; but one-man businesses that do not change their style as the business grows end up liquidated or bankrupted, the direction in which we, as stated, have been heading now for half a generation. It is urgently necessary that we begin to think about the needs and structures of a cohesive, convergent democracy relevant to the times.

A widely diffused democracy is, if the comparisons with Denmark are in any way valid, a much more *efficient* form of government than our version of democratic centralism. If so, parliamentary democracy needs to be supplemented by *local* democracy and eschew the bureaucratic mire of democratic centralism. This pinpoints one of the many fallacies about power. The more power is widely divided the greater the total power that can be mobilised in times of stress, as was shown in World War II when the degree of mobilisation for the war effort in Britain was greater than that in Hitler's Germany. And again, we can cite Mr Gorbachev's analysis of the ills of his own country and the sort of diffusion of power he proposes to bring about. Of course Britain, Germany and the Soviet Union are big countries and Ireland is very small; but smallness and scarcity also apply to the very high levels of skill required in the practice of government when the process has become so pervasive and has, as in our case, so manifestly overburdened itself.

I think the crucial concept in any approach to a new democracy is 'responsibility', the opportunities for the exercise of responsibility and self-reliance by mature citizens, to accept that the people of Ireland are, whatever their failings, mostly adults and mostly not children, to be coped with accordingly and above all to be trusted. One of the lessons to be learned since 1987 from the public response to the Fianna Fáil government and its attempts to right the finances was that the assumptions of previous years were wrong. It is *not* the handful of politicians and bureaucrats that have been shown to be the responsible ones; quite the contrary, as posterity burdened by huge debt will clearly see. It is *not* the great mass of the people who have been shown to be irresponsible; quite the contrary. Which is, of course, what democracy is all about: that in the last analysis the people are likely to know best and should be trusted. Democratic government depends, not on the concentration of responsibility in a few hands but, on its wide diffusion amongst the people as a whole. If that is to be for real there needs to be a drastic overhaul of our institutions.

This brings us back to what we have called the Crisis of our Democracy. This crisis, if it is to be coped with effectively, demands not more outmoded hand-to-mouth expedients – still less continued paralysis – but a systemic transformation to match the changes that have been occurring in society. Part of this transformation is the transition, as it has been expressed, from the main source of Big Government, the Welfare State, to the Welfare Society, where 'welfare' incorporates not only social welfare but also political welfare, the move from the centralised bureaucracy of the one to the decentralised democracy of the other, as Gunnar Myrdal foresaw a generation ago. This move, if it is to be effective, requires a set of ideas about the system of government related to its present state, to its extraordinary pervasiveness and to its likely evolution. As part of this new thinking there has to be development of thought about the requirements of democracy in our times. Just as the early and the middle years of this century saw the concentration of many of the best minds on, first, economic development and, then, on social development, so also the last years of the century call for the mobilisation and application of intelligence to the next stage on the road, the problems of political development. This requires the adaptation of our inherited set of democratic institutions to an unprecedented set of conditions, some emerged, some emerging. For this new world there is needed not just the dusting down of ideas inherited from the 18th and 19th centuries but ideas that are solutions to the new problems. At the core of these problems, Irish experience would suggest, is the issue of the distribution of responsibilities in society. Let no one be under any illusion about the difficulties of the task ahead and of the deadweight of that inertia that blocks progress in tackling our problems.

That task is radical institutional change. There may be, perhaps, some memory of the brave words of the last coalition government about engaging in substantial devolution of powers to local authorities and some people will have sensed the intense opposition of the Dublin bureaucracy to this. So, in the end, just one function was devolved. The Department of Agriculture, after, it is said, considerable and anxious heart-searching, yielded to county councils the heavy responsibility of licensing dogs under the Control of Dogs Act, 1986! The centralising forces in Ireland, those official forces that diminish personal and group responsibility, are so strong that a policy to enlarge responsibility will not be allowed to implement itself. For that there is required the mobilisation of will, intelligence and energy for the task of levelling, without derogation, the internal frontiers of the mind.

REFERENCES

AYD 1988 – *Administration Yearbook and Diary*, Dublin, IPA, 1988.

Bairoch, P & Lévy-Leboyer, M (eds), *Disparities in Economic Development since the Industrial Revolution*, London: Macmillan, 1981.

Bogason, P, 'Denmark' in Rowat, D C (ed), *Public Administration in Developed Democracies*, New York & Basel: Dekker, 1988.

Crotty, R, *A Radical's Response*, Dublin: Poolbeg, 1988.

Finance, Dept. of, *Budget, 1988*, Dublin: Stationery Office, 1988.

Fine Gael: *The New Politics*, Dublin: May, 1988.

—*A Better Health Service*, do, June, 1988.

Gorbachev, M, *Perestroika*, London: Collins, 1987.

Health, Dept of, *Health – The Wider Dimension*, Dublin: August, 1986.

Humphreys, P C, *Public Service Employment*, Dublin: IPA, 1983.

Lee, J J, 'Centralisation & Community' in Lee, J J (ed), *Ireland: Towards a Sense of Place*, Cork: University College, 1985.

Mikkelsen, P, *Public Sector Reforms in Denmark*, Copenhagen: AKF, 1982.

Mydral, G, *Beyond the Welfare State*, London: Duckworth, 1960.

OECD: 1981: *Welfare State in Crisis*, Paris: 1981.

       1982: *Employment in the Public Sector*, 1982.

       1984: *Economic Survey: Denmark,* 1984

       1986: *National Accounts, 1960-84*, Vol 1, 1986.

       1987a: *Economic Survey: Denmark*, 1987.

       1987b: *Economic Survey: Ireland*, 1987.

Russell, G W, *The National being*, Dublin: reprinted Irish Academic Press, 1982.

Rose, R *et al*, *Public Employment in Western Europe*, Cambridge: University Press, 1985.

Taxation, Commission on, *Reports I-V*, Dublin: Stationery Office, 1982-85.

Walsh, T *et al, Towards a New Democracy?* Dublin: IPA, 1985.

Whitaker, T K, *Interests*, Dublin: IPA, 1983.

Europe of The Regions

JOHN HUME

Given our island setting, our history of colonisation and our wounds of division it is understandable that so much of our political thought and approach should hinge on the nation state. The facts that the South gained independence only this century, that it had to create a stable state out of unstable beginnings and that it had to develop an economy which had little industrial infrastructure of significance have all ensured that the main focus of political and economic development would be on the 26-county context. The impact of partition, circumstances in the North and the role of Britain in that regard ensured that much of external or foreign affairs activity would relate more to the national question and less to international questions.

It is common for post-independence or post-revolution states to seek to emphasise their singularity. Such practice is necessary to justify and fulfil the effort made to secure change. A new order or a sense of it must be established but it generally must carry ancient, historic or traditional cultural associations to assert its legitimacy. Such themes are prevalent today in much of the talk about the 'new Europe', including my own! These traits were evident in the post-independence 26-counties (they were to be found in the Unionist North too). Indeed identifying gaps in this regard in the circumscribed post-independence arrangements and then meeting those needs without destabilising anything became part of Fianna Fáil's political mission in the aftermath of the civil war.

Now over half-a-century old, the 1937 Constitution, for instance, embodies much of that spirit. It asserts a historic identity of the Irish nation, pronounces rights of the citizen and identifies the democratic processes of the state. In proclaiming particular social and cultural values it conveys the urge for distinctiveness in post-independence communities which would have been more marked in the Irish context by partition and the ongoing British dimension. It has perhaps served more as a badge for particular values than as a shield for particular rights.

One example of this is the provision for the Irish language. Notwithstanding the commitments made in the constitution, the interest of government, the work of schools and the efforts of Irish language enthusiasts, the hopes for the language have not been fulfilled. I do not intend to get into the argument about whether the efforts on behalf of the language were too defensive or not sufficiently promotional. But I do believe that the efforts to protect or promote the language were in a mainly insular context ensuring that in the narrow ground of a developing Ireland it would continue to lose out to the more international English. In this context the Irish language was bound to receive dubious priority by many uncertain about its purpose or value in modern times.

I strongly believe that it is in the broader European context that the Irish language could find the recognition of its real linguistic significance and cultural value. There it can be valued with other lesser used, minority or regional languages or dialects in a Europe which wants to protect the diversity of its culture. With other such languages it can find itself a lobby and an approach which can ensure not just protective measures marking their traditional significance but which will allow these languages beneficial access to all the advances in information technology. In this setting too it will be freed from the inhibitions about being perceived to be narrow or anti-British which have made for reticence and reserve on the part of some people who have a genuine personal attachment to the language.

Greater Europeanisation providing the context for refreshing the position of the Irish language is one possible paradox of European development which I will return to later. I would also like to identify another such possible paradox. That is the potential for greater decentralisation or regionalisation in Ireland against the background of greater European co-operation and co-ordination. Rather than presenting any real threat of a centralised Europe run by Brussels, the single Europe could be the catalyst for a more comprehensive realignment of power and co-operation in Europe spanning European Community structures, national government, and the regions. In so doing it can give an impetus to practical decentralisation not least in Ireland where such a development would release local energies and allow citizens and communities to participate in the realization of economic and social objectives for their region. It is not syncretistic to suggest that European developments could yield such apparently contra-tractory power shifts.

It is not just the changes in political structures involved in creating the single Europe which will provide a background which can induce such a trend. The march of technology – both information and production – is changing the economic landscape and challenges many of the nostrums of social and economic policy to date. Unfortunately, the Right in Europe seem to have tumbled to the impact of such developments in a more alert way than the Left. Some on the Left remain preoccupied with the traditional classist and labourist approach which is less relevant in the emerging post-industrial Europe and whose primacy in contemporary circumstances will ossify the politics of the Left. In the main the Left in these islands has tended to cling on to the more statist approach to social and economic planning. But realignment is clearly under way on these issues among the new Left. The realisation is sinking in that the support for Social Democratic policies of statist development and intervention in the aftermath of World War II was a response to the devastation then apparent and the sense of national cohesion created by war and not a popular confirmation of those timely strategies as the eternal and exclusive tools of democratic socialism.

While the South has never elected a democratic socialist government much of its economic development has relied on a statist approach. Just as the Second World War created the need for state led reconstruction in other countries, the non-industrial South needed state-led construction which non-Left parties were happy to embrace out of necessity and in line with the post-independence syndrome which can see statism as an expression of nationalism. In such processes states, including the Republic, were assimilating the predominant industrial and market structures of the time which are now being termed as 'Fordism'. This whole burden of Ireland's approach to development has to be re-evaluated in the midst of transforming international economic structures. A personal hope would be that this will present an opportunity for the Left to emerge much more influentially than hitherto. The fear is real that the Right are stealing the advance in prescribing blanket privatisation and de-regulation as the answer to the obsolescence of statism while the Left fail to emerge with more appropriate and diverse forms of socialisation as a possible strategy.

The emergence of policies in this regard will interact heavily with trends for de-centralisation. They will obviously also be linked strongly to European economic co-ordination. We have already seen the lines of a European Social debate emerge between Margaret Thatcher and Jacques Delors. This argument is now on the issue of regulation in Europe, is extending to issues of interventionism and will reach into broader issues about the role and practice of the public sector as a whole. What happens in such arguments on the European level will directly shape our economic environment to a greater or lesser extent.

Politicians must be alert to the significance of all these matters. Just as business and labour is being urged to realise the opportunities and challenges of the internal market, so too must Ireland's representatives identify the ground shifts and nuances of the macro-economics of the Single Europe. Ireland cannot afford passivity in the politics of the Single Europe any more than it can afford it in the business of the Single Market.

Some might be sceptical of my hopes for a new and refreshing setting for Irish language policy in a Europe grappling with large-scale political issues and handling diverse economic problems. They might even question whether, when I have identified what the Americans call 'megatrends' relating to macro-economic and social processes, I can actually argue that the Irish language is worth attending to.

It is my contention that the issue of the preservation and development of minority cultures in Europe poses the fundamental question 'what sort of Europe do we want?' I doubt if anyone in Europe wants the centralized, bureaucratic Europe with identikit citizens (presumably sharing a homogenized culture) about which Mrs Thatcher has been at pains to scare-monger. But do we want a Europe of the nation-states à la De Gaulle as she does? Surely it will be highly centralized and uniform and will provide a growing hold on the cultural sector of the market economy deriving its profit from mass production or the levelling of cultural values? Or do we want a Europe which is much more comprehensive in its unity and which values its regional and cultural diversity while working to provide for a convergence of living standards? My choice is clearly for the latter. Such a unity in diversity would help to fulfil the deepest ideals of the founding fathers of the European Community by removing one of the major causes of human conflict – the non-recognition, undervaluing, neglect and even elimination of the identity of peoples.

The fact that there are so many regional and minority languages and cultures in Western Europe makes their position an unavoidable question for those shaping European policies. Not an inconsiderable amount of time has been devoted to their position by the European Parliament following an initial resolution by myself which led to the Arfé report. An inter-group has been formed comprising representatives from all the political groups in the Parliament. The Intergroup has had some promising meetings with the Commission to date. The energy and enthusiasm which different MEPs are bringing to bear on this issue, and the appreciation and interest they show for minority languages and cultures other than their own, have served to convince me that Europe provides a beneficent environment for lesser used languages such as Irish.

It is a familiar syndrome that rights have best been identified in the context of international fora rather than in the national context where they have often been victims of oversight or neglectful expedience until given international recognition. Europe holds out that prospect for its lesser-used cultures and languages.

In Ireland we tend to think of the continent in terms of a number of fairly homogeneous cultural blocs – German, French, Italian,

Spanish etc. We often fail to realise the extent of the linguistic and cultural diversity that still exists within the borders of the dominant languages. There are over twenty minority languages in Western Europe, the majority of them inside the EC. There are no absolutely reliable statistics but the estimates have them spoken by some twenty million people. Also very important dialectical variations exist in the major languages. Alongside standard French, German, Italian and so on, many regional and local dialects exist which can differ very substantially from the standard language. This is especially true of Italy, Germany and Belgium. Again definitive statistics are hard to come by but over 70 million people are involved. Add to all this the millions of immigrants in the EC who speak non-EC languages.

The fact is that somewhere over a third of the European Community's inhabitants practise to a greater or lesser degree some form of bilingualism or diglossia. A survey of this scene confirms that the problems caused in the Gaeltacht by industrialisation, tourism, emigration and the influx of English-speakers are not unique to Ireland. The debate on the role of television and radio in relation to minority languages and the issues involved in education through such languages are apparent in Scotland, Wales, Brittany, the Basque region, Friesland, Flanders, Catalonia, Corsica, Sardinia and elsewhere. Such issues in Ireland therefore have a practical European dimension. Government agencies and voluntary organisations working for the Irish language can learn from the experience, good and bad, of other linguistic groups. Similarly those other groups can learn from the experience in Ireland.

One of my aims in bringing forward this issue in the European Parliament was to provide properly for increasing mutual awareness, contact and co-operation between Europe's lesser used cultures. The European Bureau on Lesser Used Languages is now an important instrument in that regard. By identifying and working together, people using these cultures can provide more than mutual encouragement. In the European context they can ally to ensure better recognition and more supportive policy treatment than has been possible in the individual state setting. I have already witnessed the excitement and innovation of users of minority cultures as they get involved in this European network. They find that they can come out from under the shadow of the dominant culture in their state. They have a new synergy and are identifying in a more self-assured way the social, economic, technological and cultural dimensions of late 20th Century Europe which must be addressed and harnessed if we are to ensure that distinctive regional groups will survive in the Europe of the 21st century. Those involved have a renewed confidence that regional cultures and languages are no longer a peripheral affair or an anachronistic exception in a Europe bent on centralisation and uniformitisation.

The mobilisation to date in the European Parliament and the Commission's sympathetic responses indicate that the lesser-used cultures can make themselves into an effective European lobby. Given the European dimension which will exist to markets, the media and new technology, it is important that people using these cultures can address issues at the European level. It is also vital if we are to ensure a truly diverse Europe with a symphonic culture.

In all this there are obvious and powerful regional dimensions. Many of the issues are precisely the same as those involved in the case for more effective regional policy in Europe. If we are to protect the identities of our regions and promote their living standards then we must have policy provision and instruments of intervention which allow for the application of appropriate programmes to given regions. Effective regional policy and well-suited programmes cannot simply be ordained by Brussels or properly organised by national governments. We require much more regional autonomy in designing, securing and implementing development programmes. The Republic of Ireland is in many ways one of the most centralised states in Europe. As already stated, that is hardly surprising given the context of its birth and development. The fact that this is understandable, and has perhaps been inevitable for a variety of reasons, does not of itself commend continuing with such a centralised arrangement.

In 1987 I tabled a 'Report on the Regional Problems of Ireland' to the European Parliament. With the benefit of submissions from various groups and agencies and the observations of MEPs in the South, this report identified the regional dimensions to problems of socio-economic underdevelopment in Ireland. It highlighted that while different strengths and weaknesses exist in different regions there is no coherently regionalised development strategy in operation. In terms of EC Funds Ireland has been treated to date as one region and all applications and allocations go and come through the central Department of Finance. When I was compiling my report I came across several instances of frustration in given regions because these procedures failed to facilitate, and indeed militated against, given proposals.

Even if the arrangements which have existed to date could be justified – and there are arguments to be heard along that line – the fact is that the re-organisation of the European Structural Funds and the changes inherent in the Single Europe, require that they change.

A much larger proportion of European funding than hitherto is to be allocated to the Regional Development Fund and the Social Fund. This in turn is being concentrated on designated super-priority regions including the island of Ireland. If the funding and programmes available under these arrangements are to be fully harnessed then the regions must be enabled and challenged to bring forward programmes of their own which meet particular social, environmental, economic and cultural conditions in their region. For regional energies to be so released requires that those in the regions enjoy a much more direct interface with those coordinating European programmes.

It is also important to note that in Europe we still only have Regional Funds. We do not yet have coherent regional policy. Both as an Irish representative and as a member of the European Parliament's Socialist Group, I see the need for a comprehensive regional policy including intervention arrangements. One of the aims of the Treaty of Rome was to provide for a convergence of living standards among the regions of Europe. Less developed and peripheral regions need measures of positive assistance and intervention if they are not to fall critically behind the developed centres of Europe. A single European Market offering only a vast free market without such distributive intervention could compound relative underdevelopment in Irish regions. The case for such regional policy instruments is made compelling by the prospect of a single market. Ireland will need such processes but will not be in the best position to argue this case powerfully if it is not already adapting to more regionalised structures itself.

It is necessary to identify the need for more than a regional policy which will aid particular regions in important respects such as training, technology, communications, transport etc. We must also seek to ensure that all European policy planning is sensitive to regional disparity and includes mechanisms to ensure that policies do not sponsor widening divergence between regions. In Agriculture, for example, the prevalent theme in Europe is the need to curb price support and development assistance as a means of reducing surpluses and expenditure. The success of the Common Agricultural Policy in turning a Europe of food shortages into one of surplus has clearly gone into the realm of excess in many respects such as over-production, over-intensification of farming methods and damage to the rural environment. The expansion of the Community bringing in more Mediterranean countries has further widened its agricultural diversity and put more pressure on the CAP as we have known it.

The push is now being made for a common curb in agricultural policy – quotas and price curbs are part of this. In Ireland the reflex has tended to be opposition to such restraint and a defence of existing mechanisms. The reasons for this are legitimate given that we are much more agriculturally dependent than other countries, that we are well below the community average for development and productivity, have been developing later than other members and our land and climate give us a much more limited ability to diversify production than other countries. Is all this enough to justify Europe continuing with existing CAP arrangements? The reasons for wanting to restrain European agricultural policy are also legitimate. Surely blanket restraint is not the answer but rather restructuring using regionalisation.

A Regionalised Agricultural Policy rather than the Common one we have known can be structured to guarantee Europe the food production which it needs, minimising excess while ensuring that regions which are, economically and socially, heavily-dependent on agriculture or do have little facility for diversification can continue with their agricultural and food production development.

Regionalisation, therefore, is crucial to ensuring balanced and fair development in the Single Europe. Without it we will have much more of the 'Rich Man's Club' syndrome. The European Commission, the Greek EC Presidency of the latter half of 1988, some other member governments and European Parliament political groups have emphasised the need for a 'Social Europe' in the Single Europe. We must be careful, however, not to focus solely on pandemic regulations or intervention facilities as our means of ensuring that all share in the benefits of a single Europe and do not suffer under unmitigated market forces. Regional policy and regionalisation of policy are also essential if we are to have any hope of a common prosperity in a Single Europe.

Just as I have been encouraged by the practical commitment to lesser-used cultures, I have noted the groundswell in Europe for more regional autonomy. This in many ways reflects a re-evaluation of the trends of urbanisation, industrialisation and standardisation which predominated in Europe until more recent years. In some cases a 'neo-romanticism' has emerged in people's thinking where they no longer spurn, as their parents and grandparents had been encouraged to do, traditions of the past, the rural ethos or regional diversity. There is a more apparent willingness to acknowledge provincial and rural origins and the desire for more regionally and locally based processes is in the ascendant. This mood has been harnessed by some of the Green parties in Europe and is being reflected increasingly in Social Democratic Parties. Already some states in the Community – but certainly not the UK – have over recent years been making some moves or gestures towards decentralisation and regionalisation.

The process of decentralisation and the case for it is bound up with the changes in technology and economic processes which I identified earlier. Political arrangements, social attitudes and the public sector have reflected the patterns of industrial economic culture in a kaleidoscopic effect. We are now moving into a post-industrial or more aptly the 'Post Fordist' era and this poses questions for social and political processes. The kaleidoscope is shaking, patterns will be changing, we must plan accordingly.

If we identify industrialism in this century as 'Fordism' we can see that its features were assimilated into political culture. Centred on mass production it produced standard products for the mass market relying on well defined national markets, using routinised or mechanised task processes and flowlines, and relying on the directions and task refinement of powerful management. The 'scientific management' which it sponsored brought various behavioural and organisational theories which were readily applied in other facets of life. The emphasis on scale, on production, on uniformity and standardisation requiring mass consumption, were all reflected in the statist approach to economic development and social services. The fact is that new technology is transforming our industrial culture; production methods are much more flexible, less labour intensive and the whole process is much more market-sensitive. We have been witnessing the mass market breaking up into numerous segments according to age, income group, style, region etc. The old identifiable singular national markets are gone or going. The market is increasingly diverse requiring versatility of production and service. The mushrooming of the service sector is another symptom of this trend.

The challenge now faces us as to how we set about shaping the social and political fall-out from this in terms of its potential effects on employment levels and structures, how we provide public services and how we induce these developments into democratic processes. The macro-context of these trends means that this task cannot be tackled practically in the nation-state context alone.

It has long been perplexing to me why so many on the Left in these islands have been so resistant to providing greater European integration. More recently, however, there has at last been a growing understanding that the Left cannot hope to shape economic and social circumstances effectively if there are no political instruments at the European level. The task is to democratise these instruments by ensuring that European power structures no longer centre so heavily on the national governments through the Council of Ministers. Such democratisation clearly requires greater integration at certain functional levels. It is wrong to dismiss such functional integration as some move towards remote centralisation. When the Community is criticised for being bureaucratic or the European Parliament for being a talking-shop, the real issue that such critics are raising is not the European ideal but the inappropriate nature of existing arrangements in present circumstances. The Single European Act – not perfect by any means – at least provides for progressive development in European political structures. The job now is not to passively endorse the Single European Act or to lament it but to activate the new politics which it can offer.

Margaret Thatcher was not completely off the mark in her objections to Jacques Delors' prospectus for the Single Europe. In as far as she identified the potential for a more socialist spin to be put on economics if we pursue a Single Europe, as opposed to just a Common Free Market or anchoring everything on nation state governments, she is right.

But the trends in economic processes not only necessitate democratic politicisation at the macro-level, they also facilitate and require it at the regional and local level. I have already stressed the need for regionalisation in our political and economic development approaches. If we look at the changes in industrial trends we see that while some firms are centralising some functions because of levels of capital investment involved and processing efficiency, they are also displaying much more decentralisation in others for reasons of market responsiveness, personnel motivation, distributive efficiency etc. There is much more sub-contracting by big firms now than used to be the case; and this trend will continue as it provides the core firm with more flexibility in its own organisation, and relieves it of detailed incidental functional management allowing greater concentration on strategic planning and design etc. Modern transport and information technology assists all this.

A look at the changes under way in broadcasting should also convey some impression of this trend. We have satellite broadcasting on a continental and intercontinental scale, the growth of local cable companies, the potential for much more local broadcasting (not only in radio), narrowcasting, teletext services, video, more national broadcasting services providing much more minority interest broadcasting etc. This all marks a major growth from the generic programming of the national broadcasting service and we are provided with the potential for reaching larger mass audiences at one level but much more diverse and locally produced programming at another. The pattern is one of diffusion in broadcast production and diversification of audience at diverging levels from the old singular national set-up.

Political democracy and public services have to come to terms with this same ground-shift and perhaps similarly evolve from statism. Thatcherism in Britain and some New-Rightists in Ireland advocate privatisation, deregulation and a receding public sector as the response to this need; and their views are enjoying some ascendancy. Those of us who see the need for public services and redistributive economics (including market intervention) have to leapfrog their approach. This means overhauling the public sector so that it can respond to people better as consumers as well as citizens. It means providing for choice and flexibility as part of modern efficiency. It means allowing for more decentralisation and personnel motivation within public services. We must emphasise that only such an approach can offer people true choice with real opportunity whereas the prescription of the Rightists will confer only select opportunity, privilege rather than choice and greater social disparity.

Decentralisation and regionalisation have a vital part to play in this process. Not just decentralising facilities, services or employment but also planning and decision-making. This is all part of democratising social and economic provision

As mentioned, I have experienced the community initiative, enterprise, energy and competence that exists in the regions so much of which goes untapped. I have also continually come across the problems of administrative delays, planning oversights, legislative constipation and inadequate democratic scrutiny that marks centralised state structures. These are not criticisms of those operating inside those structures – after all they complain about the impossibility of carrying properly many of the burdens and expectations placed on them. We no longer need and cannot afford to have our democracy concentrated so heavily at the governmental and parliamentary level. To do so means that our democracy lags behind the issues which face us. It means that we unnecessarily frustrate ideas and development responses, miss opportunities and repress prospects.

Delegative national parliamentary structures emerged in circumstances where the affairs of state were very limited. Social stratification, the absence of mass education, limited access to information, people's occupation in lengthy labour and the reliance on the meeting-place for communication, all required centralism and upwardly delegative structures (i.e. the parliamentary system). But our democracy is now congested with issues and we lumber on with the same process (only with universal franchise) despite social improvement, mass education, the accessibility of information, the reduction in the amount of time spent at work and the advances in telecommunications. These all point to much more participative democratic procedures. Technological and economic trends clearly allow, and in many ways require, that services and their control be much more proximate to their 'market' – in this instance the community or region.

This all suggests greater devolution to the regions while the national fora deal more adequately than presently possible with strategic issues, finance, planning, social security, legislation and international concerns. It is almost laughable that the only prevalent proposal to have parliamentary democracy in these islands catch up with our modern technology and circumstances is to televise parliamentary proceedings. If parties seeking election can use all the technology and sophistication of today in their campaigns, why not the democracy of the country?

Without realigning democracy we cannot properly control or harness the effect of technological advance. We will find the market our ever-more dominant master and never our servant. Employment and contributive economic participation will be increasingly limited to the skilled technologists and marketers, leaving a growing social residue of unemployed, under-employed, under-consuming, under-cultured and alienated.

Only if we remould our democratic procedures can we have any prospect of ensuring that public services have their role protected and made more socially effective as well as operationally efficient, that new technology does not simply reduce industrial pay-rolls but throws open new opportunities to regions and communities (including lesser used cultures in new media facilities), that the macro-environment of European economics is conducive to improved social prosperity and equity and that local development and regional decision-making is more responsive to its communities' needs and ideas.

Some are painting a Panglossian picture of the post-1992 Europe. That is folly. No social progress rolls in on the wheels of inevitability, Martin Luther King once said. Others preach 'doomsday' about our economic circumstances post 1992 and our loss of sovereignty. There is nothing inevitable about these either. Europe's effect on us can depend on how we seek to affect Europeanisation. It depends on whether we are alert to what is really happening and seek to initiate or mitigate potential developments. It requires us to cultivate more integrated political liaisons and partnerships with others in Europe. It also requires that we strengthen the ability of our country to cope with the reality of a post-industrial Europe by re-orientating our political and development processes towards regionalism.

This is the real 'new republicanism' — the development of processes which will allow people to preserve their culture, rights and dignity; to promote their well-being and have a means of controlling the forces which will affect their lives. Rather than being any reversal of the national destiny, this will allow us better to fulfil our potential as a people; to contribute to our world; to rediscover the cultural interaction between Ireland and Europe; to reinvolve ourselves in in political relationships with those on the continental mainland and to enjoy properly the inchoate European outlook and vision which was lost in our oppressive and obsessive relationship with Britain. It maintains the necessary synchrony between the scope of democracy and economic and technological circumstances.

In Ireland, for good reason, we have always tended to concentrate on political, national and constitutional considerations. We have underplayed social, economic, technological and cultural considerations. While we have enjoyed some progress in synthesising these considerations, we must develop this further and absorb the European dimension to all these. On that basis we can provide for a social, regional and Irish dimension to our Europe. It depends on our political vision and will whether we want to make of the single Europe simply a dilution of national sovereignty or a dilation of democracy. The peoples of smaller countries like Ireland, because of the common interests and identification with regions across Europe and within the larger Nation States, will wield a much greater influence in shaping that Europe and in developing their own distinctiveness in a Europe of the Regions rather than in a Europe of the Nation States.

Ireland in Europe 1992
Problems and Prospects for
a Mutual Interdependency
MICHAEL D. HIGGINS

Writing at a time when billboards invite one to reflect on the message, 'are you ready for Europe?', or challenged with the image of oneself as an insecure driver at a level crossing as the barrier goes up, one cannot but be struck by the reactionary character of the advertising campaign for the Single Europe of 1992. The suggestion is that one has to wake up or be condemned to an eternal sleep. Rip van Winkle's last chance has come, it seems, for an advance to the modern and the normal.

The similarity with the myth of progress in the nineteenth century is striking. There is a comprehensive, intellectual capitulation to an idea of inescapable progress not rooted in time, or history, or social classes. The idea of a single option for the future, crafted externally to one's present and past experience, assumes the character of a myth. Reading the media hype for the Single Market, the literature of the Cargo Cults floats before my eyes. Listening to the rhetoric, I can recall the recorded speeches of millennial preachers. 'There is but one golden future. Are you ready for it?'

It is not, of course, in the history of ideas, the first transposition of a religious or mythic canopy of symbols to the world of commerce. The much debated connection between the personal values of Calvinism and the rise of a commercial bourgeoisie is but one obvious example. As with all myths, the myth of the Single Europe has produced its unique intolerance. To question something as transcendentally defined as the myth of the Single Europe from the perspective of nationality, history, or, above all, the philosophical tradition of egalitarianism, brings down on one's head the charges of being isolationist, traditionalist, nationalist or even jingoist.

Yet, such an exercise as questioning what values will prevail in the Europe of 1992 is important. Mythic excursions fuelled on fantasy, even if such fantasy is monetarily inspired, can lead to disaster unless hubris is exposed and some element of critical choice made possible. Let us be very clear. The debate in Ireland about Europe 1992 is not about choice. It is about the desirable or undesirable

58

consequences of a state towards which we have drifted. It is not about the consequences of a decision we took in terms of options elicited, compared, evaluated and consciously rejected or accepted. If one needs evidence of this, all one need do is contrast the information campaign prior to the Referendum on the Single European Act with the present advertising campaign. An advertising campaign inevitably distorts and seeks to evade the totality of what it is selling. What is important is the attractive packaging of the perceived fantasy of the new European consumer. Thus emigration, a national problem is translated into a labour mobility problem at European level. Unemployment and poverty, national problems, become problems of adjustment between the regions at European level. The release of market forces is real. The rhetoric of regional and social adjustment, a politically required apologia.

It is appropriate then to tease out some of the assumptions lying beneath such rhetoric.

I: The Dilemma of Regional Policy

It seems to me that there is a major clash between what was seen, up to now as two not easily reconciled sets of aspirations. One set of aspirations was for a market without barriers, the other was for a Europe of productively employed workers. I find it hard to see any attempt at reconciling these aspirations. Certainly, the more explicit references to 'Regional Policy', or 'Cohesion' are there: but they are vague, in sharp contrast to the quantifiable effects of a barrier-free market. The documentation from the Commission is a neat example of this, eg, the Cecchini Report does not explore the ideal of a Europe moving towards equality.[1] It deals with the cost of trade barriers in an economic block in competition with the USA and Japan.

This raises such simple questions as: can Regional policy be an adequate check to the logic of capital investment attracted to the location of greatest profit and least cost? Are we talking of a new form of capitalism that takes the egalitarian aims of social and regional policies as a restraint on itself? Can it achieve such a metamorphosis and yet be an aggressive opponent of the trading blocks of the US and Japan?

In an address to the Socialist Group of the European Parliament in 1987, I addressed such questions at some length. I set out the problem as follows:

---

1. The Cecchini Report deals with the costs of a non-aligned market. Irish parliamentarians have noted the absence of reference to inequality or regional disparity in briefing documentation from the European Community. Reference is rarely made to such publications as exist outside the Commission such as that of Kreble, Owens and Thompson: *Centrality, Periphery and EEC Regional Development*, CAP, 1981.

The concept of *Regional Policy* has assumed a new significance within the European Community with the formal reference to economic and social cohesion in Article 23 of the Single European Act.

This latest reference comes after earlier commitments at the level of the Community's basic documents, many would call them charters, to the elimination of regional imbalances in living standards, productive capacity and social provision.

The Draft Treaty establishing the European Union, in Article 9, declared it to be one of the objectives of the Union to attain 'the progressive elimination of the existing imbalances between the Regions.'

Article 58 expanded in detail on this theme.

The Regional Policy of the Union shall aim at reducing Regional disparities and, in particular, the underdevelopment of the least favoured regions, by injecting new life into those regions so as to ensure their subsequent development and by helping to create the conditions likely to put an end to the excessive concentration of immigration towards certain industrial centres. The Regional Policy of the Union shall, in addition, encourage trans-frontier co-operation and shall comprise:

- the development of a European framework for the Regional Planning Policies pursued by the competent authorities in each Member-State;
- the promotion of investment and infrastructure projects which bring national programmes into the framework of an overall concept;
- the implementation of integrated programmes of the Union on behalf of certain regions, drawn up in collaboration with the representatives of the people concerned and, where possible, the direct allocation of the requisite funds to the regions concerned.

There is therefore, a new formal commitment, preceded by a myriad of aspirational references. There is, too, available to us the realities of actual regional initiatives and transfers and, above all, the human evidence, the economic indicators and the social conditions that we can use to answer such questions as – have the references to Regional Policy constituted an expedient political rhetoric, a cynical sop to soften the inexorable logic of free market competition under conditions of industrial capitalism, a genuinely held but often fallacious expectation that moral concerns can check the cold logic of market location decision-making by firms, many of them transnational?

I raised questions too about the use of the concept, the tool, of Regional Policy within the European Community.

The debate about Regional Policy and Regionalism has a long history but that history has not given *precision* to the concept. Where is the economic theoretical evidence that could show that Regional Policy has impeded, corrected, or undone the inequalities of capital concentration, or the social diseconomies of human agglomerations, created by the *coercion* that capital investment and industrial location represent? Capital decides the location of workers. Workers do not decide the location or forms of usage of capital.

Can it be assumed that the beneficiaries of existing structures of economic production, capital investment with its vicarious relationship to a labour force of ever-increasing unemployment and, in some cases of technological impact, unemployability, have decided to sacrifice their structural benefits in favour of new structures tending towards harmonization in living standards in all Regions of the Community? Have I missed a conversion at the level of capitalist investment decision-making?

These questions cannot be dismissed by pointing to the actual spending of the European Regional Development Fund, that in the period 1975-1986 the ERDC helped 21,500 investment projects with total grant expenditure standing at over 9,000 million ECU or that the Fund's share in the budget of the Community has risen to 8.7% in 1983.

The questions can only be answered by relating such activity and such expenditure to the overall process of the Community and its Member States in economic, social and, indeed, cultural terms. That process has been one of growing inequality, wider gaps in participation, sharper divides in probabilities of being employed, being below the poverty line, being excluded from education, being excluded from full development of personal capacity.

Almost two decades ago, I was writing, with other regionalists, of the case for the concept. We wrote of the case from a 'rights' perspective, some of us. The right of every citizen to participate in growth where it existed or in development potential where it was promised. We were in a minority. The majority wrote of regionalism from the perspectives of undoing diseconomies or of the benefits of infrastructural provision so as to release the productive capacity of factors that were underutilized.

I still read these arguments in a new context where Europe has gone politically to the Right and where the most dated liberal market theories are enjoying a revival. They seem hollow as political strategies. My colleagues take refuge in the suggestion that they were contributions on the *technical* aspects of planning. But what is happening to planning if it is ever removed from its political framework? I respond. The apolitical regionalists continue hoping and writing that those who benefit from the present mobility of factors of production, from the disestablishment of State initiatives in employment protection and creation, will one day break into what would have to be an unparalleled deviancy in the history of economic thought, acceptance of the radicalism of a Regional Policy. Their faith is in the long-term self-interest of the strong, in making consumers and producers of the weak in such numbers as to ensure the reproduction of the economic, social and cultural hegemony of the powerful in the richer regions. It is a faith in long-term self-interest. In this the European economy is a microcosm of an exploitative world economic order.

But the issue of the relevance of Regional Policy is not an academic one. I will add but one more question of a theoretical kind. Can the arguments of those economists who have examined the decision-making process of multi-national corporations, whose studies have shown that location decisions are made more within the logic of multi-national corporations than within the logic of any regional industrialization plan a State may have, be accepted and at the same time a discussion on Regional Policy be meaningfully sustained? Socialists have a particular problem with concepts like Regional or Social Policy within structures that are unequal.

Have socialists refocussed their consideration and use of the concept of Regional Policy within the framework of what is surely obvious, a new international division of capital and commodities and, above all, a new international division of labour?

In my address to the Socialist Group of the European Parliament I attempted a response to such questions. I argued that to approach the subject of Regional Policy in the new conditions of theoretical analysis of the International Division of Labour requires that socialists move back from the fallacy of a benevolent, reformable capitalism; that they draw from what is real and human – the actual and historical experience of the regions in question. However susceptible to mythic selectivity and reconstruction – there is a history of peasants, workers and the exploited. Their struggles against often apparently insuperable odds created the impulses that delivered the parties that made all the political careers of us present actors within the Socialist Movement possible. Our present solidarities are weakened if we forget that common history of class society, of economic exploitation, political manipulation and cultural destruction.

The ahistorical appeal to pragmatism and to a contemporary practicality within an unequal society is the correct philosophy and strategy of conservatives and liberal market theorists of the Right.

For Socialists, such views represent little less than a betrayal of those who won the space for our discourse. It castrates us intellectually in terms of our world responsibilities to the people of the planet struggling for survival, for bread, literacy and participation.

As we head for completion of the internal market by 1992, what is it we mean by *cohesion* – the new word to carry the old aspiration of undoing regional inequality? It cannot be reduced to some kind of residual guilt payment to the weaker regions when the benefits to capital of the free movement of goods and services has been established.

If this was accepted as a version of Regional Policy, it would mean simply that the Fund would be the location of a war between the poor for the concessions of the rich. To those who would argue that any such help would be better than none, an advance on the existing situation, I reply that that is the argument Racist supporters of South Africa would use, saying that the lowest discrimination-based pay in the white-owned companies that loot the mines of Africa is better than the income available to the migrant worker in his home village.

No. The European idealists have suggested that Regional Policy is co-equal with the process to complete the internal market. Can this be so? Will the Regional allocations, and far more importantly, the *process of regionalism*, be allowed to pursue the fine sentiments of the Founding Treaty?

It is, above all, in a colloquium with Socialists that one can look for hope; but it is socialists that will have lost most if they cannot succeed in integrating the social and regional processes so thoroughly within the decision-making of the Community so as to not only undo the existing inequalities but to mitigate and undo the obvious tendencies to the further inequalities of a completed internal market.

The glib statement of the Information Offices of the Community that a large completed market with free access will automatically benefit all Member States and regions is as pertinent as the statement that all Irish people have access to the best hotel in Dublin.

Unless there is a centrality given to the egalitarian thrust of a genuinely regional policy process, not only aspiring towards but achieving redistribution, then the electorate of Europe, including Ireland, has been conned.[2]

I have seen nothing since I expressed these views in 1987 that might convince me that Europe in 1992 will do anything other than

2. In my paper to the Socialist Group of the European Parliament, 'Regional Policy: Rhetoric, Illusion or Socialist strategy for undoing inequality', September, 1987, Dublin, I examine these issues in the context of an evolving Regional Policy discussion. A shorter version of the paper was published in the *Irish Review*, Spring, 1988.

increase inequality between regions and classes.

II: Towards a New International Economic Order
Above and beyond the pessimistic tendency of observable facts in relation to the undoing of inequality at national or Community level, there exist some other questions that go even deeper, such as: what will be Ireland's international role in the nineties and in the next century? What concept of interdependency will prevail? Will it be the interdependency of constituting a breeding ground for a common labour pool? Will such an interdependency constitute the final rejection of any aspiration toards a planetary interdependency? Which option is being facilitated by Irish Foreign Policy? Put more bluntly, is the interdependency of a trading block aimed at defeating the challenge of US and Japanese trading blocks reconcilable with such a wider concept of interdependency as might follow from an extension of the better ideas involved in Overseas Development Aid? If Europe 1992 handicaps, rather than facilitates, our approaches towards undoing inequalities in Ireland and Europe, what does it do to our voice on world hunger, issues of aid, trade and debt?

While it may be argued that individual countries such as Holland and the Community as a whole, have been more generous than Irish governments in sustaining their commitment to Overseas Development Aid, the reality is that such aid is not directed towards an equality of participation in world trade or economic power. It is not a case of our being asked to abandon a comprehensive policy, I would emphasise. It is a case of abandoning a debate that so many of us had hoped would take place on the principles, practice and evolution of Irish Development Aid. I saw such a debate as looking towards a mutual interdependency at planetary level, engaging such issues as the shift of resources from armaments to development, the building of peace, the development of cultural pluralism as an antidote to residual colonialism, the establishment of a New International Economic Order, the advancement and extension of Human Rights into the economic and social sphere, above all, the elimination of the threat of recurring famines.

It is perhaps worth reflecting on how far our consideration of Development Aid has gone and the options we might have taken. I wrote of such options five years ago on the occasion of Trocaire's 10th anniversary.[3] I was obviously optimistic and did not anticipate the destruction of the Aid Programme by a cut of 26% in 1987, the closure of our embassy in Nairobi, the abandonment of our Aid

3. Higgins, M. D., 'Irish Government: Saint or Sinner?' in 'Ten Years of Action for Justice and World Development', Trocaire, Dublin, 1985, pages 40-53; a more comprehensive history of Irish Overseas Development Aid is presented, together with a critique.

Office in famine-stricken Sudan. Drawing on the work of colleagues within the Labour Party, I wrote of some principles that might inform an adequate Development Aid Programme. I stated that self-interest plays too great a part in the Irish Aid effort. Untied Aid must be given a greater priority in future. Development depends upon the cohesive activity of nations, internally and internationally. It cannot, and must not, be left to the free play of market forces which will, inevitably, lead to inequality – with riches for some and poverty for others. The world community as a whole must face up to its duties to guarantee an acceptable minimum standard for each and every citizen within the overall framework of equality in basic human relations. This will require planning in a comprehensive sense.

The strategy of development must aim to:

1. satisfy basic economy and social needs;
2. eradicate hard-core poverty;
3. achieve reasonable educational standards for all;
4. encourage self-reliance in individuals, groups and nations;
5. tackle problems at local, national, regional and international levels, and
6. secure social justice through the positive exercise of public power.

The search for a New International Economic Order – to which the member states of the United Nations are formally committed – must be based upon a positive and progressive definition and understanding of development.What is at issue goes far beyond the conventional indices of economic growth to encompass a whole range of goals in such areas as education, health, life expectancy, human rights and cultural advance. Development implies the liberation of people and nations from exploitation, dependence, need and powerlessness. Above all, it must involve freedom both for the individual and for the community or nation. The developing nations must be permitted, and actively encouraged, to develop in line with their own political, economic and social aspirations. They must be guaranteed freedom from all forms of intervention of a political or commercial nature.

A new stimulus to the debate on the New International Economic Order is needed in the light of the present North/South stalemate. This could come about through a political initiative designed to launch action on a number of specific issues within the context of an overall plan. Theory and practice must be linked in a sensible programme. (See my 'Appendix' to this essay, below.)

To return to the question of Irish policy and practice. Apart from voluntary effort and certain obligatory multilateral aid contributions, Ireland had no meaningful policy on world development issues until the early 1970s. Since then, interest in and discussion of the question has increased for a number of reasons, including Irish entry into the European Community and a greater political awareness. Development co-operation still does not command adequate public attention and the level of public information and awareness is inadequate. This fact poses a major challenge to all progressive political forces.

With the National Coalition in power, the Government, in 1973, made a commitment to achieve increases in Official Development Assistance in line with UN targets. A goal of 0.35% of GNP was set for 1979 – the 1970-73 average level being 0.04%. The target has not been met. Both the National Coalition and Fianna Fáil administrations have reneged on their policy commitments and the aid allocation in the 1980 Budget amounted to less than 0.2% of GNP. In 1975, Michael O'Kennedy firmly committed Fianna Fáil irrespective of budgetary or balance of payment problems, to achieving the 0.35% target within five years. In fact, the aid target has now been effectively scrapped. Only Labour and the Left are committed to the attainment of the UN goal of 0.7% of GNP within a maximum of ten years from 1979, with implementation guaranteed in budgetary terms and specific provision for the carry-forward of all funds not spent in any one year.

Ireland has concentrated much effort on building up bilateral aid through the Bilateral Aid Fund, the Agency for Personal Service Overseas and Disaster Relief. This approach was appropriate for a small country like Ireland which cannot make any decisive input at the world level but which has resources of skill, technique and experience capable of being used in a constructive manner through bilateral projects.

Bilateral aid was concentrated in projects in Lesotho, Tanzania, Zambia, Sudan and India. The first three countries have been classified by the UN as least developed. The amount of the funds available had been severely cut in 1980. Much of this aid is tied to the procurement of goods and services from Ireland.

APSO sponsors Irish personnel to work on social and economic development projects in Third World countries. About 250 persons were sponsored in 1979. This work is of increasing value and must be supported and facilitated, for example, by ensuring proper conditions at home for returning volunteers.

Ireland's bilateral aid programme should be strengthened on the basis of clear developmental principles and no longer on a restrictive 'tied' basis. There is need for the establishment of a state agency for planning and co-ordinating all bilateral aid activity. This agency is essential and working with the National Council for Development Co-operation will cut across the bureaucratic obstacles associated with the varying approaches of different departments.

Up to 68% of Ireland's ODA is obligatory — arising from the terms of membership of the EEC (60%), the World Bank and the International Development Association. Because of the very high ratio of ODA going through EEC channels, Ireland's relationships with the Third World are disproportionately under the influence of Brussels. This situation can only be remedied by the allocation of a significantly larger proportion of GNP to development assistance purposes. About 70% of this country's bilateral assistance is effectively tied to procurement here. Of the £1.98 million in the Bilateral Aid Fund in 1978, almost £1 million was actually spent in Ireland and a further £0.8 million channeled through Irish firms. Self-interest plays altogether too great a part in the Irish aid effort. Untied aid and assistance must be given greater priority in the future.

Policy on development co-operation and its administration must receive far greater attention in future. It is essential that:

(a)   national policy should be based upon coherent principles, openly stated, regularly updated and translated into an action programme;

(b)   a separate Minister and Department of Development Co-operation should be established to give this vital area of policy appropriate weight in government and in the civil service machine;

(c)   the programme decided on by the government should be financially secured for five-year periods to avoid 'stop-go' situations.

The establishment in 1979 of the Advisory Council on Development Co-operation was a step forward. Such structure is necessary to assess national effort and to advise government.

A much stronger and more influential body is required and, accordingly, I propose the setting up of a National Council on Development Co-operation, representative in character and charged with the tasks of: (a) advising the government on all aspects of development co-operation; (b) conducting and publishing independent research; (c) working closely on matters of policy and programme development with the Bilateral Aid Agency and APSO; (d) conducting programmes of public education and information dissemination.

The Council would be equipped with all the necessary staff and resources to do a worthwhile job on an independent basis.

Ireland's activity at international level is of increasing importance in relation to development co-operation. It is essential that this activity should be entirely founded on development principles. Legitimate commercial activity, while necessary for the good of the economy, must in no circumstances become confused with development co-operation efforts.

The main emphasis in international activity must be on: (a) the creation of close working links with developing countries and with the Non-Aligned Movement in pursuit of correct policies at world level; (b) the creation of similar links with progressive developed states to press for correct policies within the world; (c) the pursuit of stronger and more effective EEC policies.

The state sector must play an increasing role in the development co-operation field. This is all the more necessary when consideration is given to the necessary leadership responsibility of state enterprise in the Irish economy in future. Issues such as that of economic restructuring will be successfully tackled only with a major state sector input. The present role of DEVCO, which tends to place too much emphasis on purely commercial activity in Third World countries, must be reviewed with the intention of clearly defining the different characteristics of commercial activity and true development aid programmes which are not pursued for gain. Ground rules and criteria for state involvement in world development, including a basic code of practice for state agencies and semi-state bodies, will be established and enforced. The potential of the state bodies in the field of technical assistance is very great and must be fully realized.

Non-governmental organizations have a long and honourable history in Ireland's limited development co-operation story. This contribution must be enhanced, in quality as well as in quantity, in the years ahead. I envisage a major role for voluntary organisations and for bodies such as the trades unions and co-operatives in the overall structure of Ireland's development programme and also in the area of development education at home. Practical support for the work of these bodies must be forthcoming as part of the state's commitment. How realistic are such ideas? There is a danger here, I admit, of being too optimistic in that such principles might be accepted by those whose self-interest lay in their very opposite.

Such a danger, however, simply means that we must redouble all efforts to ensure that the developed nations accept that the logic of world development demands of them quite radical economic restructuring as trade patterns and industrial investments provide new and essential opportunities for the developing countries. This whole area calls for careful planning, positive government intervention and the full participation of the working people of each country. There is urgent need for a constructive and planned approach to this matter at the level of the European Community, taking fully into account questions of regional balance. What may appear to be an imminent and unacceptable threat can, with proper planning, become an opportunity for positive and progressive structural advance.

The concept of development co-operation should be extended to encompass the fullest possible encouragement of collaboration and joint efforts between the developing countries themselves. The emergence of regional self-reliance groups is to be actively supported as one of the best means of ensuring that development take place to the true advantage of the local populations and that lasting structures are created for the sustained progress of the nations in question. The developed countries must be prepared to support such efforts in a practical fashion.

Colonial exploitation must not be permitted to be replaced by economic and political domination of the developing countries. This can be guaranteed only by a balanced approach in which political freedom is matched by the creation of effective and acceptable systems of administration and education and the provision of an economic infrastructure enabling people to have control of all aspects of their own affairs.

The achievement of a New International Economic Order will greatly depend on international organisations through which the world development issues are debated and tackled in practice. These are the indispensable channels for future progress and for the monitoring of this progress.

The United Nations and its affiliated bodies – UNCTAD, the World Bank and the International Monetary Fund – are central to the whole process. It is essential that these organisations should be appropriately structured and that their policy orientations should take into account legitimate interests of the developing countries.

Economic relationships on the world level must be based on a clear set of values. Central to these values must be an acceptance that development relates to the welfare of the human beings and not to the dictates of capital. The IMF must conform in practice to this principle and must ensure that its programmes of financial support fully respect national integrity and impose only those conditions which are in line with the goals and possibilities of development policy.

President Nyerere of Tanzania has made pertinent observations on this question: 'The World Bank and the IMF . . . were set up by . . . and are still controlled by, the rich nations of the world. Whether they are now effective in serving the purpose for which they were established, is, I would have thought, questionable. But what is quite certain is that – apart from the IDA, subsidiary of the World Bank – they are not instruments for attacking world poverty and dependency. The IMF, in particular, endorses and serves the present international financial structure, rather than in any way acting as a corrective in its injustices. Further, although it is a creature of the developed nations, these hide behind the IMF when they find it convenient. They pretend it has a special expertise and is politically neutral; when a poor country seeks credit, it is therefore told first to reach an understanding with the IMF. This approach must be ended and replaced by a system which will support development and not crush it as in the current deplorable case of Jamaica.'

The world monetary system must be reformed so as to fight instability and speculation and to meet the urgent trade and economic needs of the developing countries. Worldwide monetary instability is leading to changing economic relationships and to distortions in markets for the basic commodities on which so much of the prospects of the developing countries still depend.

The rapidly growing role and power of a small number of commercial multinational enterprises must be recognised in any programme for world development. The achievement of the new International Economic Order should result in adequate provision for surveillance and control of these organisations based upon the principle that uncontrolled or uncontrollable power, either political or commercial, poses an unacceptable threat to true development. In line with the stated views of the ICIFU Development Charter, the control of multinational companies should be extended to:

- legislation covering the activities within particular countries;
- binding international covenants, involving all parties;
- bilateral and multilateral industrial co-operation agreements between the governments of developing and industrialised countries;
- extension of the transnational activity of the trade union movement;
- implementation of effective workers' control in industry.

Policy must be directed towards narrowing the gulf between the rich and poor countries in terms of prosperity, knowledge and power. The EC should adopt a firm and progressive position in the continuing international dialogue between the poor and rich nations and, in particular, in the discussions on the creation of a New International Economic Order. It is crucial that the Community develop its own policies in this area of urgent control, including the recognition and strengthening of the Lome Convention; appropriate foreign trade and agricultural policy development; updating the whole range of development co-operation programmes and preparation of a structural plan for the member states which will take account of the true long-term needs of the developing nations. The community will also have the task of seeking to promote and co-ordinate the policies of the individual member states and of the voluntary development agencies, in the area of development co-operation. This means accepting that the development of the Third World be based on the utilization by the developing countries of their own resources. Aid should not be tied to the guaranteed supply of raw materials to the developed countries.

III: Towards a World of Mutual Interdependency

The Brandt Report has been correctly described as '. . . one of the last and most important attempts to avoid the danger of confrontation between developed and the developing countries by means of reform and common effort'. Facing up to the reality of the world development situation and recognising the political challenge it poses, the Report states clearly that, if the world community rejects the necessary and radical steps needed to bring about lasting change, 'it will be forced upon us all through the unfolding of the events over which the international community will have little control'.

Two themes which establish the reasons for a new world order are at the centre of the Report: *morality* and *self-interest*.

The priority given to the concepts of self-interest and mutual benefit arises out of the recognition that our world is one of interdependence, increasingly faced with common problems, such as unemployment, the arms race, ecological problems and the depletion of energy and mineral resources. There is a great urgency to look beyond parochial national boundaries and interests, accepting that solutions to these problems will inevitably become internationalised.

To avert a major catastrophe and to ensure mankind's survival, a restructuring of international relations and a plan for action is needed immediately, involving a massive transfer of resources from the industrialised to the developing countries.

A new international order will take time to achieve, says the Report, but, since the present world crisis is so acute and dangerous, it is imperative to draw up an emergency programme for the next five years. This programme has to be seen as part of a longer-term strategy involving four vital areas in which drastic changes have to be implemented immediately.

These are: a large-scale transfer of resources to developing countries; an international energy strategy; a global food programme and major reforms in the international monetary system.

In addition to the emergency food programme, an action programme is proposed comprising emergency and longer-term measures to assist the poverty belts of Africa and Asia and particularly the least developed countries. Such a programme would require additional financial assistance of at least £2 billion per year for the next two decades at grant or special concessional terms, assured over a long period and available in flexibly usable forms.

The members of the Commission conclude with the statement that 'whatever the differences, there is a mutuality of interest between North and South. The fate of both is ultimately connected. The search for solutions is not an act of benevolence but a condition of mutual survival. We believe it is dramatically urgent today to start taking concrete steps without which the world situation can only deteriorate still further . . . '

It is imperative that the findings and proposals of the Brandt Commission should be taken fully into account at the level of world decision-making. In its wide-ranging recommendations and in particular in the terms of its extremely practical and urgent Programme of Priorities the report provides a blueprint for action based upon sound principles and painstaking study of present prospects and possibilities.

Any programme of action for just development at world level will require fundamental and lasting changes in public attitudes. It is essential that the fact of Third World existence, the reality of inter-dependence and the inevitability of economic restructuring within the developed countries are fully appreciated. It is equally impor-tant that people are helped to understand the nature of the forces of injustice and exploitation which are at play within the world's economic and political structures and which profoundly affect the fortunes of the peoples of the developing countries.

Development education is increasingly recognized as an inherent part of any meaningful national programme of development co-operation. In all aspects of a programme for accelerated world development, the attitudes of the people – and the voters – of the developed countries will be of the utmost significance.

It is therefore most important that priority be given to schemes for development education at home and in the community, by means of which the facts, the issues and the policy options will be explained to a wide audience. Above all, it is essential that people be brought to understand the true meaning of development and to appreciate the fundamental interdependence of the nations of the world. A real commitment is needed to provide the resources needed for the preparation and implementation of well-researched schemes of development education.[4]

Such principles, it seems, do not inform Irish foreign policy. There is a consistency of support for them derived from an involved

4. Since I wrote of such hopes three years have passed with no progress. The reverse has happened: eg, Political and Social Studies, for which a Curriculum had been designed that included Development Education, was shelved as a reform by the present Minister for Education, Mrs Mary O'Rourke.

sense of compassion. The next step to a conception of justice has yet to be made. The galvanizing connection between issues of inequality at home and at world level exists but for a few. Liberation theology abroad is combined often in a grim paradox with authoritarianism at home. Such a paradox is made possible by a spirituality colonized by denominational prosletyzation – a spirituality deeply anti-philosophical in character.

However, the challenge, even if neglected, remains.

Does Ireland in a Single European Market after 1992 mean then that we can progress on issues of poverty/inequality at home and abroad or does it mean we are to regard such conditions as natural? The present mythological tendency supports the latter.

I am certain, however, that we must continue to define an Ireland without frontiers in terms of a mutual interdependency beyond the confines of a Single European Market. We have to pursue a planetary interdependence. This will be necessarily painful in a number of areas. For example, pursuing the logic of the majority – the poor – means more than the acceptance of liberation theology. It means abandoning denominational prosletysation in favour of cultural pluralism. It means abandoning the schizophrenia of a liberation theology for the Third World and an antiquated authoritarianism for the so-called First World. In economic terms we are challenged to think socially at planetary level when we have failed to do so even at national level, our value system suffused with the values of the private and of an amoral familism that negate any moral concept of the community or of the social. We are challenged to accept the consequences of losing our hegemony of exclusion so that our fellow humans might participate. We are challenged as the provocateurs of ecological destruction to re-think our responsibilities in the mutual ecosystem. It is in being *of the planet* rather than in being *of an integrated European Market of 1992* that I see a moral challenge.

In the end will Europe of 1992 act as some catalyst for Irish business, for the multinationals, or for ourselves? I see no evidence that it will facilitate the examination of the values I have listed, that it will enable us to know the world in depth any better, know ourselves, examine the facilitating factors and obstructing factors towards the establishment of a genuine mutual interdependency or the recasting of personal morality in terms of a truly social responsibility.

Finally, to return to a distinction already made between *choosing* a Single Europe and *drifting* towards an integrated European Market, I feel it incumbent upon me to justify this distinction beyond the simple contrast of the present advertising campaign and the one prior to the Referendum.

The truth is that the preparation for the Single European Act and the process of European Political Co-operation took place in an atmosphere of near unaccountable secrecy. This has to be understood in a wider context. Irish Foreign Policy is a pragmatic amalgam of positions on issues of the day decided by the executive arm of diplomacy rather than a representative assembly. Almost unique in its lack of a Foreign Policy Committee, the Irish Oireachtas is viewed with suspicion by the permanent mandarins in the executive.[5]

A motion proposed in Seanad Éireann on 10th December 1986 to establish a Foreign Affairs Committee was defeated by a well orchestrated mandarin lobby. A dedicated European, Professor Dooge, used the conservative Report of Dr P. A. J. M. Steerkamp, President of the First Chamber, the Netherlands, to a European Speakers Conference to effect in order to demonstrate the merit of containing foreign policy formulation within the ranks of professional diplomacy rather than the robust emotionalism of parliament or public opinion, as he saw it. Dr Steerkamp was quoted as saying:

Undeniably, a contrast began to emerge between the emotional approach by part of public opinion (often fed by pacifism and moralism) and the business-like approach of the Government aiming at the feasible.[6]

Professor Dooge's arguments won the day and I was defeated with my motion. Since then I have not succeeded in getting any commitment from the present Government for discussion on such a Committee. Indeed, the Joint Committee on Development Co-operation has been abolished.

To conclude, in a political and philosophical atmosphere where moralism and pacifism are construed as emotional, unaccountable secrecy is defined as pragmatism, where the State is eroded as an economically accountable instrument for employment creation, where the market is to be completed and employment creation left as a residual effect, inequality is to be explained as 'natural', then it will not be in Europe of the 1990s that we will be struggling for the advance of mutual interdependency. The alternative location of the liberation struggles of the poor and excluded is surely more attractive. Or is it?

Our challenge, it seems to me, is to read the myth critically. The question for an Ireland without frontiers may well be an academic

---

5. Higgins, M. D., 'The Case for an Oireachtas Foreign Policy Committee', *Studies*, Dublin, Spring, 1988. In this article I give the case for and against such a Committee as debated by Professor Dooge and myself, and the decline of the idea.

6. Streenkamp, Dr P. A. J. M., in Report of a *Conference of European Speakers*, Copenhagen, June, 1984; published by the European Centre for Parliamentary Research and Documentation, Brussels, 1984.

one if we simply replace the musty psychic boundaries of a badly defined middle class nationalism with the even more inhuman dreariness of being the breeding ground, a source of labour supply, for a depeopled, dehumanized, integrated market.

The myth of Progress of the Colonizer returns in a new form to seduce the colonized who see themselves as consumers rather than independent humans. To construe such an invitation as modern, or post-modern, is an invitation I must reject. There *are* real victims of these processes. The battlefield has changed and it is wise to know that. The issues I have raised, such as the prospects for an accepted mutual interdependency, are perceived as 'soft' issues in the Ireland of 1988. The completion of the internal market is perceived as a 'hard' issue. This very dichotomy of thinking, relegation of the philosophical and political aspects of European integration, the unbridled hubris of short-term market dominated, and indeed jaded, economic thinking, represents a prospect of the development of the very worst features of contemporary Irish society.

The intellectuals have run off the field or joined the army of Progress. As always in the history of the abuse of academic freedom, there is a time for uniforms. The fashionable distraction is the part of Europe that will commercially challenge Japan in 1992. The challenge is the world. The neglect of the latter for the former redefines a peasant status for us.

In the end, the integration of life and thought, of reason and imagination, of reflection and action, of philosophy, politics and economics, would be our best preparation for Europe 1992, as part of the world. It is more likely that the divided version of ourselves will prevail – and to all our loss. It would be nice to be totally wrong.

APPENDIX

Development Strategies

The concept of the New International Economic Order must be made concrete (in terms of clearly realisable short and medium term actions), effective (in terms of measurable results) and sustainable (in terms of a degree of mutual benefit for developed and developing countries). Nonetheless, the New International Economic Order will involve fundamental changes in structures and economic relationships and these must be fully researched and defined. It will also involve a discernible shift in power throughout the world and this must be accepted by the nations of the developed world.

Aid to the developing countries will continue to be a central and necessary element in any world-wide programme. A substantial, real transfer of resources is required through policies of direct grant-aid, through project work and through the financing of economic and trade activities. More and more, attention should be directed towards arrangements for aid and development co-operation which involve the collaborative efforts of both developed and developing nations. The model of the Lome Convention may be cited with qualified approval in this connection. The solemn duty rests upon all developing nations to take the steps necessary to meet the existing international targets in respect of official development assistance.

Employment
Unemployment is a deep-seated and terrible scourge of all the developing countries. All aspects of a co-ordinated development programme should, therefore be directed towards the creation of viable jobs. What is now essential is a more rational and fair international division of labour. This will call for measures of a radical nature applied both in the developed and developing countries. Job creation in the Third World will demand a balance between industrial, commercial and agricultural development. Balance is achievable only through a planned approach involving all sections of the economy and stressing the appropriate application of modern technology.

Food and Rural Development
The question of agricultural and food policy and rural development policy must be brought into a more balanced relationship. An international food and rural development policy is required which will result in secure food supplies – of money and of technical assistance – into rural community development projects. The concept of a World Food Reserve must be given practical expression and good aid programmes should be developed under combined international administration. Particular emphasis must be placed on control of the common distribution of seeds for food production.

Access to Markets
The linked questions of access to markets and of the terms of trade for the developing countries must be faced up to. What is really at issue here is a totally planned approach to the restructuring of world markets with an overall increase in world trade, assuring real opportunity for the emerging productive capacity of the developing countries without unacceptable dislocation of the developed economies.

Commodities
The search for a new and more effective world system for trade in commodities has continued since the onset of the oil crisis. Attention should be concentrated on the achievement of an integrated commodity policy based upon a realistic version the controversial and long-delayed Common Fund. The objectives of such a Fund should be the stabilisation of the price system, the guarantee of export earning levels for the developing countries and the orderly structuring of a world commodity marketing.

Debts
The crippling nature of the present debt burden in the developing countries is now fully recognised. It represents not alone a threat to further development but a potential source of stagnation and economic decline. There must be an early agreement on a policy of easing the present debt burden. In the future, a positive debt policy must be joined with a more urgent search for rationality in world financial and monetary arrangements and should provide for a planned reduction in the level of indebtedness.

Transfer of Technology
The present patterns of technical assistance and transfer of technology require to be radically changed if the real needs of the developing countries are to be met. This is particularly true at a time of dramatic technological change and advance to microelectronic and related developments. At present, much of the technical capacity introduced into Third World countries is inappropriate and likely to create dependency. Technology itself is not necessarily the enemy of employment and human values. Its application is, however, often wrongly motivated and implemented. All technical assistance must be designed and planned to produce genuine progress towards agreed economic and social goals.

Population Policy
The rate of population growth around the world remains a challenge to overall development policy. Population policy should aim at a reduction of the rate of natural population growth, but this can be acceptable only in the context of programmes which are honestly geared to real progress in the developing countries. Any suggestion that population policy is a disguised form of colonialism or exploitation must be avoided by the strict adherence to principles of development which respect the aims and cultural integrity of the developing nations and the inherent human dignity of their people.

Aid to the Poorest Nations
In any programme, special attention must be devoted to the particular needs of the poorest and least developed nations. Aid, technical assistance and other schemes should be specifically designed to take into account the circumstances of countries where almost all aspects of economic, social and political life are characterised by acute underdevelopment.

Disarmament and the Arms Trade
The fact that over £200 billion was spent in 1980 on weapons of destruction represents, at once, a threat to peace and a barrier to world development. The alarming dissemination of nuclear technology, at one extreme, and the sordid trade in conventional weapons, on the other, must be seen as among the most negative aspects of the present world situation. The trade in arms to the developing countries is a reflection of the greed and immorality both of governments and of the arms industry in the rich countries and of the seriously incorrect priorities of many Third World governments. No strategy for world development can be in any sense positive if it is not paralleled by a programme of disarmament and arms control. The continuing efforts of the United Nations, which is dealing as a matter of priority with the prospects of disarmament, takes on a particular urgency when its work is related to the obvious imperatives of World development. The importance of the Strategic Arms Limitations Treaty (SALT) and Mutual and Balanced Force Reduction (MBFR) talks between the major world powers must be stressed and our commitment to success in these negotiatons is imperative.

Women in Development
A vital component of developmental strategy, rooted in a fundamental concept of justice, must be a guarantee of the rights of women. In such areas as the removal of legal inhibitions and discrimination, equal opportunity in education and work and adequate family planning provisions, the position of women must be advanced. This should be regarded as a matter for positive action rather than negative protection.

Ecology and the Environment
The protection of the environment and the wise and planned utilisation of scarce raw materials must be taken fully into account. In all aspects of this question, including the pursuit of a balanced world energy policy, the legitimate aspirations of the developing and less affluent countries must be given full weight as against the historic actions of those nations which have been selfish and profligate in their use of the world's resources.

Ireland in the 1990s – North and South

PAUL BEW AND HENRY PATTERSON

Any attempt to speculate about the future of Northern Ireland is a grim task. When the Anglo-Irish Agreement was signed in 1985 there was much hope and euphoria – significantly though this was mainly in London and Dublin and not in the capital most intimately affected, Belfast. Opinion polls revealed that the majority of people in Northern Ireland expected an upsurge in violence and they have not been disappointed. This gut emotional response proved to be considerably more accurate than that of optimistic savants elsewhere.

By the end of 1988 it seemed clear that the Anglo-Irish Agreement – direct rule with a green tinge – had ushered in a more unstable form of direct rule. Death from political violence rose steadily from 56 in 1985 to 64 in 1986, 93 in 1987 and seems set to be at least as bad in 1988. Nor was this a matter of 'bad men' frustrating the effects of a beneficial initiative which was eroding their support base – the broad pool of sympathy for Sinn Féin was unaltered by the Agreement itself. Sinn Féin had an 11.8% share of the Ulster vote in 1985 on the eve of the Agreement and in 1987 it still retained 11.4% share. Support for loyalist paramilitary violence also seemed to have increased significantly. When this is taken alongside the intensifying emigration of middle-class talent and continued decline of the 'real economy', there is a clear picture of a gradually deteriorating environment. The principal restraint on deterioration is the massive British subvention and the entirely reasonable determination of the majority in both communities to lead largely privatised lives. But it is a worrying fact when one can point only to the widespread war weariness as the best hope for the future rather than to any serious political strategy on the part of the major players.

Many people will be upset by such a negative prognosis. True, they will say, the Anglo-Irish Agreement gave Dublin a say in the affairs of the north for the first time and upset the Unionists. But does not the Agreement make provision for devolution which will return real political influence to the two communities, if they can only reach agreement? The problem here is that the Unionists can not 'knock out' (as Mrs Thatcher once inaccurately put it) the

Agreement by agreeing to some form of internal power sharing. As one of the most passionately committed devolutionists, V. Galloway, has explained in *The Irish Times*, (6 September 1988):

> 'not even the most moderate Unionist will ever accept devolution within the terms of the present Agreement, which makes it quite clear that even in the event of devolution in Northern Ireland many powers of intervention in Northern Ireland will be reserved to the inter-governmental conference.'

Or, as the *Belfast Newsletter* puts it, on the same day:

> 'Stepping out of the frying pan into the fire is not a course of action that would appeal to sensible people.'

There is, in short, insufficient incentive for any significant section of Unionists to make a deal with the SDLP. Anyway, the continued political strength of Sinn Féin makes it difficult for the SDLP to enter into any settlement which Unionists would have to portray as largely internal and the 'last concession'.

Whilst the Unionist leadership remains in the hands of Paisley and Molyneaux there is, therefore, no significant possibility of devolution short of totally unexpected concessions from London and Dublin. Paisley is still an opponent of power sharing: though it is worth noting that both he and his party appear to be declining in electoral appeal. Molyneaux is still more interested in moves towards integration (he would welcome an Ulster grand committee at Westminster, for example) than any form of devolution. In so far as he is interested in devolution it is at a very low level. Both have asked therefore, for symbolic concessions. Paisley has insisted that the Maryfield secretariat be closed. Molyneaux has asked that an Agreement be designed which loses its exclusive six county focus by dealing with the rights of the Irish minority throughout the UK. In this way, he hopes to strip the Agreement of its anti-Ulster Unionist symbolism – as a structure which applies to them but not to other UK citizens – and resurrect his policy – which prior to 1985 had been quite successful – of creeping integration. As these proposals have been public for over a year without eliciting any explicit favourable response from London or Dublin it may be presumed that they are non-starters. Yet the *Fortnight* poll of Spring 1988 appeared to show overwhelming Protestant support for the position taken by Paisley and – more particularly – Molyneaux. Also, the IRA's late summer campaign of 1988 created more sympathy for the Unionist position in the British media and political class than at any time for some years. This in turn effectively reduced the pressure on the Unionist leadership to make 'political progress'.

The two governments find it very difficult to agree to any alteration of the structures agreed at Hillsborough. In part, this was
because they were so hard to arrive at in the first place. At the very
least, the British believe the Accord guarantees a better international hearing for their policies. There are also two inconsistent
impulses within the current British political leadership, both of
which keep the Agreement alive. Mrs Thatcher sees the Agreement
primarily as a device (or necessary concession) to win greater
security cooperation from Dublin. On the whole, she has been
disappointed with the results thus far but she intends to continue to
exploit the device with even greater vigour. Sir Geoffrey Howe in
the Foreign Office, on the other hand, is keen gradually to reduce
the British stake in Northern Ireland and thus is mainly concerned
that the Agreement, as as first step in this process, is kept in being.
Much will depend on which tendency wins out. In the short term,
given Thatcher's resolve, the republican movement with its talk of
'one last push' may be making a serious miscalculation. Despite
Howe's uncertain future, it is less clear that they are doing so in the
long term. The scene therefore seems to be set for further deterioration because there will in all probability be no 'historic compromise'
and therefore continued uncertainty. There will also probably be
economic decline which will soon have significant effects also on
young working class Protestants who will find themselves in the
same morass of unemployment which affects so many in the
Catholic ghettoes dominated by Sinn Féin.

We have talked so much about the poor prospects for power
sharing devolution within the Anglo-Irish Agreement not because
we are opposed to it in principle – we have repeatedly argued
elsewhere that *any* constitutional shell which might reduce the
divisions in Ulster ought to be considered seriously – but because
today unrealistic projections on this topic are the new 'opium' of the
'thinking classes' in Ireland. 'The heart of a heartless world' such
dreams may be but they are not the basis for a realistic politics. NIO
ministers continue to believe that five or ten years from now the
Unionists will be worn down. It is true that Paisley and Molyneaux
are old men but both are – barring unforeseen circumstances – likely
to lead into the 1990s and no probable replacement is likely to
change the stance on the Anglo-Irish Agreement. The Unionists
have had to accept the Agreement but they are never likely to take
action which sanctifies it – by agreeing to devolution within its terms
– while the IRA continues to be a considerable force. The republican movement clearly faces difficulties – the most important of
which is the number of deaths of 'innocents' (even in its own terms) it
has caused. There is also a problem of exaggerated expectancy
within its own ranks. Nevertheless, Adams has taken care to move
the movement away from a dangerous radicalism on a number of

issues – which put them excessively at odds with the Catholic church, Fianna Fáil and the SDLP. The current Sinn Féin leadership is determined to ensure that their movement will not be isolated by the Anglo-Irish Agreement – and there was no more graphic illustration of this strategy than the seven month long dialogue with SDLP leader, John Hume. It is worth recalling also the fact that *An Phoblacht* (25 June 1987) sees any power sharing deal post-Hillsborough as further evidence of the IRA's ability to crack unionist resistance.

All this poses the question: is there any more positive way forward? Within the current framework certain limited improvements are possible. With certain rare exceptions, the current UK ministerial and official team handling the Northern Ireland question is highly unimpressive; a sweeping change of personnel would not make matters worse. The Agreement has signally failed to provoke a reconsideration by Unionists of their place within Ireland – as the *Fortnight* poll has shown, the only option which is gaining popularity is that of integration. On the other hand, expectations have been raised in the nationalist community which have not been satisfied – in part, because of the Agreement's focus on the symbolic and cultural basis of national alienation rather than the economic and material basis. The clue may be to separate questions of creeping unification from questions of internal reform. There are clearly means of reassuring Unionists – some moves towards improving the handling of Northern Ireland business at Westminster combined with reintroduction of a border poll – which do not affect the Agreement. At the same time, a greater commitment of material resources to challenge mass deprivation within nationalist areas would be of decided benefit.

Of one thing, however, we may be certain: the Sinn Féin leadership believes it has received indications from the British in the various 'negotiations' of the 1970s – culminating, as Gerry Adams has recently reminded us, in his 1979 meeting with Douglas Hurd – that its demands are at some level on the agenda of the UK state. Sinn Féin fears the security cooperation which might result from the Agreement – though currently it must be said that the figure of those being charged with republican violence is well down on 1986, despite a substantial rise in IRA activity – but Adams praises the Agreement's disorientating effect on the position of the Unionists.

In short, the IRA believes that it is working with the grain of history – as one of us has argued at length in *Fortnight 264*. The most recently advocated panacea from within the terrorism industry – the proposed application of the Italian repentancy laws – merely dramatises the difference between Italy and Ireland. In the absence of a serious political strategy, the Provisionals will set the agenda for the forseeable future. But there are those who argue that the marked lack of real support for Sinn Féin's objectives and tactics in the Republic will prove fatal to the movement in the north. This raises the acute question: what is the real status of the supposed modernisation of southern Irish opinion? In a bitter leader on 7 September 1988 the London *Times* denounced Mr Haughey for showing no evidence at all 'that he is willing even to attempt to educate public opinion in the Republic'. This 'education' would, of course, be directed against the tenets of militant Republicanism. But was such an expectation on the part of the *Times* ever a legitimate one?

The rapidity of economic, social and cultural change since the 1950s has not been, until very recently, clearly reflected in the Republic's political system. Is it an exaggeration of the extent of these changes to claim as Brendan O'Leary has recently done, that 'The Irish party system has undergone a major shock-wave, confirmed in the February 1987 election . . . there are good reasons for supposing that the February 1987 election portends greater Europeanisation and re-alignment'?[1] Central to this claim is the emergence of the Progressive Democrats with 12% of the votes and fourteen seats, replacing the Labour Party as the third largest party in the Dáil.[2] The PDs put forward a coherent neo-liberal response to the economic crisis – tax cuts to be financed by a comprehensive programme of cuts in public expenditure and privatisation. A lesser but still significant theme was the reform of church-state relations through a lessening of the confessional nature of the state in the Republic.[3]

Brian Lenihan's response to the emergence of the PDs demonstrated the clear dangers which Fianna Fáil saw in its approach: 'The only end product of right wing radicalism is destabilisation of the political system leading to class antagonism, which we have never had here. It's based on extreme laissez-faire, selfish materialism which takes no cognisance of the weak, deprived and less well-off in our society.'[4] It is true that class antagonism had never threatened to fundamentally disrupt the political system, but this was not because of the non-existence of class antagonisms and conflicts in Irish society. In fact as we have shown elsewhere, a large part of the success of Fianna Fáil as a mass party lay in its ability to take up and domesticate demands and grievances which had their

1. Brendan O'Leary 'Towards Europeanisation and Realignment?': The Irish General Election, February 1987' in *West European Politics*, vol. 10, no. 3, July 1987, p. 461.
2. *ibid.*
3. See Thomas Lyne, 'The Progressive Democrats' in *Irish Political Studies*, vol. 2, 1987.
4. Quoted in Dick Walsh *Des O'Malley a political profile* (Dingle 1986), p. 92.

roots in the conditions of life of small farmers and urban workers. Fianna Fáil's radicalism as it was developed in the inter-war period was dependent on a clearly conservative regime in power and then from a reactionary challenge from the Blueshirts i.e. it derived as much from its conjunctural location as from the substance of its economic and social policies. It also benefited from the role which the Catholic Church played in confining the legitimate scope of ideological debate within narrow limits. Irish Catholicism's deep roots amongst the masses, extending back to the penal period in the eighteenth century, gave it the ability to play a deeply conservative role in the evolution of the new state. The Church contributed powerfully to the forces making for a national consensus which lasted into the fifties and was characterised by a complacent and stagnant conservatism, reinforced by stringent censorship which ensured a stifling cultural isolation.[5] In an important sense, Fianna Fáil's radicalism in this period consisted in an avoidance of the excesses of a rabid anti-communism indulged in heavily by the Free State government and the Church. While some of its opponents would use anti-communism as a weapon against even the mildest proposals for economic and social reform, Fianna Fáil was careful to champion the cause of reform while at the same time distinguishing its legitimate social concerns from attempts to 'import' what was referred to in the Hierarchy's pastoral condemning the socialist republican organisation Saor Éire in 1931 as 'sinful and irreligious' doctrines. In his excellent account of the deportation from Ireland in 1933 of the radical socialist, Jim Gralton, Pat Feeley provides a vignette which crystallises Fianna Fáil's 'radicalism' – the minister of Justice who presided over his deportation was Paddy Ruttledge, a man who Peadar O'Donnell regarded as the most radical member of the government.[6] It was because the popular aspirations, however inchoate, for a society which would see an end to emigration and the increasing desolation of rural life, and which the party had tapped powerfully in the twenties and early thirties, would be frustrated, that there was a retreat into an increasing reliance on the integrating ideologies of Catholicism and Nationalism in the 1940s. It was Sean Lemass who clearly realised that such instrumental use of these ideological resources would, in the continued absence of economic development, be ultimately counter-productive.

Because of the radical shift in economic policy he initiated, the themes of national independence and unity together with commitment to a Gaelic and Catholic culture which remain central to Fianna Fáil's persona, are increasingly in some dislocation with the

---

5. See Thomas Boylan, 'Versions of Community and Economic Change: Consensus or Conflict?' in M. A. G. Ó Tuathaigh ed. *Community, Culture and Conflict* (Galway 1986), p. 34.
6. Pat Feeley, *The Gralton Affair* (Dublin 1986) p. 39.

realities of life in the Republic.

Catholicism is still a major force in Irish life, but its grip on the population has weakened substantially. Economic growth created the conditions for a radical shift in demographic patterns with population growth and a (temporary it now appears) ending of emigration, producing a marked alteration in age structure which has given the Republic the youngest population in the EC. At the same time the liberalisation of the economy was accompanied by an opening up of an involuted culture with the advent of a national television service in 1962. Unlike the tradition of the national radio station where most programmes were home produced and any material which went against Catholic principles was self-censored, from the start RTE provided for the wide dissemination of American and British programmes. It was also estimated in 1961 that over 30% of potential television homes in the Republic were already receiving British television, and by 1984 66% of Irish homes were receiving good quality signals from British television and the 'denationalising' influence of this medium has since been substantially added to by the onset of multi-channel cable television.[7]

The practise and discourse of television – the heavy emphasis in many imported programmes and in an increasing number of home produced ones on the situation and problems of urban individuals instead of portrayals of Catholic ruralism – challenged the dominant forms of discourse in De Valera's Ireland. It accompanied a limited growth of a more iconoclastic, critical and investigative type of television as the Republic was very directly influenced by the backwash of 1960s radicalism.[8] Economic growth, urbanisation, a younger population, improvements in the general standard of formal education, the gradual disintegration of an insular culture under the pressure of television in particular, all contributed to an attenuation of popular Catholicism. The survey carried out in Ireland for the European Values Study Group in late 1980 showed a country that was still heavily religious in European terms – 82% of the sample claimed to go to church once a week or oftener compared to 52% in Northern Ireland, 14% in Britain and a 25% all Europe average.[9] Arguably the continuing significance of experiences and memories of a more disciplined and monolithic Catholicism encouraged a degree of exaggerated religiosity amongst some respondents and experienced observers tend to believe that the rate of attrition is considerably higher. The survey showed that the group with the lowest percentage of weekly attenders was the

7. Martin McLoone & John MacMahon, *Television and Irish Society* (Dublin 1984), p. 7.
8. *ibid.*
9. M. Fogarty, L. Ryan & J. Lee eds, *Irish Values and Attitudes* (Dublin 1984) Table 1 (ii), p. 126.

unemployed – 65%[10] and reports from some priests in working class Dublin parishes estimate that only 10% of their parishioners go to Mass every Sunday.[11] It is also important to note that amongst those who attend church regularly there is an increasing number who do not accept the Church's definition of sin – particularly in that area with which the Church has been obsessively concerned-sexuality. [12] The growth of a more critical and individualistic type of Catholicism amongst sections of the urban young and middle class was also encouraged by the impact of Vatican II which as Ó Tuathaigh notes, 'contributed significantly to the dissolution of the solid consensus of the nineteen fifties.[13]

Another important force for change was the worsening situation in Northern Ireland which encouraged the development of a debate on the need for a more pluralist society in the Republic as a means to help reconcile the Protestants of Ulster to eventual unity. As Ó Tuathaigh puts it, ' . . . arguments in favour of internal social change have become inextricably bound up with or subsumed in the larger debate on the relations between the two parts of the country, between the different traditions, and on the political structures most likely to lead to peaceful co-existence between the different communities in Ireland.'[14] Garret Fitzgerald was a central figure in this debate. In 1972 he had criticised the policies of previous southern governments, particularly Fianna Fáil for being based on the 'simplistic theory that Ireland is one nation with a single neo-Gaelic, Roman Catholic culture, to which all citizens north and south should conform.'[15] As movements towards pluralism he was prepared to argue for the deletion of the constitutional ban on divorce, although he disputed the need to actually introduce divorce in the Republic – it would be sufficient to allow the north to retain its own divorce legislation in a new federal Ireland. He also proposed a liberalisation of the laws on contraception and censorship, although with the proviso in the former case that any such liberalisation would provide for 'safeguards and limitations on free sale'.[16] This was a cautious liberalism which had nothing to say about such fundamental bastions of the Church's social power as its large degree of control in crucial areas of education, health and welfare. As the decade progressed his timorous liberalism was consolidated and encouraged by evidence of a growing component

10. *ibid.* Table 4 (ii), p. 132.
11. Peadar Kirby, *Is Irish Catholicism Dying?* (Cork & Dublin 1984) p. 37.
12. Tom Inglis, *Moral Monopoly: The Catholic Church in Modern Irish Society* (Dublin & New York 1987), p. 27.
13. G. Ó Tuathaigh 'Religion, Nationality and a Sense of Community in Modern Ireland' in Ó Tuathaigh, *op cit* p. 74.
14. *ibid.* p. 79.
15. Garret Fitzgerald, *Towards a New Ireland* (London 1972), p. 175.
16. *ibid.* p. 152.

of public opinion willing to consider changes in the areas of contraception and divorce. He was also impelled towards the declaration of a 'constitutional crusade' by the increasing difficulties of the social democratic component of his strategy for resuscitating Fine Gael. His declaration of the need for such a crusade in a radio interview in September 1981 was an honest and self-critical statement for an Irish nationalist to make:

> We have created here something which the northern Protestants find unacceptable. I believe it is my job to try and lead our people to understand how it is that we have divided this island . . . . If I was a northern Protestant today, I can't see how I could aspire to getting involved in a State which is itself sectarian in the acutely sectarian way Northern Ireland was in which Catholics were repressed.[17]

Unfortunately for Fitzgerald the real, if limited liberalisation of attitudes on a range of issues which had developed from the sixties, had begun to encourage a traditionalist response. For if the breaking down of an insulated political culture had helped liberalism, international developments were also closely attended to by Catholic fundamentalists. The example of the efflorescence of new right pressure groups, particularly of a 'pro-life' sort in both Britain and the USA, would be noted in the Republic where fundamentalists feared that the liberalism of the sixties would lead to secularism and abortion. Fitzgerald's own doubts about the degree to which liberalised attitudes had acquired a rootedness in Irish society had become clear earlier in the year when, during an election campaign, he was the first party leader to give a pledge, to the recently formed Pro-Life Amendment Campaign, to introduce an amendment to the Constitution against the introduction of abortion. Although when the amendment was eventually put to the electorate it was drawn up by Fianna Fáil and opposed by Fine Gael on a number of obscure technicalities, the party did not campaign against it and a sizeable section of the party clearly supported it. Two thirds of the 55% of the electorate voted for the amendment. The 'yes' vote was highest in rural constituencies in the west and lowest in urban constituencies with a sizeable middle class population, five Dublin constituencies rejected the amendment by a small majority. At the time some consoled themselves with the notion that the result was a pyrrhic victory for the Church since despite mobilising all their resources and with the active support of the

---

17. Quoted in John Cooney, *The Crozier and the Dáil: Church and State 1922-1986* (Cork & Dublin 1986), pp. 7-8.

18. See Brian Girvin, 'Social Change and Moral Politics: the Irish Constitutional Referendum 1983', *Political Studies*, 34:1, p. 81.

dominant party, there was a failure to mobilise a more substantial proportion of the Catholic electorate.[18] It is true that the vote demonstrated the existence of a substantial liberalised minority, but this interpretation would soon clearly be seen to have underestimated the power of traditionalism.[19] In 1986 Fitzgerald's government would suffer a major rebuff in its attempt to amend the constitution to allow for divorce. Although opinion polls had demonstrated clear majorities in favour of removing the ban, the government's proposed amendment would be defeated in a referendum with a result which was almost an exact replica of the abortion vote: 63% rejected the proposal in a turnout substantially higher than in 1983, 63%.[20] Again with Fianna Fáil and the Church ranged powerfully against, the government's own commitment was seriously undermined by the fact that many Fine Gael TDs were known to be opposed to divorce and the Fine Gael contribution to the campaign was virtually negligible. Part of the substantial shift to the PDs from Fine Gael in the 1987 election may be explained as a protest by sections of the liberal middle class and bourgeoisie and the debacle of Fitzgerald's 'constitutional crusade'.

Fianna Fáil's total embrace of traditional values is clearly related to certain problems it faces. In an urbanising society, the strong traditional affective ties between voters and parties are weakened. Its hold over its voters is greater in the more rural and peripheral areas, and this section of its support base is the most conservative on moral issues in the Republic. At the same time this is a shrinking section of the electorate – the proportion of the population living in urban areas has increased from 42% in 1961 to 56% in 1986. By 1981 almost one third of the population of the Republic lived in the greater Dublin area and the proportion of Dáil seats elected from the Dublin area increased from 20 to 29% between 1961 and 1987 while that from Connaught Ulster fell from 25 to 19%.[21] It might appear that a Fianna Fáil commitment to traditional values would put it dangerously out of touch with long term social trends, whatever its short term advantages. However, whilst it may be the case that its position on the referenda may have alienated some bourgeois and middle-class support, it is far less obvious that it will damage it amongst the working class. For it represents an alliance with an institution which, through the health and education apparatuses, is deeply involved in working class existence. A traditionalism which presents itself as based on deep communal values and concerns as opposed to an unrepresentative 'cosmopolitan' and liberal elite, can hope to mobilise working class support.

19. C. O'Leary & T. Hesketh 'The Irish abortion and divorce referendum campaigns', *Irish Political Studies*, vol. 3, 1988 provides a useful overview.
20. Inglis, *op cit* p. 88.
21. Peter Mair, *The Changing Irish Party System* (London 1987) pp. 78-79.

When liberalism is clearly a coherent doctrine for market-led growth and separation of church and state, as to an extent it appears to be with the PDs, it will not have a ready appeal to large sections of the working class. There is no tidal wave of modernisation in the Republic and Fianna Fáil's espousal of traditional values does not put it dangerously out of touch with urban Ireland. In a society so marked by inequality, with a large unemployed and poor element in the working class, the appeal of ideologies of consolation, amongst which traditional nationalism figures as well as religion, should not be underestimated.

It has become increasingly difficult for Fianna Fáil to maintain a corporatist strategy towards the working class. There is little sign that experienced observers of the Irish economy expect 1992 to have other than a negative effect on Irish indigenous industry, thus exacerbating the problems already apparent. High levels of unemployment and emigration appear to be becoming a permanent feature of the economy. In such circumstances, the appeal of the neo-liberal radicalism of the PDs to the bourgeoisie and sections of the middle class and skilled working class is understandable. Fianna Fáil's volte face in government and its implementation of a relatively serious programme of retrenchment has temporarily dis-orientated both the PDs and Fine Gael, who were forced to give effective 'critical support' to the government's economic strategy. The problem for Fianna Fáil is that while such policies may well bring back middle class defectors to the PDs, there is a real danger of an attrition of working class support to Labour and the Workers' Party. There is little sign that the government has worked out an economic strategy that can seriously respond to the problems of Irish industry in an unfavourable international environment, and at the same time maintain its base in the urban working class. Its capacity to continue on a course of retrenchment must be doubted, but the deep structural problems of the economy do demand radical action. A form of modulated and, if possible trade union sanctioned, moderate retrenchment is perhaps what will emerge. It will be sold as a less unpleasant alternative to 'full-blooded' Thatch-erism à la PD and will in some ways be little distinguishable from the revivified 'social democratic' pose of Fine Gael under Alan Dukes. However, it will have the advantage of the subsidiary supports of Catholicism and nationalism.

The small Irish left faces a future with some real opportunities. If Catholicism is still a major force, it is a religion of consolation more than the hysterical anti-communism of the 40s and 50s. The domin-ant bourgeois party faces conditions which clearly undermine its capacity to generate economic growth and sustain all its working class support. The emergence of the PDs has allowed for a clearer demarcation of basic strategic alternatives in the economic and social life of the Republic. The dominant response of Fianna Fáil and Fine Gael may well be to attempt to fudge these issues. Their success here will depend to a large extent on the interaction between the domestic and international economy. Continuing and even deepening economic problems will however provide no inevitable increase in the left's constituency. Past failures to challenge the clericalist and nationalist consensus in the south have contributed to a situation where the left vote is a protest and often clientelist one rather than one for any coherent vision of a different type of Irish society. The necessary radical initiative on constitutional and moral issues has been largely coming from forces outside and even hostile to the left. Sections of the left still hanker for a lurch towards an 'anti-imperialist' strategy aimed at getting Britain out of the north and the country out of the EC. Amongst those more in touch with reality there is no clear consensus on key issues like Northern Ireland and economic strategy. In the Republic, as in Britain there are some who realise the need for serious strategic thinking but many who are still enveloped in moralising and posturing. The real evidence of severe problems for Ireland's ruling class, of a weakening of the hold of traditional parties and institutions, of dealignment of the electorate, merely demonstrate an increased 'availability' of sections of the electorate for alternative policies. There is no sign that these policies need be of a leftist sort. In the 1960s the hope of those who foresaw a weakening of the hegemony of the major parties was that this would inevitably lead to a socialist 70s. The weakening was hailed prematurely. Now that there is in fact some real evidence for it, there is little prospect of the nineties being socialist. However, there is a prospect of a small but growing socialist and secular challenge to a society increasingly polarised, with a large and growing 'under class' of permanently unemployed, and a dominant party, still Fianna Fáil, but a party long since bereft of any claim to a real strategy for economic development, opportunistically prolonging its life by increasingly virulent appeals to the most reactionary currents of nationality and religion.

Hopes for an impetus to modernisation and realignment from the effects of 1992 are probably misplaced. Already nationalist politicians like Seamus Mallon are claiming that the move towards a single European market makes partition 'irrational'. Perhaps, but politically the effects of such 'irrationality' are more open-ended than he thinks – it could equally justify the call for a move towards some greater federation of the two islands. We do not, of course, think this very likely, we simply make the point to demonstrate the futility of reading off some inevitable recasting of political allegiances from prognostications of economic change. Politicians in the nationalist camp have had some success in using the language and symbolism of Europeanism to market a product whose basic features are fundamentally traditional. One major instance of this success was the Hillsborough Agreement. Whatever the objectives of the Coalition government in negotiating this, and both Fine Gael and the Labour Party have often expressed support for a modernisation of politics and ideology in the Republic, its effects have been to stimulate a resurgence of traditional nationalism. This was likely given the central ambiguity about the exact role which the Agreement gave to the government of the Republic in the governance of Northern Ireland. Expectations of influence and major change have been raised in the Republic and their inevitable frustration fuels resentment and a recrudescence of anti-British feeling. Membership of the EC together with the rapid change in the economic and social structure of the Republic in the last three decades has produced a ruling class, which although it faces major economic problems and the social malaise of unemployment and emigration, can at least congratulate itself on weathering the past thirty years much more successfully than the Protestant ruling class in Northern Ireland. This objective weakening of the material basis for Ulster Unionism, mirrored in the disdain with which it is treated by elite opinion in Britain, Europe and the USA, has unfortunately encouraged a triumphalist and inflexible tone in Nationalist attitudes to northern Protestants. Economic development and modernisation has not had the emollient effects on traditional nationalist and unionist ideologies that its champions like Garret Fitzgerald had hoped. The economic basis for partition may well be removed by the twin effects of 1992 and the Thatcherite immiseration of the 'privileged' Unionist population in Northern Ireland. However, without a fundamental reassessment of the continuing power of the Catholic and Nationalist components in the political culture of the Republic, there will continue to be a deep and bitter division in popular culture and attitudes.

Thinking Globally and Acting Locally

ROSEMARIE ROWLEY

The last world war was the last possible world war which could be won. The explosion of the first nuclear bomb, and the creation of opposed power blocs through an information war, has given us since then, an atmosphere of constant global crisis.

In the West, the 1968 generation whose twentieth anniversary is upon us, were the first who grew up after the war, and the first to stop a war through protest. However, they are remembered more for their excesses than for their success as a peace movement. Disaffection and alienation from the system has continued in the form of pop culture, ersatz rebellion, and a search for personal happiness through love, though ambition is now respectable among the young, chiefly because of the intense competition in a shrinking job market.

The political ideas of 1960s radicalism have been largely incorporated into an unprecedented many-faceted pragmatism, the shadow play of left and right, Thatcherism being a successful model of popular capitalism with pride in house ownership hiding distressing realities like unemployment and inner city deprivation. In Western culture generally, the idea of personal happiness through love has been linked to consumerism, in the iconography of the happy couple who have responsibilities only to each other and their careers – one is never sure in which order, since the answers will surely depend on how feminism will develop as many men still refuse to consider options like house-husbanding – even with a limited time span or part-time structures.

Gorbachev remarked that 'sixties radicalism had communal character'.[1] However, in our part of the world, it is through ignoring the idea of community that a mass exploitation of the earth's resources, facilitated through the potent image of the couple in advertising, has been carried out from the seventies onwards. The calls to privatise everything in the public sector (even the water supply in England!) shows how far some tendencies are moving away from community.

Community and privatisation stand at opposite poles of human responsibility. Social responsibility in the East bloc was compul-

---

1. *Towards a Nuclear Free World.* Moscow English language edition, 1986.

sory, reflected in art and politics and public life as social content. In the West the idea of responsibility was minimal and personal. The East bloc, which professed to find form corrupt, lived in a godless world where transcendence was a bad word. Understanding was vitiated by the paradox of revolutionary freedom working deterministically (although now with Glasnost the possibility of airing problems in public has created a new understanding between East and West).

The endless replication of form in the West, the flux and flam of idols for the popular show, challenged the definitions of vacancy and meaninglessness, rendering even such definitions bankrupt. In the world of political reality, a polarisation was evident which allowed of little development but caused plenty of anxiety since there was little evidence of mutual understanding.

An advance out of the stalemate was first put forward by thinkers like André Gorz, in the mid seventies, following on Illich and Schumacher. Gorz eschewed the polarisations of East and West, capitalism and communism, and found that what they had in common with each other, their centrist and growth economics, was incompatible with the survival of the planet.

'Each man for himself and God for all' suited capitalism admirably. The contrasting communist slogan 'From each man according to his ability, to each according to his need' gave too much power to the state to define talents, and even the person. And we know the fate of those people who refused to be defined. Gorz' credo, 'The only things worthy of each are those which are good for all' – strikes a balance.

Macro economics, with its destruction of individual and local autonomy, the lack of control over the workplace, and its substitution of energy-consuming systems for personal input and responsibility, has been seen to tear the fabric of society, replacing the model of community and neighbourhood with faceless individuals who shop in one place, work in another, and exist in another, using technology and energy wastefully. It is clear many industrial societies, East and West, bear such marks. Human culture, the planet itself, was heading for disaster. The role model for economic expansion was the male explorer/exploiter. Could a model for cooperation be found in the female, notwithstanding that woman as consumer, with her newly acquired purse, was complicit in eco-destruction? Feminism (albeit with the emphasis on cooperation and nurturing), was perceived to be a healing power for the planet, along with grassroots ecology and non-violence movements – a real politik where the relationship to community and place were recognised, and not abstracted to a central idea or aspiration. Women in the community, in the interpretation of their history of wise cooperation, were more keyed to survival than the male with his conveniently eponymous history.

The German Greens (*Die Grünen*), for example, with women very much to the fore, arrived on the map elected to the Bundestag in 1981 through success at local elections. The Ecology parties in Sweden, France and other European nations have since followed suit. On the agenda for the first time anywhere is the call to counteract the huge threats facing the planet, the global nuclear threat, and the danger to the environment. With their electoral success at grass roots level, these matters were taken up by the media, who adopted mostly a bemused stance to the politics.

As has happened in all countries since, the environmental concerns, polluted water, scarcity of resources, even the threat of nuclear power stations, were usually portrayed in isolation from the factors which produce them, the macro-economic systems. In our own country, there have been advances – the anti-pollution legislation, the Hanrahan victory in July 1988 in the Supreme Court against the multinationals, the concerted Government campaign against Sellafield in particular. These concerns developed out of an awareness about the environment, and out of the environmental direct action groups rather than out of party politics.[2]

Commendable as they are, and perhaps more necessary at the moment than political ideology, Earthwatch and Greenpeace attack the symptoms rather than the disease. The Government are in the unfortunate position of proposing anti-pollution measures with one hand, while the other beckons industry onward. Economic expansion may never again be possible. As we have seen, the main political parties have reacted to the pressure of ecology groups by policies of environmental concern, such as unleaded petrol and CFC aerosols, but again such reforms have taken place, not overnight, despite compelling evidence as to their harm, but in relation to a time span which gives too much regard to the purely economic concerns of the industries which produce them. Lead in petrol, at first suspect, and now known to cause brain damage in children, has only slowly been tackled since the motor car industry has needed time to phase out the old models, many of which only needed a cheap adjustment. Ireland obtained a derogation in 1981 which meant for a long time, five years, we had the most leaded petrol in Europe. The government was more conscious of the Whiddy oil industry than its greatest resource for the future.

The success of environmental and ecology movements throughout Europe may indeed lie in putting these things on the agenda, and forcing the central powers of government and media to accept them. Yet the prognosis for the future cannot but include the

---

2. For example, the setting up of An Bórd Pleanála, 1976, the Water Pollution Act, 1977, and the recent Industrial Safety legislation, which made provision for chemical pollution and workers' health.

possibilities offered by feminism and ecological lifestyles, and the radical idea of placing power at the local level, a web instead of a system. (In a web, all the parts relate to each other and to the whole in harmony, while in a system the parts can be sacrificed to the whole.) However, while there are Greens, in the Bundestag, and in the Swedish and European Parliaments, it will be some time yet before their real political influence, in terms of changing the system, will be seen.

The European Community was founded in the first order as a means to peaceful relations between countries, at a time when the limits to growth economics had not been imagined, save by the prophetic few. Although largely with structures which favour industry and wealth creation it has been a community in which resources and wealth have been shared, human rights recognised and indeed where peace has prevailed, save in the tragic conflict of Northern Ireland. Much of the positive legislation affecting women in this country, such as equal pay, has come directly from Europe rather than from a nationalistically conceived utopia – which in Ireland, would be unlikely to be a woman's utopia (as the anti-SEA and referenda campaigns indicate).

In fact, it is feminism, in the broad sense, with its history of cooperation, its respect for the other, the understanding of oppression and its call to wholeness, which may offer a solution to post-industrial problems, particularly in the interim when macro and grassroots solutions must go hand in hand, and indeed in the foreseeable long term too. The policies of regionalism and regional aid provide a direction for community cohesiveness, and an answer to the problems of centrism and large corporations.

Mr John Hume's report to the EC on the 'Regional Problems of Ireland' (1987) should be read in conjunction with the main report (third periodic report) on the regions of the enlarged community. Mr Hume's proposition, No. 11, when he wishes to take full advantage of the possibilities offered by European Community practice and legislation to establish a number of programmes, including integrated operations to enhance the endogenous potential of regions, and to involve local authorities and the Regional Development Organisations in the preparation and implementation of these programmes, seem particularly timely and appropriate. Mr Hume, in his paper, advocates that the regional authorities should have executive, administrative and planning powers which would give the local community a considerable say, an input, and the benefit of such authorities. Along with the establishment of regional bodies in Ireland, which are to be successfully promoted internationally, many of the Green measures, such as feminism, active concern for the Third World, and a society sustainable on ecological principles, would be workable both in the short and long term. Mr Hume's emphasis on regional autonomy would fit in with the Green idea of decision-making at the lowest possible level. Indeed the Greens have been strong supporters, in Strasbourg as elsewhere, of a Europe of the Regions.

In the meantime, perhaps some of the Green ideas could go along with the macro economic structures in a way which would make use of present personnel and resources to create the means to a just, ecological society. I have found Green ideas adaptable and I would suggest the following.

1.   As a working measure, capital aid programmes, and a socially responsible theory of capitalism, should go together. For example, a multinational franchise should go hand in hand with a community project model.[3]

2.   The right to basic income linked to a 5 year mandatory work programme, could be recognised. Simple administration of Social Welfare (to be renamed Citizens' Dividend), could mean all resources could be redirected usefully. Control at local level for basic income would help avoid centrist power abuses and bureaucracy. Bus-driving, housework, river cleaning, garbage collecting, and other socially useful jobs would after the compulsory stint, yield basic income for life. Certain spin-off effects would mean (a) Work would not be a privilege; (b) Rigid class distinctions based on manual work would be softened; (c) No one person would be a slave for life; (d) People with special talents or needs, such as artists, or parents, would be free to deploy their time and talents without the strain of economic hardship; (e) Because everyone in the community would have practical experience, people with academic inclinations would be less enamoured of theory and the whole of society would benefit.[4]

3.   Work and cultural educational exchange programmes, now being made possible through the new legislation for 1992. Respect for cultural diversity such as language.[5]

---

3.   Ms Anita Roddick runs her Bodyshop on ecological principles, which means her products are not based on animal experiments and her containers are refillable. The Bodyshops in Dublin run a hospital visit programme and are supporting work on Alzheimer's Disease.

4.   For example, children in the tower blocks in Ballymun have absolutely no playing area, save a small space on the landing. There would be less neurotic mothers and children if there was more practical thinking. An article 'What women want from housing' developed similar points, *Woman's Way*, July 29, 1988.

5.   This respect for national or regional language should not, however, prevent an examination of the communication possibilities in artificial languages, such as Esperanto which seem to avoid ideological confrontation. China has developed

4.   Rejection of corporate image-making with the establishment of European cultural bodies (e.g. on the model of Aosdana) who may have a social function of scrutinising the mass media for injurious propaganda, with the establishment of counter-advertising on matters of community interest. Television should provide a platform, with radio and the printed media, for all people and should not be the province of vested interests or the narrow deterministic interpretations of social engineers. Of great importance is education for the media by the media and by the community.

5.   A reform of the banking system would create a role of social responsibility for the banks. A strict supervision of how they use their resources would help defeat the conditions which have created the world debt situation. Although some of our banks have made exceptional provision[6] for the Latin American debt, who is sure what the exact result is? In future, governments should be discouraged from borrowing. The present repayment of our national debt should include the interest as part of the capital repaid. Since it is a national emergency with health services being threatened, how, in relation to the Constitution (Article 45.2 iv) can the banks be understood to have no social responsibility? Perhaps our banks would consider a fixed administrative charge until the national debt is cleared.

Credit is best for housing needs, but purely speculative paper money must be tied to resources to avoid the 'Black Monday' syndrome and the depletion of resources directly linked to people, jobs and housing.

6.   'Housekeeping' agencies for the control, distribution and recycling of precious and natural resources,[7] should be set up, with in-built controls to prevent these becoming cartels.[8] The economist, Richard Doutwaite, has suggested we think of our national resources as capital, with a sparing withdrawal attitude, and our extraction costs equivalent to the bus-fare to get to the bank.

Esperanto because the European languages were felt to be suffering from a colonialist world view. At the level of European organisation, the adoption of an artificial language could even lead to vast savings in trees!

6.   See AIB accounts ending 31st March, 1988, p 29.

7.   Known resources at present rate of consumption may be exhausted within 25 years, while the discovery of an oil-like bacterial substance 2-3 miles below the sea could mean a new source of energy, but it may be a pollutant. Satellite and new technology (they are now extracting gold by cyanide, which is ecologically destructive) means that previously non-commercial metals may become a commercial proposition. I am grateful to Mary O'Donnell of Earthwatch for this information.

8.   The European Community has legislated against cartels. Article 85.

In the long term, an adaption to a low-energy, low-resources community of communities, where local industry and work are rescheduled to include part-time work as well as full-time work in cooperatives and small businesses, socially necessary work, flexitime, working from home, proper use and sharing of tools and resources, the recognition of special talents, aptitudes and concerns which are not essentially monetary, but vital to human wellbeing, such as parenting, art, community theatre and dancing, and a development of what is common to us, locally and internationally, including the celebration of diversity.

The crux is to have local input at supranational level, and to create at the same time a power divide which favours the local, but which respects the universal application of human rights.[9] The present possible progression from District Court to European Court of Human Rights expresses this state of affairs in law. The challenge is to implement such a transitional model at all levels of our society in the 1990s.

---

9. In the Green coordinating group, to which I was the Irish delegate for 1985/86, the Greens anticipated the work of the Moscow summit in calling for disarmament. Their approach was to break down the blocs. The log-jams in East-bloc West-bloc thought were becoming very apparent at that time of crisis. I helped edit the collection of essays 'From Two Blocs Towards One World' which was circulated to the US and USSR embassies here in Dublin. Founded in 1981 as the Ecology party of Ireland, the Green Alliance/Comhaontas Glas has, however, made little impact to date. The reasons for this are circular. A certain amateurism seems to have been indicated from the start. To be an amateur is perfectly reasonable in a non-party party but informal leadership may be in danger of creating an invisible influence, not open to checking tendencies for centrism or censorship. In the same way, Greens who can finance their own election campaigns may be seen as counter to democratic ideals, yet a really radical candidate may not attract supporters. (Aristotle discusses the problem in 'Laws'. According to George H Sabine, in *A History of Political Theory* this perennial dispute in political ethics, the conflicting aims of oligarchy and democracy made Aristotle abandon his search for the ideal state and take up the more modest problem of the best government for the most states. We have seen the results!)

They made little impression on the media, since Carnsore was scrapped in 1979, and it wasn't until the government took up the Sellafield issue after Chernobyl that the party was reckoned to exist at all. However, the direct action groups were more prominent and achieved more. In a media which is heavily dependent on advertising, the non-consumer ethic of Green politics was lampooned more than once. Candidates with little relationship to real-life problems such as unemployment, did not advance the cause, particularly at election-time. Credibility in Ireland is linked very much to past traditions of politics and the cult of leadership, with clientelism almost a mode of parliamentary action, so that the PDs advanced through the system because all these networks were open to them, and not to the new Green party in Ireland.

However, the Irish Greens have made an important contribution to the thinking on consensus (although the woman largely responsible for this was forced to resign with Green anarchists in 1986, when the party failed to resolve the tensions between grassroots input and political organisation). Its healthy positive approach to the Irish language is commendable, and the same group has been initiating recycling projects in the local area of Fingal and an organic community farm project.

Greens are up against formidable opposition, not only from within in their lack of political experience, but from the powers of industry and the media, who of course try to reduce everything to fodder for the moneymaking enterprise they essentially are in these hard times. Animal Farm may be on the wane, but Organic Vegetable Farm will need a lot of hoeing to keep out the weeds.

BIBLIOGRAPHY

The Nuclear Barons, P. Pringle and J. Spellman, Michael Joseph, London 1982.
The God that Failed, ed. Richard Crossman, Gateway Editions 1983.
A Matter of Life or Debt, Eric de Mare, Veritas Publishing Company Australia (reprinted) 1986.
Piecing it Together, Feminism and Non-Violence Study Group, Devon 1983, and War Resisters International, London 1983.
Ecology as Politics, Andre Gorz (trans.), Pluto Press 1975.
The Right to Useful Employment, Ivan Illich, Marion Boyars 1978.
Small is Beautiful, E. F. Schumacher, Abacus 1973.
A History of Political Theory by George H. Sabine, reprinted Harrap and Co. 1960.
Hanitg Keir Merck on Ireland, Green Action News Group, Dublin 1984.
The Windscale Experiment (Sellafield), Dr. Rupert Blackith (TCD) and Dublin Clear Seas Campaign 1984.
Writers and Politics, a Partisan review reader, Edith Kurzweil & Wlm Phillips, eds, RKP 1983.
Blueprint for a Green Planet by J. Seymour and H. Girarder, Dorling Kindersley London 1987.

Towards a World Community of Communities

DESMOND FENNELL

The real independence of Ireland, and the means of attaining and maintaining it, must always be our first priority, and any thinking about Ireland and Europe in the years ahead which ignores these matters is of no positive use either to the Irish or to Europe. I will expand briefly on that statement, give voice to those Irish people who would pooh-pooh it, and answer them. Then I will suggest how we can work realistically through the 1990s towards a really independent Ireland.

By 'real' national independence I mean something quite modest. I mean sufficient independence for a nation to be the shaper, by and large, of its own worldview, life and international relationships. Everyone agrees that this is a fundamental human good, that it is wrong for a nation to be deprived of it, and that a nation without it is a nation only in name. It is a human good because a nation is a unit of mankind with a particular history, existing in specific, concrete circumstances, and it is only by having effective control of its life that this group and its members can realise their specific humanity, collectively and personally, and thus contribute their due share to the inherent and enriching diversity of mankind – or of Europe, if they are a European nation. By the same token, mankind, and Europe specifically, need the real independence of their constituent nations in order to *be mankind* and to *be Europe*. But real independence is also the primary practical good of a nation, for the good reason that none but itself and its members can identify and advance its interests, and they need independence to do this. Consequently, however one views the matter, the real independence of Ireland is an imperative for the Irish and a necessity for Europe.

Standing, however, in opposition to these truths and realities is the obvious fact that we live in a world which is unfavourable to the real independence of small nations, and particularly to that of a small nation such as Ireland which shares a common language with its two powerful neighbours, one of whom is immediately adjacent to it and its coloniser and controller for centuries. Both in our own case, and in that of many nations, a proposition once believed in as

99

dogma has proved to be untrue; namely, that for a small nation to have real national independence, it is sufficient for it – barring overwhelming armed invasion – to possess a state of its own. Since the Second World War, developments in communications, and in the international organisation of industry, finance and commerce, have brought about a situation in which major states, or more precisely, world power-centres, can control small nation-states, or decisively limit their freedom of action, without recourse to military invasion or occupation. Empire can now be, and is, exercised at a physical remove and by indirect means.

From this obvious conflict between the present state of the world and our need in Ireland for real national independence, two things follow logically. In the first place, a vision of Ireland in the years ahead, if it is to be of any positive use to ourselves or to Europe, must include realistic thinking about how we can achieve and maintain real independence. Secondly, we share a common interest with all other small nations, and particularly with those which labour under such extreme disadvantages as we do, in re-shaping the world and its power structures so that they will be less unfavourable, and ideally, favourable, to the independence of small nations, ourselves included.

There are many in Ireland today who would demur at those two propositions. I am talking about people who are actively concerned about the independence of Nicaragua, Honduras, Cambodia, or Namibia, as the case may be. But they would demur, these same people, at the suggestion that what we Irish most need is independence to shape our own worldview, culture, polity and external relationships.

Ireland, they believe, is for one reason or another, an exception to the general rule – which applies to Nicaragua, Honduras, Namibia, Zimbabwe and so on. What Ireland needs most, they say, is to be more like other countries, especially Britain and America, but selectively of course in both instances; and to be able to provide a decent living for the Irish who stay at home, and useful education for those who go abroad to take up jobs in Britain, on the Continent, in the USA or the Middle East. We are, after all, in the EEC (or the EC as it's now called), and that opens endless opportunities for our young people, and makes independence to do our own thing, shape our own life, play our own role in the world, superfluous. France, West Germany, Britain, Italy? Well, yes, but they're big countries, we're a very small, tuppence-halfpenny country on the outer edge of Europe. As for our 'sharing a common interest with other small nations in re-shaping the world', that does sound a bit pretentious not to say unrealistic. A common interest, perhaps, with some of them, the democratic ones, the neutral ones maybe. But rather than 're-shaping the world' – some enterprise that! – we should be thinking of getting the most we can out of it as it is.

I think it is fair to say that opinions *about* Ireland in the Republic today are divided between that sort of view, which does not take Ireland seriously as a nation, and another view which does, and which I share. I reject the first view because it implies that, as an Irishman, I belong to a failed project – a nation that has given up. It treats as unimportant the fact that we have not yet in history created a state; that we feel constrained to live in a British-made state which we are afraid to reorganise to suit us; that our culture from our political institutions and language to 'For He's a Jolly Good Fellow' and horse-racing is largely derivative; that our journalists belong to a British trade union and the stock exchange in Dublin is a section of the London Stock Exchange; that our thought and hence our worldview are largely borrowed from London and that we have therefore not contributed anything of significance to the thought of our time; that when we import ideas or practices we seldom digest and re-think them so as to transform them into something marked by ourselves; that our industrial exports are mainly those of foreign firms in Ireland which repatriate their profits; that we have failed to generate, out of our own enterprise and resources, an economy sufficient to maintain ourselves; that we collaborate with Britain in suppressing rebellion against British rule in Ireland and, in betrayal of our neutrality, have allowed the Republic to be integrated into the British military and military surveillance systems; and that we lack both an independent foreign policy and its principal fruit – foreign alliances created by ourselves to serve our interests.

All of those things, which are of no importance to the view of Ireland which I have outlined and reject, are of importance to me. They are the evidence which shows that we have no real independence, and are not, therefore, living up to our nationhood or, simply, to our practical potential as four million well-fed, intelligent and imaginative people. Those Irishmen who tell us in effect to ignore this because it does not matter are, in fact and willy-nilly, collaborating spokesmen of the imperial propaganda which would have us believe just that. Insofar, moreover, as they are members of our political and administrative elite – whether of the national or the Euro kind – the thwarting of Ireland's independence is, indeed, a matter of practical indifference to many of them personally, because quite irrespective of its condition in the world, the Irish nation-state provides them with jobs, careers, influence and formal status.

Patriots who cite the list of social dependencies and inertias which I have cited above often do so in order to exhort us morally: they urge us to get up off our backsides or our knees and show more spirit, pride, enterprise and the like, as ordinary citizens or as politicians. I do not say that because I believe that, for the most part, those dependencies, inertias and servilities merely illustrate the predictable effect on us of a world so organised – around Ireland and within it – as to prevent the independence of small nations, Ireland included. And there are, to my mind, only two honourable and effective ways of dealing with this situation, mitigating its disgrace, and lessening its damage. We can call off our separate Irish project, become by acts of will and law British or American, and throw all our frustrated talents into making a splendid success of the United Kingdom or the United States. Or, recognising that we share a common interest with other small nations in re-shaping the world and its power relationships to make them at least less unfavourable to our project and theirs, we can start thinking how that might be done, and gradually move from thinking about it to sustained and intermittent action. This is my choice, and consequently, my hope for Ireland in the 1990s is that at least some among us will be doing this thinking, and that it will be taking practical effect.

Identifying the Real World
It will start, necessarily, by rejecting – losing faith in – the prevalent image of contemporary reality, and by identifying how things really are and how they came to be that way. The established 'view' of the world, the world-image which is presented to us and by which we largely see the world, is, needless to say, the tranquilising propaganda-image disseminated by London and New York. Its purpose is to represent the Western world – both as it is, and as it impinges on the rest of the world – as benign, natural, normal and inevitable. Regardless of how you or I, personally, regard this system of power and control, the fact is that it depends for its existence, not on nuclear bombs or standing armies or accumulated wealth, but on the faith of hundreds of millions – including four million Irish – in that imperial world-image and its message. It follows, then, that as we rid our minds of this illusion and construct another, truer, and inevitably subversive image, the constricting system weakens a little, and we begin to get hints and glimpses of a different, possible, less unfavourable world. We can start with nation-states.

The world is made up of states which call themselves nations and purport to be nations. A few centuries ago there were very few of these 'nation-states', but, as every nation wanted to be like Britain or France, or to a lesser extent Spain – these were old nation-states offering models for others to follow – there came to be nation-states all over the world. When we look closely at the three states which served as models, we notice that they are each made up of several nations and (in the case of France and Spain) parts of nations; for example, part of the Basque nation in Spain, parts of the Basque, Catalan, German and of other nations in France. In each case, to begin with, an imperial core-nation– English, Frankish, Castilian – hammered together into a single state a collection of national communities and ethnic groups and called them a nation. The resulting 'nation' – a sort of umbrella-nation or state-nation – was originally a fiction, but through schooling and inter-state wars it was made into a sort of accepted fact, coexisting among the subject nations and ethnic communities with their own thwarted communal lives and consciousness. Not surprisingly, then, as the habit of making nation-states took on and spread, many of them were similarly multinational conglomerates, culminating ultimately in the monster nation-states of the USA, the Soviet Union and China.

If we look again at the three original models, we notice that, from an early stage, the chief city of the core-nation – London, Paris, Madrid – came to dominate the entire nation-state, *including* the core-nation. Drawing strength and wealth from the communities it was subjecting and destroying – as it replaced the collection of communities with a mass of uprooted and isolated individuals and nuclear families – it attained in fact an imperial status and exercised an internal imperialism. Ancient Rome did the same in Italy while building its empire abroad, and these modern European capitals also built empires abroad. It has been a convenient fiction of the Modern Age to speak of the British, French and Spanish empires, when in fact the empires in question, at home and abroad, were those of London, Paris and Madrid, with the inhabitants of their respective nation-states working, as empire-builders and favoured clients, to increase, in the first instance, the power of these imperial power-centres. So great was their power, relatively, that, together with other centres of similar power, such as Vienna, Berlin and St Petersburg in their heydays, they became *world* power-centres; London and Paris have remained that even after 'losing' (a relative term these days) most of their empires abroad.

The upshot of it all was that, over the past two centuries, as more and more new nation-states emerged, each with its imperial power-centre, major or minor, the world arranged itself, not, in the first instance, as an assembly of nation-states large and small, but in the first instance, and effectively, as *great hierarchies of power-centres*. New York-Washington (or New York for short) is now the chief world power-centre. Through its dependent power-centres it holds dominion directly over the USA and indirectly over the rest of the American continent, Western Europe and further afield. Moscow, controlling the Soviet Union and much outside it through another hierarchy of power-centres, vies with New York for the top place. Beneath New York stand Chicago, Los Angeles, Dallas, Boston, Bogotá, Rio de Janeiro, Tokyo, London, Paris, Brussels, and beneath each of these its satellite power-centres – Dublin being one of London's. This is the New York empire.

An important thing to understand about the power-centres, major and minor, is that they are castles as much of mutual fear as of actual or would-be domination. As they came into existence, they frightened each other into existence – each of them concentrating as much power within itself as it could, so that it might withstand, and possibly overcome, its threatening rivals. And standing now, confronting each other competitively and fearfully, they maintain each other in existence. By an intricate system of interaction, London towers as high as it does over Ireland, England, Scotland, Wales, because, in their various ways, New York, Moscow, Beijing, Tokyo, Paris and Frankfurt compel it to tower high – as they compel each other, mutually and collectively, to tower high. Meanwhile, Dublin does its best, with the resources available to it in Ireland, to be our local London.

When I use a city-name to name a power-centre, I am referring, in the first instance, not to that mass of individuals – no longer a real city community – and the radiating force which its sheer mass and its economy generate, but rather, to the decision-making and controlling powers which exist there, and the accumulated resources, human and material, which they have at their disposal there. But of course the power exercised by a power-centre does not all issue directly from it. It issues also through a network of attached agents and collaborators 'in the provinces', and is increased by these. When the power-centre is of world status its provinces are far-flung and include many legally 'independent' states; and in each of these is a 'national' power-centre with its provinces; and in these again, in some states, sub-national power-centres, each with a province of its own.

Attached, therefore, to the hierarchies of imperial power-centres are hierarchies of dependent provinces; and these rank higher or lower roughly in accordance with the ranking of their national power-centre. In short, we live in a world of empires and provinces; more precisely, in a world of provinces depending on hierarchies of power-centres which, within their respective dominions and collectively, rule the world. Ireland is a province of the London region of the New York empire, and is dependent also on the Brussels confederacy which a group of major West European power-centres dominate.[1]

I have been using the word *province* in its qualitative sense to mean a society which is generally dependent and derivative – mentally, culturally, economically and politically. Patrick Kavanagh, describing a typical member of such a society in the mental aspect, wrote: 'The provincial has no mind of his own. He

---

1. Much of what I am discussing here is dealt with more fully in my book *Beyond Nationalism: The Struggle against Provinciality in the Modern World* (Ward River Press, Swords, 1985), especially in Ch. 5 on nationalism.

does not trust what his eye sees until he has heard what the metropolis – towards which his eyes are turned – has to say on the subject'. Imagine such a mentality multiplied by millions – or even by thousands in a provincial elite – and it is clear that the life which follows from it must be generally dependent and derivative. A province is the opposite and the negation of a *community*, whose hallmark is autonomy and autonomous life – springing from the distinct discourse and worldview which the members of the community have fashioned together.

Communities are the natural form of human social existence. They are made up of persons and – if they are of more than the smallest size, which comprises a number of nuclear families – of other communities also. Provinces are communities (or communities of communities) disempowered, disintegrated, and transformed into atomised, dependent 'individuals', who, in each province respectively, fall into two malleable masses, one considerably smaller than the other. This smaller mass, the 'provincial élite', provides the collective directorate in the provincial power-centre.

Latently, then, our world of empires and provinces is a world of communities, national or sub-national, old or embryonic, which are negated and thwarted in this manner. All of them, though maimed and muffled, are more or less conscious of themselves, feel themselves as *'we's*, as nations or ethnic groups, or urban, regional or neighbourhood communities, but are unable to realise that communal consciousness as autonomous life. Their more conscious and spirited elements try sporadically or persistently to do so, but they are continually counteracted by two forces: on the one hand, the dinned-in imperial image of the present world as the normal, humane and inevitable world; on the other, the attachment of the masses, rulers and ruled, to the goodies labelled The Good Life which the imperial system delivers and promises, with the constantly reiterated assertion: *'These are to be had only in these shapes and packagings, and delivered by this system on these terms'*. Which is a lie.

Imagining a Favourable World
That, roughly, is the nature of the world which is preventing Ireland and other small nations from having the independence they need; and, as I said above, identifying this real state of affairs is the first stage in thinking about how it might be transformed into a state of affairs less unfavourable to us. The second is, by a leap of mind, and without thought of ways or means, to imagine this present world changed into a world that would positively facilitate an Ireland in which we are no longer copy-cats, parrots and catcher-uppers living by laws, working in factories, lodging in a state, and accepting a worldview, which others have prescribed or financed or made, but

have become again, as we once were, a people creating our own sufficiency of wealth and our own unique worldview, life and culture.

What would that world be like which would favour this? The empires and provinces have been replaced by a world community of communities – the world in its natural human shape. Big Ben still chimes and Westminster Bridge still stands, but London's usurped powers of government and wealth-production, and many of its inhabitants, have returned to Scotland, Wales, Mann, Cornwall, and the regions of England. The Seine still flows through a Paris that has lost its fat, and it is still a lovely city in the spring; but Brittany, Normandy, Occitania, Corsica, Alsace and Picardy have come into their own again. California, New England, Dixie, Texas, the Sioux, Apaches and Hopis, and many other nations – one along the Hudson – whose names we don't yet know, have replaced, on its home territory, the New York empire. Armenia, Azerbaijan, Uzbekistan and Kurdistan, Estonia, Lithuania, Ukrania and Georgia, in their own full right, under their own governments, contribute once again their uniqueness to the world, and Siberia is astonishing the world with its new song. Zulus, Afrikaners, Masai, Yoruba and Ndebele, the absurd colonial boundaries and the Pretorian empire cast aside, join with Ngoni and Xhosa in the assembly of African nations. In short, the world is much as the map reproduced on pages 108-109 shows; it was made by Peter Broberg of Malmö, Sweden, who has a similar vision.

Technology is no longer such that it seems to compel bigness of organisation and of institutions; in all its forms it is available for effective small-scale use, so that the choice between large-scale and small-scale can be made, and is made, pragmatically, in accordance with the individual and collective needs of communities and persons. States are no longer marshallers of peoples, but the pragmatic instruments and agencies with which they manage, respectively, their common affairs and their formal international relationships. Desires for wholeness, integrity, omnipotence, absolute justice, are expressed by other means.

Many groups of small nations adjoining a large nation are linked as confederations, balancing the weight and influence of the large nation. While the nations of North and South America speak, for the most part, English or Spanish, most nations worldwide speak their own individual languages and use them in their educational systems, while also using, as a *lingua franca*, some other suitable language – often that of a large nation adjoining them. In the British Isles, what should have happened centuries ago, and would have given all these peoples a happier history, is now fact: Ireland, Scotland, Wales and Mann, each speaking its own language while using English as a *lingua franca*, are linked in the Confederation of

Mann, balancing the weight of England.

The United Nations Organisation is in good health, with a greatly increased membership, and its headquarters in Mauritius. A universal upsurge against the massacring technology of modern warfare has resulted in the enactment by all nations of the Law Against Massacre, and the establishment of a United Nations police force, with worldwide detachments and unlimited inspection rights, to supervise its enforcement by national police forces. The Law lays down that anyone found possessing or manufacturing a lethal or disabling device capable of killing or disabling, by its single use, more than one person, will be executed; and any nation found conniving officially in a breach of the law will have its frontiers, airports and ports sealed for a period of three years.

Making the Present World Less Unfavourable
Such a vision will serve as a guide and goal in the third and final stage of thinking about how the world and its power relationships might be made less hostile to the independence of Ireland and of other small nations. This final stage issues directly in practical action, and is consequently the kind of thinking which I hope we will be implementing in the 1990s. Aiming at the transformation of the world into a de-imperialised, deprovincialised, and disarmed community of communities, it will identify the immediate courses of action which, while gradually increasing our freedom in the present, will nudge the world towards that future state. As these lines of action are identified, they are combined in an active foreign policy with political, economic and cultural dimensions.

This policy is likely to have four immediate aims.

1. Alliances which would strengthen us against London, in the first instance, against New York in the second.

2. The reconstruction of the European Community as a grouping not of nation-states, but of national and regional communities – the national communities to include all those nations, such as Scotland, Wales, Brittany, Corsica, Euzkadi and Sardinia, which at present have no representation.

3. The encouragement by one means or another of the break-up of large states, and of autonomy, or greater autonomy, for nations and regions within large states.

4. The promotion by one means or another of the abolition and effective suppression of weapons of massacre.

When the Republic and the Six-County Irish, in the early part of 1988, had to endure a series of grave provocations from London, such that the Irish government responded repeatedly with

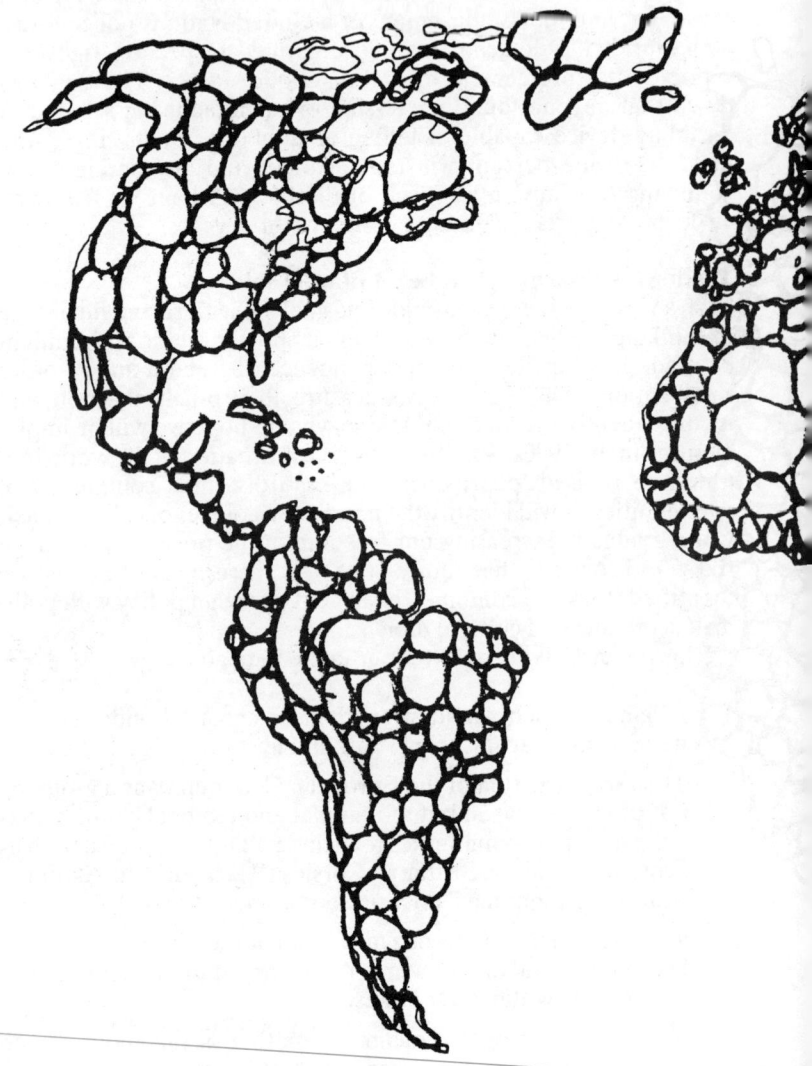

A WORLD COMMUNTIY OF COMMUNITIES

measured anger, the remarkable fact became apparent that Ireland has no allies. No other government, no prominent person or group in a foreign country, spoke out on Ireland's behalf. To be without allies who take its side in international disputes is an anomalous condition for a state or nation. Even before Irish independence, our nationalist struggle against London sought and found support at different times from Spain, France, Germany and the USA. Since the forging of alliances is one of the normal priorities of a foreign policy, and specifically of a Department of Foreign Affairs, this current isolation of Ireland suggests that we are without an effective foreign policy or Department of Foreign Affairs.

The isolation I am talking about is not of Irish people as individuals: never before have so many Irish people been in direct or indirect contact with such a wide extent of the world. It is an isolation, rather, of our nation, our collective life, our body politic, none of which reflect or exploit, in its international relationships, the far-ranging involvement of individual Irish people in the present-day world. On the contrary, our government gives the impression that, apart from our membership of the EC, it is somehow illicit for us to be allied with other nations.

Self-debarred on principle from being members of the British Commonwealth, it seems that we cannot be members of NATO because we are neutral, nor of the group of European neutrals because we are members of the EC, nor of the group of non-aligned nations for the same reason. But when we have a row with London, neither the other EC countries as a group, nor some of them, intervene on our behalf. Nor is the case any different when, quite apart from our disputes with London, matters affecting the Irish interest arise in the European Community. It seems that we have no special alliance with anyone in the Community, say, with the smaller countries, or the agricultural ones, or France, or Spain. Yet we cannot, it seems, ally with Third World countries because we are developed, nor with Middle Eastern countries because they are not respectable, nor with postcolonial, anti-imperialist countries because that might seem Provo, nor with China because that would seem far-fetched, nor with Cuba, though its geopolitical position *vis-à-vis* New York is very similar to ours *vis-à-vis* London. Meanwhile the only active support offered to the Irish in their dispute with London – the support from militant Irish-Americans, Libya, the PLO and the Basque ETA – is unacceptable to the Republic of Ireland because it is extended to the IRA; or alternatively, goes to the IRA because Dublin has no use for it.

Is there some hangover in all of this from our days as 'Catholic Ireland in a pagan world'? Some notion that Ireland, that is, official Ireland, is so pure, different, noble, moral, ethereal, that it is not of this world, and that therefore any conceivable alliance or special relationship which would serve the earthly interests of our national independence is not appropriate for us, would sully us? Better perish than be defiled – or judged not respectable by our superiors? Whatever the reason, this scandal of our political isolation must be looked at and discussed, its motivations rejected, and decisions taken to form alliances which will lessen our mental, political, economic and cultural dependence on London and New York, and our subjection within the European Community to the collective interests of the major West European power-centres.

Within Europe, to go no further, we are characterised by history and present circumstance in two ways which offer us advantageous linkages: by inheritance we are a 'Celtic' country, and in terms of the power relationships of Western Europe we are a 'peripheral' region. We are, moreover, the only one of the Celtic countries which has the rank of statehood, and were until this year – when Greece and Portugal became single regions of the European Community – the only peripheral region of the Community with state status. On the face of it, that would seem to have fitted us to assume a leading role in both these categories. But since the end of the de Valera era – which was marked by several initiatives towards the other Celtic countries – we have largely ignored the Celtic aspect of our Europeanness; and since joining the European Community we have ignored, and failed to exploit, the peripheral condition within it which we share with other regions and nations extending from Sicily and Sardinia through Andalusia and Brittany to Scotland and Jutland.

During a period when things Celtic have been in vogue throughout Europe, when traditional Irish music has been acquiring a worldwide following, and people of Celtic sentiment and culture in Brittany, Wales, Mann and Scotland have looked to independent Ireland for leadership, we have allowed the major annual Celtic cultural festival – attended by hundreds of Irish performers – to be established in Lorient, not Dublin, and we have no Irish cultural information centre, let alone a consulate, in Wales, Scotland or Brittany. In the 70s some Bretons founded the biennial Conference of European Maritime Peripheral Regions, with its headquarters in Rennes, and a membership extending from the Mediterranean through Ireland West and Mid-West to Northern Norway. This, as it happened, gave me the idea of an institute, located in Ireland, for the interdisciplinary study of European peripheral regions. Assuming that EC funding might be available, I proposed it first to University College, Galway, then to the Irish Council of the European Movement and the Irish Commissioner in Brussels; but none of these showed interest, and I felt, in the case of the latter two, that they regarded the notion as at best hare-brained, at worst subversive. Neither then nor since have we had any Irish institute devoted to any branch of European studies. Of course, an institute for the study of European peripheral regions was only one of the ways in which Ireland, the only member-state which was also a peripheral region, might have marshalled the periphery of the EC to assert its interests *vis-à-vis* the dominating centre – the Birmingham-Milan-Hamburg triangle and its supporting governments. In the event we chose no way.

What we see here under both heads, Celtic and peripheral, is a shunning by Ireland of her place and reality within the British Isles and within Europe – a place and reality which, if asserted, would be very much in her interest and would give her a leading role. And this shunning of our real location in the cultural heritage and geo-politics of Europe is symptomatic of our general refusal in today's world to 'be ourselves', and therefore first-rate and strong, in favour of 'being not ourselves' and therefore weak, second-rate and failing. Instead of embodying, forcefully, within the British Isles and Europe, the Celtic idea and the peripheral interest, and gathering allies around itself under both heads, the Republic of Ireland has chosen to hover shiftily, in isolation from all but London, a sort of mini-England with an interest in agricultural prices and subsidies.

In effect I am suggesting that the Republic of Ireland play as creative and self-interested a role in the restructuring of the European Community as the Irish Free State did in the restructuring of the British Commonwealth; and I am arguing that, for the successful maintenance of our body politic and a lessening of our dependency, it is imperative that we do so. With the Community structured as it is, and with partial free trade among its member states, the economically stronger regions have grown stronger, and the weaker ones relatively weaker, with a resulting increase in dependency and emigration in the latter. It is reasonable to assume that, under the conditions of full free trade which will operate from 1992 onwards, this process will intensify unless effective counter-measures are taken. 'Europe' will be integrated, but it will not be Europe, because many of the autonomous social personalities – including Ireland – which have gone to make Europe will have ceased effectively to exist. The 'pro-Europeans' among us who are not concerned about this are not pro-Europeans, but enemies of Europe and of Ireland who are serving an anti-Irish, anti-European and anti-human idol – a nothing-god of geography and power economics.

Yann Foueré, a Breton who settled many years ago in Connemara, published a book in 1968 called *L'Europe aux Cent Drapeaux* (Europe of the Hundred Flags).[2] The title speaks for itself. Foueré argued that the construction of a European Union on the basis of

2.   Presses d'Europe, Paris.

Professor Northcote Parkinson's suggestion of 'The Little (United) States of Europe' in *Profiles*, Brussels, 1975.

the existing nation-states would – because of the operation of the centre-versus-periphery process – result in the final destruction of most of the nations, ethnic and regional communities, which the larger states contain. To prevent this, and to construct a unified Europe which would both preserve Europe, and revive its rich diversity, he advocated first, the transformation of the big states into federations of region-states, together with the adjustment where necessary of existing state boundaries to restore the integrity of split nations or ethnic groups such as the Basques, the Flemings or the Tyrolese; secondly, the establishment of a Community government based on the region-states, and giving their delegates, collectively, the power to decide the norms on which the Community would operate.[3]

I believe that, in our own interest, and without waiting for 1992, we should adopt this programme, canvass and organise support for it throughout the European Community, and demand that the assembly of the (real) nations, ethnic communities and regions of Europe have the right to look again at the Single European Act and all other Community measures, and take all future decisions about the shape and trading regulations of the Community. Naturally, it would take time to bring about this transformation of the Community, but the support for it would be such that we could reasonably hope that, by the mid-1990s, Ireland would belong to a European Community which would not be inimical to her national and social interests.

Already three of the big West European states have begun to lay the foundations for such a Community. West Germany is a federation of eleven states which lead vigorous autonomous lives. Italy has twenty, Spain seventeen, devolved regional assemblies with considerable powers. In Eastern Europe, Yugoslavia, in one of the boldest constitutional ventures of modern times, is a federation of six very autonomous republics and two autonomous regions. The diversity of its nations and cultures shakes it continually, but it persistently retains respect for this, preferring the difficulty of coping with it to the simplicity of domination by the biggest city of its biggest nation.

It is in our national interest to encourage throughout Europe and the world at large all decentralisation of power within large states, whether this be by way of granting autonomy (federal or devolved) to distinct nations or ethnic groups, or similar autonomy to regions within the same nation. Even more so, it is in our interest to encourage national breakaways from large multinational empires. All such developments would involve diminishing the power of one or other of the major power-centres, thereby lessening, as by a chain reaction, the felt need for power in others, so that, by one means or the other – direct or indirect – the power-centres directly dominating us would become less dominating. But our interest apart, all domination of nations or regional communities, whether within states or across state boundaries, is imperialism, and it is therefore not only self-interested, but in keeping with our anti-imperialist tradition – and a continuance of it – to take this line, pursue this policy, and let it be known and advertised worldwide.

If a small nation such as Cuba can pursue its own brand of anti-imperialism, even to the point of military involvement, in countries

---

3.   Under this arrangement larger nations, such as the English and French, would have larger representations than smaller ones. England and the French part of France, divided respectively into, say, eight regions, would each have eight times the representation of a nation possessing only one region-state.

distant from its shores, so can we, by diplomatic means and propaganda, without going so far as to dispatch regiments. Of course we could do this with a better conscience if we decentralised *ourselves*: if we set about reorganising our own country as a federal state of four or five units, and prevailing on Britain and the Ulster British to aid and abet this with regard to Ulster. I have had much to say about this elsewhere.[4] But even without doing that, and simply as a small nation in whose interest it is that power be deconcentrated in the world around it, we can make this a foreign policy aim with a good conscience and our heads high.

It is in our interest that Estonia, the other Baltic nations of the USSR, Armenia, Georgia and Uzbekistan, successfully assert their national rights *vis-à-vis* Moscow. It is in our interest that the native American nations of the USA, having already proven their legal right to be recognised by Washington as 'governments', go on to secure the recognition of their independence and their territorial integrity, thereby beginning the transformation of the USA into an assembly of independent nations. It is in our interest, again, that Tibet regain autonomy from China, that the Kurds divided among three countries acquire a state of their own, that the Zulus separate from South Africa, the Vietnamese withdraw from Cambodia and Laos, and that Scotland becomes independent. Once we have got used to seeing our interest in these and similar terms, the means of encouraging such developments – by every means from the supportive telegram or delegation to the vote at the United nations or the provision of technical assistance – will occur to us as each case arises.

Finally, there is the matter of our interest in working actively for world disarmament. It is clearly contrary to the interests of a small nation that powers which can reach it should possess weapons of massacre, whether these be bomber planes, or missiles capable of delivering nuclear, chemical or biological death. It is not, in the first instance, a matter of such powers actually using these weapons against us, but of the intimidatory force which their possession of them gives to their demands on us and indeed to all their dealings with us. But weapons of massacre are also grossly immoral, and it behoves us, as a nation so taken by morality that our public discourse is mostly moralising, to be much more active in getting rid of them than we have been hitherto. A world, moreover, numbly sickened in the hearts of hundreds of millions by the horror of

---

4. See, for example, my *Sunday Press* column 1969-72, 1980-84; the booklet, *Sketches of the New Ireland* (The Association for the Advancement of Self-Government, Galway, 1973); *Beyond Nationalism* (cf note 1), Chs. 3 and 4; and the chapter, 'A Federal Ireland' in *Options for a Divided Society: Proposals for a way forward in Northern Ireland*, ed. John McGarry, Oxford University Press (forthcoming).

modern warfare, is waiting for leadership in this matter far more radical than any that has yet been seen. We could give it that leadership, and it would give a dignity and constructive content to our professed neutrality which at present it sadly lacks.

We could begin by ending our surreptitious integration into the British military and military surveillance systems which, apart from their application to Northern Ireland, are concerned largely with preparations for a nuclear war. We could then – and how strange and telling that this suggestion is shocking to the contemporary Irish mentality! – call a conference of small nations on disarmament, not confining the invitations to their governments. What Ireland could and should do afterwards would emerge from that.

I believe that the elements of a foreign policy which I have sketched here would fit together coherently, and that the resulting policy, executed in political, economic and cultural terms, would not only serve our national independence – which is what a foreign policy is supposed to do – but would also make Ireland again, both in the minds of many of its inhabitants and in the world's eyes, an interesting, rather than a boring country.

– PART II –
SOCIAL AND ECONOMIC PERSPECTIVES

Ireland's Economic Welfare in a
Barrier Free Europe
EITHNE MURPHY

It would be difficult to think of a year that has been mentioned more often than 1992. As a reporter for *The Economist* magazine said '1992 has become a state of mind'.[1] The reason for the general level of excitement is that the last day of 1992 is *supposed* to herald the completion of the internal market, an event which should have a profound impact on the economic wellbeing of all of us who live and work within the European Community (EC). I emphasize the word 'supposed' because, like anything that is subject to political forces, it must remain a matter of speculation whether the measures deemed necessary to complete the internal market will actually survive the political process. The aforementioned measures are contained in the European Commission's White Paper to the European Council[2] and are approximately 300 in number. (It is rather interesting to note at this juncture that 20 or more measures have since been dropped.)

The objective of this article is to assess some of the likely economic implications for Ireland of the completion of the internal market. I am of course assuming that we will see the creation of an internal market in which goods, services, people and capital will be free to move without restriction. This assumption may be unrealistic but, given the vagaries of the political process, it is the only workable scenario with which to proceed.

One could justifiably question the efficacy of writing about an event on which a decision has already been taken. We as a nation have already decided constitutionally in favour of strengthening the European connection. Discussion is a valid and useful exercise if it

---

1. Nicholas Colchester, 'Europe's Internal Market', *The Economist*, 9-15 July 1985.
2. Commission of the European Communities, 'Completing the Internal Market', White Paper from the Commission to the European Council, Milan, 28-29 June 1985.

can have a bearing on the outcome. In this instance it is probably safe to assume that, although we have ratified the Single European Act (SEA), the economic outcome for Ireland of the process that has been set in legislative motion depends, to some extent, on the response of Irish people and the Irish government to the opportunities and threats confronting us in a barrier free EC. It does however place the onus on commentators to appraise realistically the issues. Much of what has been passing for economic debate at a political level is little more than ex post economic rationalisation. Such rationalisation is of little use in helping us face a post 1992 world, unless of course our political leaders believe that it will help engender a positive national outlook and thus improve our chances of economic success.

The economic rationalisation that politicians have used to justify our support of the SEA has usually proceeded along the lines that, since Ireland is a small open economy for whom exports constitute the engine of our growth, then the internal market by enhancing our export potential should be a positive force in helping us to realize greater economic prosperity. The problem with this kind of reasoning is not what it says but what it fails to say. Undoubtedly the more we export the greater will be our gross domestic product (GDP) and presumably this will have a positive impact on our level of national economic welfare (assuming of course that most of the population get the chance to share in it). However the completion of the internal market is designed to ensure that goods, services, capital and people are free to move within the EC. The dangers for Ireland are that this could result in more unemployment, emigration and capital outflows. The above phenomena are related and will be dealt with in greater detail later in this article.

When referring to economic prosperity I am assuming that the indicators of same for Ireland are: gross national product (GNP); GNP per capita; low unemployment; and some minimum income threshold for the poorest section of society. I accept that not everyone may assess national economic progress in the same way. For the true Europeans the word national is probably anachronistic. They presumably would not view emigration (or internal EC migration if you prefer) in a negative way. If one agrees with that perspective, then the relevant indicators of economic progress are not the Irish values of the aforementioned variables but their EC values. In this article, the economic performance of the EC as a whole is considered to be relevant only insofar as it has an impact on the Irish economy.

Barriers that Divide the European Community
Title II of the Single European Act contains provisions amending the Treaties that established the European Communities. The

objective of the Treaty of Rome (one of the aforementioned treaties) was the establishment of a common market. In economic textbooks, a common market is usually defined as an area in which goods, services, people and capital can move freely. Although the EC succeeded in liberalizing trade between Member States, it manifestly failed in its objective of creating a common market. It is not as easy to transport goods from Munich to Paris as it is to transport goods from Munich to Hamburg. Similarly, it is still easier for a person to travel within a country than between countries. This has nothing to do with the distances involved, rather it is a product of national boundaries. The Treaty of Rome may have succeeded in removing almost all tariffs and quotas on intra EC trade, but this is not synonymous with the creation of a common market. The barriers that remain have been classified in the Commission's White Paper as physical, technical and fiscal. All add to the cost of transporting goods between one Member State and another, and, in some instances, they actually prevent trade and the movement of people and capital. They are symbols of a fragmented Europe and it is the removal of these barriers to which Member States have committed themselves.

Removal of physical barriers is dependant upon: the removal of remaining duties and quotas on intra EC trade (monetary compensatory amounts, national steel and textile quotas plus bilateral voluntary agreements negotiated between individual Member States and non member countries); the removal of underlying technical and fiscal barriers; finding new means of carrying out functions that were previously performed at international borders. It will mean Member States having to harmonise their legislation on drugs, armaments and the treatment of refugees. It will mean devising new methods of collecting trade statistics and indirect taxes. It will not be an easy process, its implications for national sovereignty are too great.

Technical barriers exist within countries. Examples of same are: national standards as to product specifications, whose aims are ostensibly the protection of the consumer and of the environment; restrictions on trade in the financial services sector; and a non recognition of professional and vocational qualifications acquired in other Member States. *Mutual recognition* and *harmonisation* are the means by which the plethora of technical barriers that still exist will be removed. The former means that provisions in existence in one state must be recognised in another. This approach recognises that the underlying objective of such standards is usually the same in all Member States, even though differences may exist as far as the specifics of national rules are concerned. Recognition of vocational and professional qualifications will also be a feature of the internal market. In certain instances, harmonisation of legislation will be necessary to ensure a good or service unrestricted mobility within the EC. Such legislative harmonisation will however be much less detailed than previously existed. It will confine itself to essential requirements with which national legislation must comply.

The most difficult barriers to remove will undoubtedly be fiscal ones because of the extent to which they impinge upon national sovereignty. The level of indirect taxation in a country has fiscal, distributional and public health consequences. The Commission has proposed the establishment of two bands for value added tax (VAT), a standard rate of 14 to 19 percent and a reduced rate of 4 to 9 percent. The standard rate will apply to most goods and the reduced rate to basic goods and services. All goods and services will be included in the VAT base. Excise duties will be harmonised at approximately the EC average rate. Tax will continue to be applied according to the destination principle. In other words the same rate of indirect tax applies to the same products regardless of their origin. The tax revenue due to the national exchequer will still depend on the level of domestic consumption. However, instead of using the border to give tax refunds on exports and to levy domestic taxes on imports, a clearing house mechanism has been devised to replace borders. For example, an Irish manufacturer selling goods to a German importer will include VAT in the selling price of the good. The VAT paid by the German importer will be refunded to him/-her by the German exchequer, while the VAT collected by the Irish exporter must be refunded to the Irish exchequer. The latter amount must then be paid by the Irish exchequer to its German counterpart. German consumers will continue to pay the same rate of VAT on goods regardless of their origin, thus preserving the neutrality of the system. Of course funds paid by one national exchequer to another will be executed on a net balance basis.

This proposal will not be subject to majority voting in the Council of Ministers. It is difficult to imagine it getting the approval of all Member States. Britain favours unlimited cross border shopping without any formal EC harmonisation of VAT and excise duties. They want the narrowing of indirect tax rates to be a consequence of free market forces. France favours a longer timetable for the changes scheduled to be completed by the end of 1992. Other countries such as Ireland and Denmark will suffer a considerable loss of revenue if they are obliged to adopt the new indirect tax bands. In addition, the clearing house system does seem to be rather unwieldy and there will be greater scope for fraud.

Other Potential Developments that could
Further the Process of European Integration
Two potential developments that are not included in the European Commission's White Paper on completing the internal market but

that have been discussed by the Commission are, the harmonisation of company taxation and the development of a monetary union. Both developments would be necessary in the creation of a genuine common market.

Differing rates of company taxation can distort the flow of capital to the detriment of overall productivity in the EC. Capital would not necessarily migrate to where its marginal productivity was greatest. Harmonisation of rates of company taxation would be one means of removing such a distortion in a market where capital flows were fully liberalized.

Exchange rate stability and capital liberalisation are not compatible except in some kind of monetary union. Hence, unless progress is made in the direction of a monetary union, freedom of capital movements will lead to increased exchange rate instability and ultimately undermine the European Monetary System (EMS).

Completing the Internal Market – An Aggregate Perspective

The SEA was motivated in part by the political objective of furthering the cause of European political union but primarily by the pragmatic lure of revitalizing the economy of the EC. The EC has not been performing as well as its main economic rivals, the United States and Japan, in terms of growth, employment and technological development. Being political entities, the latter countries have the benefit of large barrier free domestic markets. The internal market mission is based upon a belief that there is a causal link between a genuine common market and economic growth. If the EC could be welded into a market in which no barriers to the free mobility of goods, services and resources exist, then as the world's largest common market with 320 million consumers, it could form the basis for a more prosperous EC.

Trade theory supports the link between free trade and economic prosperity. In its traditional guise, trade theory states that countries trade because they are different in terms of resources, technology and taste. According to the law of comparative advantage if each country specializes in what it does *relatively* best, then their overall level of productivity will increase to the benefit of all countries concerned. These gains are sometimes labelled the static gains from trade, i.e. the once off gains associated with a more optimal use of resources.

Contemporary trade theory stresses the gains to be got from specialization as a result of economies of size. A larger market facilitates the growth of large firms. If economies of size exist, then the larger the scale of operation the lower the unit cost of production. This further enhances productivity. Whereas trade based on traditional comparative advantage tends to be inter-industry in nature, with countries specializing into or out of whole industries, trade based on size economies tend to be more intra industry in nature, with countries exporting and importing products belonging to the same industry. The former is more common between countries at different stages of development, whereas the latter is a feature of trade between industrialized countries who tend to be similar in terms of resources, technology and taste. The two theories are complementary rather than competitive. In fact economies of size merely add to the overall gains that are afforded by trade. One distinction between the two theories of trade in terms of their effect is that, according to the comparative advantage view of the world all countries stand to gain from trade, whereas this is no longer necessarily the case if the basis for trade is economies of size. In the latter instance, despite enhanced gains afforded to the integrated area, all countries may not necessarily gain, especially if they end up specializing in industries where economies of size are absent.

Another theory designed to explain why trade stimulates increased productivity is the x efficiency theory. According to x efficiency proponents, lack of competition can result in a less than optimal use of resources within firms. Hence the creation of an internal market, by increasing and intensifying the competition that firms face, force from them a higher level of productivity. This is popularly known as the cold shower effect.

Free mobility of resources within an internal market should serve to enhance still further the productivity of resources, since it allows resources to migrate to where their earning power is greatest. Assuming that earning power reflects productivity levels, this can only serve to boost output levels.

All the aforementioned effects should ensure a greater level of economic activity than would exist if markets remained small and fragmented. However, as stated in the Commission's White Paper, the objective is not just to ensure a single market but also one that is expanding, not static. The issue at stake is whether an internal market will simply move the economy of the EC on to a higher plateau of economic activity or whether it will ensure that continuous growth will be a feature of the new arrangement. Growth does not just depend on a more optimal use of existing resources, it requires continuous investment in order to expand the resource base and improve on its performance. A common market should serve to reduce uncertainty as to other countries' commercial policies, which in itself should be conducive to investment. Likewise, since a larger market means a greater potential demand for the products of research and development (R+D), this should stimulate innovation. If the internal market results in the rationalization of industry, as is expected, then this could also have a positive effect on R+D, assuming of course that economies of size exist in R+D. In the latter instance, one would expect expenditure on

R+D to be greater in an internal market consisting of large firms than in a more fragmented market where the average size of firms is smaller.

At a theoretical level the positive association between a large common market and a greater level of economic activity is unambiguous.

In March 1988 the Commission of the EC under the chairmanship of Paolo Cecchini published a report[3] in which they attempted to estimate empirically the economic benefits that would ensue from the creation of an internal market. According to the aforementioned report, a completed internal market would increase EC GDP by between 2.5 to 7 percent, depending on whether one assumes macroeconomic policy is going to be passive or active. The price level would fall by approximately 6 percent and 2 million additional jobs should be created. (That represents an increase in the initial employment level of nearly 2 percent). Of course such figures are only very approximate, being the product of very approximate information, certain economic assumptions and judgement. For example, two important assumptions underlying the empirical estimates are: that it will take 5 or more years to realize the large part of the effects; and that micro and macroeconomic policies will ensure that the resources released as industries adjust to increased competition, will be productively re-employed. This ignores the possibility of an adverse political reaction in some countries to the short-run adjustment costs, which will initially include increased unemployment as industries undergo rationalisation and restructuring in response to stiffer international competition.

Completing the Internal Market – The Distributional Consequences
This is the issue of greatest concern to a country like Ireland which is peripheral to Europe both geographically and economically. It is also an issue that has not been adequately addressed at Commission level, notwithstanding the fact that the structural funds are due to be doubled, an issue that will be discussed below. In fact the Commission's White Paper mentions that one of the objectives in completing the internal market is to ensure the flexibility of markets so that resources can flow into the areas of greatest economic advantage.

Such a scenario would not necessarily be to the advantage of a country like Ireland which, at its present state of development, cannot ensure a return to resources comparable with the returns available in regions of greatest economic advantage. Subsequently, the White Paper does make reference to the inherent risks involved for poorer regions when resources are free to move without obstacle

---

3. Commission of the European Communities, 'The Economics of 1992', European Economy No. 35, March 1988.

to the areas of greatest economic advantage, but it is suggested that this is a problem for which a solution must be found on the basis that frontiers will have been abolished. It is suggested that the structural funds need to be used in an imaginative way in order to prevent regions in the EC from diverging further.

The Cecchini Report, which attempted to estimate the magnitude of the expected gains arising from a barrier-free Europe, made no attempt to measure the regional distribution of the gains on the grounds that such a task would be extremely difficult. However they do state that neither economic theory nor economic history can point to any clear-cut pattern of likely distributional advantage or disadvantage, although analysis of trade between industrialized countries tend to favour the theory of more balanced or indeterminate outcomes between regions. (The problem for Ireland is that our level of industrialisation is not comparable to that of other Member States). After admitting to a certain degree of uncertainty as to the spatial effects of integration, the report then proceeded to make the totally unsubstantiated claim that smaller countries have proportionately the biggest opportunities for gain from market integration. Such claims, for which neither theoretical nor empirical support was given, are not just careless and misleading but quite dangerous, especially when used as propaganda weapons. If we are to stand a credible chance of prospering economically in a large barrier free common market, then we need to be realistic about the threats that will confront us.

Issues of Concern to Ireland
The issues of concern to Ireland in terms of their immediacy are: the government's fiscal problem if the proposed harmonisation of indirect taxes is implemented; increased competition that many domestic sectors will encounter; and the longer term threat of a decline in our resource base due to emigration and capital outflows.

These threats are not mutually exclusive. The response to the fiscal crisis will undoubtedly have a bearing on the competitiveness of industry, while the success or otherwise of Irish industry in the 1990s will influence resource migration.

Harmonisation of Indirect Taxation Rates
The Commission is proposing that both the base and rates of indirect taxation (value added tax and excise duties) be harmonised by 1992. As mentioned previously, this is an area where reform will prove to be most difficult. Ireland has accepted the Commission's proposal in principle yet, according to government sources, if the proposals proceed unaltered it would mean a loss to the national exchequer of IR£420 million in the first year and further annual losses of IR£350 million thereafter. Independent estimates have put

the loss at approximately IR£198 million.[4] Even this figure may indeed be an overestimate, given that the study did not take into account the secondary expenditure effects that would ensue as a consequence of consumers disposable income having increased. However, though one may quibble about the extent to which indirect tax revenue would fall, the fact remains that the decline would be of sufficient magnitude to be a matter of concern to the national exchequer, especially in these days of fiscal rectitude. Unless some compensation is received at Community level, making up the shortfall would leave the government with politically unpopular options; increase direct taxation; levy some kind of property tax; cut public expenditure. These options would also have adverse economic and social consequences. The Minister for Finance has indicated compensation will be sought from the EC to make up the losses. Increased funds accruing to Ireland under the structural funds should not be acceptable as a means of making up the shortfall, since their purpose is developmental not the subsidisa-tion of a country's national exchequer.

The rates of tax applying to goods and services tend to influence consumption patterns through their impact on relative prices. At 25 percent Ireland has the highest standard rate of VAT in the EC. This applies mainly to luxury type goods. In addition excise duties on drink, cigarettes and petrol are the highest in the EC. However our VAT base is also very narrow and many items are zero rated, namely food, children's clothing, rented accommodation, fuel and books. The Commission's proposals would lower the tax on so called luxury items and increase the tax on necessities. Such a development could be claimed to be regressive in its impact insofar as it would have the greatest adverse effect on those who spend the greatest proportion of their income on basic necessities. Also, one could question the desirability of the consequences for public health of a big reduction in the price of cigarettes and alcohol.

The Competitive Position of Irish Industry
Ultimately the success or otherwise of the Irish economy in the 1990s will depend on the strength of Irish industry. Certainly consumers will gain from competitive prices, but this must be balanced against the effect on their earning power of greater competition.

Export Market
In theory Irish companies should stand to gain from a reduction in barriers protecting the markets of continental Member States.

---

4.   Irvine, I., Thom, D. R., and Walsh, B. M., Department of Political Economy, University College Dublin. Unpublished report.

Because of our peripheral location Irish exporters have more frontiers to cross, all of which add to the cost of exporting. Hence one would expect the proportional savings to Irish companies to be greater than that enjoyed by their continental rivals. Also, if the completion of the internal market results in greater national prosperity for the EC as a whole, this could have a positive spin off effect for the Irish economy, to the extent that it results in increased demand for our exports.

At present most of our exports to continental Europe are accounted for by foreign owned firms operating in the high technology sector. Since much of this trade is intra-firm (sales from one subsidiary to another) in nature, and since decisions regarding market expansion are taken by the parent company, the prospect of these firms expanding their exports in any significant way in response to lower barriers remains in doubt. Indeed O'Malley in his survey of Irish industry mentioned that many of those companies who registered a negative response to overseas expansion were in fact foreign-owned subsidiaries operating in high technology sectors.[5] Of course it must be remembered that an increase in exports accounted for by foreign owned subsidiaries located in Ireland can also occur as a result of an increase in the number of such firms located here. If the completion of the internal market improves access to the rest of the EC, thus making Ireland less peripheral, then Ireland becomes a more attractive location for foreign investment. However, having said that, the benefit of increased exports to the domestic economy is greater when the activity is undertaken by indigenous companies, since the latter usually have much greater linkages to the rest of the economy and are less likely to repatriate profits abroad.

The problem to date is that indigenous companies have not proved to be very successful in exporting to continental Europe. One would suspect that this is primarily a consequence of our general lack of proficiency in foreign languages and poor marketing skills. Overcoming this very definite market barrier is an area where government education policy can play a role. In recent times there does seem to be increased awareness among third level institutions about the need to make progress in this area. Some are now offering for the first time combined degrees in business studies and a foreign language. Whether the effort to improve our linguistic skills will be sufficient to enable indigenous companies to venture into continental European markets to a greater extent than heretofore remains to be seen.

Export-oriented indigenous companies have mainly concentrated their marketing effort on Britain and the United States. The

5. Chris O'Malley, *Over in Europe*, Orchard Press Ltd, Dublin 1988.

British and Irish markets are reasonably well integrated due to historical reasons. Therefore the removal of the remaining non-tariff barriers is more likely to benefit our continental rivals to a greater extent than Irish companies.

Much can also be done unilaterally to improve our market position in both the British and continental markets. Better infrastructure and an improved trade clearance system would reduce the delays and consequent increase in costs suffered by Irish exporters. Ireland has not yet computerized its system of import and export clearance, despite the introduction of the Single Administrative Document (SAD) which is meant to be processed on computer. The SAD is designed to simplify customs procedures, by replacing the plethora of documentation previously required by exporters and importers with a single document. From a policy point of view, the dilemma faced by those responsible for taking a decision on whether or not to computerize customs procedures, is whether such a measure will be rendered redundant by future developments. In a genuine frontier free internal market customs posts will not exist as far as intra-EC trade is concerned. Hence the SAD would also be redundant. A computerized system would only be of use as far as non-EC trade is concerned. On the other hand, if the 1990s does not herald the completion of the internal market (a distinct possibility when one considers the political hurdles that must be overcome before it can become reality), but rather results in the EC becoming a more integrated albeit still incomplete common market, then it is definitely in our economic interests to improve customs procedures.

Domestic Market
Just as foreign markets will be more open to competition so too will the Irish market be more open to penetration from foreign companies. A wider range of products at cheaper prices will be of benefit to the domestic consumer but will present Irish industry with new competitive challenges. From a national economic welfare point of view, resources made redundant by foreign competition represent a cost to the domestic economy for the length of time that they remain idle. The importance of the domestic market to our economic wellbeing should not be understated in the drive to achieve new export markets. Firstly, domestic companies serving this market are usually indigenous, employ relatively more people than the average and have greater linkages with the rest of the economy than foreign-owned export-oriented companies. Secondly, the domestic market has an important developmental function, since very few new companies are in a position to start exporting before first gaining experience in the domestic market. Finally, to the extent that Irish products sold on the domestic market replace imports, they save us foreign exchange, which is as

economically significant as an equivalent amount of foreign exchange earned.

The sectors most dependant on the domestic market for the bulk of their sales are: drink and tobacco, paper and printing, non-metallic mineral products, food, timber and furniture. Some of these sectors like the drink and tobacco industry and the paper and printing industry are dominated by relatively large (by Irish standards) companies while in other sectors, namely the wood and furniture industry and the mechanical engineering industry, Irish firms tend to be small. Apart from certain sectors within the food industry, Irish industry in the aforementioned sectors weathered Ireland's entry into the EC quite well, although owing to their level of dependence on the domestic market, they suffered in the 1980s due to depressed domestic demand. A worrying feature about some of these industries is that many have low profit margins and are particularly sensitive to increases in costs.

The clothing and footwear sector is an example of one of those industries that was decimated by foreign competition in the aftermath of our entry into the EC. Since then the industry has become much more export oriented. Consequently one would expect the latter industry to be more streamlined and capable of withstanding even greater competitive pressure in the future. O'Malley in his survey of Irish industry confirms this optimism as to the survival prospects of those industries that took such a hammering in the 1970s. Most have since moved upmarket into the less price sensitive more image conscious niches of their respective markets.

It is difficult to predict just how well Irish manufacturing industry will perform in a single market of approximately 320 million consumers. Some commentators claim that since the costs associated with non-tariff barriers have a greater proportional impact on smaller companies, the same companies should benefit most from their dismantlement. On the other hand it needs to be remembered that one much quoted benefit arising from the creation of a true European common market is the opportunity it will afford firms to expand and exploit more fully economies of size. Although the EC as a whole may benefit from the creation of industrial giants that are capable of taking on the Japanese and the Americans, this is small comfort to Irish companies who, because they are on average smaller than their European rivals to begin with, may not be in a position to compete with the big conglomerates. Our principal hope is that Irish companies will be able to specialize in specific niches in the market, preferably in the high value added less price competitive niche.

Service Sector
This sector merits separate treatment, in part because of the revolu-

tion it is undergoing due to technological developments, and also because legislative reforms proposed both within the EC and in the wider forum of the General Agreement on Tariffs and Trade (GATT) promise to have a greater than average impact on this sector. The sector classification is really rather misleading since it covers such heterogeneous activities as hairdressing and the development of computer software. For convenience it is desirable to categorise services into those that are internationally tradeable and those that are not. The non-traded service sector tends by and large to be engaged in the provision of consumer services rather than producer services. It is usually labour intensive and its economic importance is very much dependant on the level of national income. The catalyst for the development of this sector is the development of the underlying internationally tradeable sector, which is traditionally associated with manufacturing and agriculture. However, owing to the revolution in information technology and in telecommunications, it is now becoming possible to export services that previously were not tradeable. This is because the need for face to face contact has been replaced, in many instances, by computer networking. Hence, traditional services such as banking, insurance and mortgage finance can now be sold across national borders without necessarily locating in the country of sale. Publishing is another example of a service sector where technological developments have had a major impact. A person in New York can now buy the *Financial Times* published in London on the same day as a Londoner. O'Malley claims that the services sector has been neglected by policy makers in the formulation of development policy and, that as a high growth market whose success depends on labour skills, technology and market contacts, it could be one area where Irish companies could have a comparative advantage. I must admit to reservations about the potential of the service sector to lead us down the road to increased economic prosperity. I accept that one major traditional handicap of Irish industry, the distance from principal markets, should be of less consequence when the product being sold does not have to travel across geographical space but rather can be beamed by satellite or networked through a computer link-up system. Similarly, we would appear to have a suitable resource base for this kind of service. However, if one looks at the evidence it would seem to suggest that the threat of losing domestic market share is probably greater than the opportunities to expand our foreign market share. In the insurance sector Irish concern is so great that the government requested that special provision be made for the Irish insurance industry as far as the application of new EC rules is concerned. In the area of banking and mortgage finance, the major fear is that of increased competition from larger conglomerates who will not even need to locate a branch in this country. Economies of size apart, large financial firms have the capacity to engage in predatory pricing in order to capture market share. Much of this competition could come from British financial institutions who would be attracted to the Irish market because of its similarity to the British market. One handicap that Irish banks and building societies face is that they are more regulated than their potential competition. Given that home country control will prevail, this will have to be rectified if Irish financial institutions are to have any chance of competing with their foreign rivals.

Subsidiaries of foreign owned manufacturing companies, whose financial needs are at present catered for either by Irish banks and insurance companies or by foreign banks located here, will, in a post 1992 world, be able to avail of the services of a financial company which will not necessarily be located here. The financial services sector would also appear to be an industry where economies of agglomeration are important. By economies of agglomeration I mean a tendency to centralize activities in one place. Witness the concentration of the financial services sector in London. The danger associated with the proposed financial services centre in Dublin is that foreign firms that might be induced to locate there will engage in transfer pricing in order to reduce their tax burden.

According to export figures supplied by Coras Tráchtála, the greatest share of the service export market is accounted for by agricultural services followed by transport services and construction services. (Tourism is not included). One important feature of our service export trade is that major markets appear to be either less developed countries or Britain (Guinness Peat Aviation is of course a notable exception). The challenge of the 1990s is to increase the export of services to continental Europe. Our poor track record in this area must make one sceptical about our chances of success. Indeed it is in this sector, even more than in goods trade, where language skills are a must if we are to stand any chance of developing this market. A tangible product is, to a certain extent, self explanatory, a service relies more on communication to reveal its usefulness.

Public Procurement
This is an area of economic activity that has been traditionally subject to protectionism in the form of the revealed preference of the public sector for the output of domestic firms. The Commission's proposals, designed to open up this area of economic activity to increased competition include, improving existing directives in order to ensure greater transparency and the extension of present directives to include energy, transport, water and telecommunications. Ireland has not been as guilty of protectionism in this sector to the same extent as other Member States, due mainly to the fact

that we do not have a large defence, aviation or motor industry. The principal domestic suppliers to the Irish government sector are in the construction field and they already operate in a competitive environment. In fact export opportunities probably exist here for Irish companies if the governments of other Member States genuinely open up this market to increased foreign competition.

The Implications for our Resource Base of the Completion of the Internal Market
Ultimately a country's growth potential is constrained by its resource base, that is its stock of physical and human capital, its technological knowhow and its supply of labour. The greatest fear that we as a country face is that the creation of an internal market, by allowing resource mobility, will result in the depletion of resources in peripheral, more disadvantaged areas as those resources are attracted to the more prosperous centres of Europe. The reasons are both economic and social. The social infrastructure is more developed in prosperous areas thus reducing the cost to firms of such overheads as electricity, communication and transport. There is a greater depth of ancillary services (legal, financial and consulting) available at a lower cost. Access to skilled labour and capital is better in large, well developed, densely populated markets. That vital commodity information is also more easily obtained when firms are in close proximity to each other and to the centre of political and administrative power. All serve to make well developed centres attractive locations for investment. It is also easier to attract high quality labour and skilled managers to prosperous regions which usually offer an attractive range of educational, health and entertainment facilities. For a country like Ireland, that is peripheral both geographically and economically, the threat of autonomous outflows of people and capital is ever present and can only be alleviated when the gap between us and more prosperous countries is narrowed. However, an even greater threat is that of induced resource outflows resulting from the adjustment process that will be an inevitable part of completing the internal market. Even the Cecchini report acknowledged that the short-term impact of the restructuring of industry will be unemployment. It is not sufficient to say that the long-term equilibrium situation should see more employment, because for a country like Ireland the process of adjustment influences the ultimate outcome. Hence, instead of idle resources eventually finding employment in some productive sector of the Irish economy, history would lead one to expect that the response is likely to be emigration.

**The Role of Industrial and Social Policy
in the Development Process**

The objective of industrial policy is ostensibly to further the process of development. Indicators of development include national income, the level of employment, the distribution of income as well as certain social and health related indicators. Lack of resources acts as a constraint on the effectiveness of regional and social policies in poor countries. The Commission of the EC in recognition of the fact that poorer regions of the Community could suffer as a result of the completion of the internal market, proposed that the structural funds be doubled in order to help regions overcome their relative backwardness. The structural funds consist of the European Regional Development Fund (ERDF), the European Social Fund (ESF) and the Guidance Section of the European Agricultural Guidance and Guarantee Fund (EAGGF). Lest we get carried away by such munificence, it is worth remembering that in 1986 the regional fund and the social fund accounted for 7.3 and 7.5 percent of the EC budget respectively and that the budget of the EC was approximately 1 percent of the GDP of the EC of 12. So relative to the size of the economy of the EC the amount being allocated to help disadvantaged regions is very insignificant. Of greater significance to Ireland is the fact that up to 75 percent of the cost of a project can now be financed from the Regional Fund. This eases the burden on the national exchequer.

The constraints on Ireland's economic development are: the size of our domestic market; our geographical remoteness and our inadequate infrastructure. Our domestic market is small because of our small population and low income. This limits its developmental potential as a catalyst for small companies. It also inhibits our industrial policy to the extent that it is oriented to attracting overseas investment. Foreign companies do not locate here in order to exploit our small market, their market is the rest of the EC. As a base from which to service the EC market, especially the continental EC market, Ireland is at a distinct geographical disadvantage; we are an island behind an island. Hence in order to get foreign companies to locate here we have to offer them financial incentives to do so. Finally our inadequate infrastructure serves to exacerbate our remoteness. It adds to the cost of producing and transporting goods to other Member States.

Our industrial policy should be oriented towards overcoming our developmental constraints. Success in this regard is dependant upon financial capacity, appropriate use of funds and the proper selection of policy instruments in order to implement policy decisions. For a country like Ireland whose public expenditure is severely constrained by lack of financial resources, it is imperative that regional spending in the EC is accorded a high priority and that this is reflected in the size of the structural funds. Increased regional and social spending may be a necessary condition for regional development but it is far from being sufficient. If regional funds are used to subsidize inefficient industry or to retard adjustment then they are of little developmental significance. Improving the stock of national infrastructure should have a positive impact on society socially as well as economically, since the stock of these immovable capital goods affects the quality of life of individuals as well as the competitiveness of industry. The infrastructure of greatest significance to industry is in transport, telecommunications and energy. Infrastructural development is a necessary, albeit insufficient, condition for national development. The nation's stock of capital also includes its stock of human capital, which is dependant upon the level of general education and the skill level of its population. The ESF presently provides support for vocational training measures and the creation of self employed activities to help the long term unemployed. It is in Ireland's economic interests to have these funds not only increased but also extended in scope to cover support for general education. Apart from the economic significance of investment in education for the national stock of human capital, the high level of emigration of highly trained people from this country represents an unrecouped economic cost to us and an economic gain to the countries to which they emigrate. To the extent that such emigration is internal migration within the EC, and, bearing in mind the fact that increased economic integration is likely to lead to increased labour mobility within the EC, it would only seem appropriate that education be financed at a supranational rather than at a national level.

Improving the national stock of infrastructure and the skills of our population will improve the competitive position of our industry in general, by reducing costs and improving the productivity of our resource base. It is difficult to say whether this would be sufficient to bridge the economic gap between this country and the more prosperous centres of the EC. Additional measures designed to promote economic development include direct assistance to industry. As far as targeting sectors for development is concerned, an attempt should be made to identify those sectors where our potential comparative advantage is greatest. Given our locational problem, this must be in sectors where the cost of transportation is not a crucial factor as well as being suited to our human, physical and technological resource base. That would appear to bias us towards high value added low bulk sectors, sectors in which the distance shrinking effect of technological developments, a high level of labour skills and the use of domestic raw materials are important. Using the appropriate policy instruments to develop these sectors is also important. For example the factors needed to develop indigenous industry differ, to some extent, from those needed to encourage foreign firms to locate here. Indigenous industry tends to take the domestic location with all its inherent disadvantages as given (even the more successful indigenous companies who have expanded their overseas operations usually maintain a presence in their home country), and concentrate on overcoming that disadvantage through their marketing, price and product strategy. Multinationals on the other hand, with a variety of possible locations to choose from, will finally pick a location on the basis of cost considerations. The policy of offering low corporation tax as means of inducing foreign companies to locate here has been criticised on the grounds that such a policy encourages the practice of transfer pricing (the setting of prices on sales between subsidiaries of the same company in order to maximize the profit of the subsidiary in the low tax zone) and discourages linkages between these companies and the rest of the economy. One could however question whether those linkages would be established in any case. In particular, it is difficult to imagine any large corporation locating its research activity in a peripheral country, even in a tax climate that did not positively discriminate against such an activity. Also, in order to continue to attract foreign companies, it would be necessary to replace the incentive effect of lower corporation taxes with other financial incentives, such as increased grants, which would be much more visible and thus less likely to be politically acceptable. It is difficult to envisage means by which foreign companies located here can be encouraged to make a greater contribution to the national economy than they do at present without discouraging them from locating here altogether. The more pertinent policy issue is the extent to which foreign companies as opposed to indigenous companies should be seen as the engine of our economic development. Developing the latter entails identifying the barriers that hinder them, and tailoring policy instruments to overcoming those barriers. Providing assistance through grants or subsidies for marketing, training and research and development as opposed to capital grants, is more likely to address the relative weakness of Irish industry.

Conclusions

The process of economic integration is one which involves the erosion of the policy making autonomy of national governments. The integrative process involves the harmonisation of national economic policies or the relinquishing of responsibility for those policies to a supranational body. Differences of opinion obviously exist as to the desirability of that process but those differences of opinion are usually based upon differences in value judgement. For individual countries, the process of integration contains a mixture of benefits and threats. That economic integration is a positive sum game from the overall perspective of the integrated area is unquestionable. More open to debate is the sharing of those benefits between different regions of the integrated area. Some regions may gain more than others, some may even lose. Predicting the regional consequences of integration is almost impossible. Certain measures can be taken to minimize the possibility of certain regions lagging behind, such as targeting the structural funds on those areas in greatest need, but whether that proves to be sufficient is something that can only be judged in hindsight. Indeed the more market oriented economists would view regional policy as being merely an inefficient means of income redistribution, which retards aggregate economic efficiency by interfering with the market mechanism. This view is open to debate and depends upon the assumption that market imperfections do not exist and that the economic location of industry is in some way pre-ordained. Rejection of the aforementioned assumption means accepting that the structural funds are a necessary condition for development, even if they do not prove to be sufficient.

Regardless of whether or not regional policy is deemed to be effective, there is still a case to be made in equity for the transfer of funds into lagging regions. If integration means loss of national policy making autonomy, then it would seem logical that responsibility for the consequences of integration rest at supranational level. The transfer of funds into lagging regions should be automatic and not discretionary, similar to what exists at present in most countries. It should be additional to transfers made under the structural funds which are essentially discretionary in nature and whose purpose is economic development. Fiscal relief to ease the adjustment problems of depressed regions within countries takes the form of reduced taxes emanating from those regions and increased spending into the regions. In an EC context, this can only be achieved if the fiscal authority of the EC is increased and if the institutions of the EC take responsibility for certain areas of social expenditure that presently come within the purview of national governments. Economic integration has political, social and economic consequences that cannot be ignored at EC level, since the power of national governments to deal with these consequences is circumscribed by the very process of integration. The risks for peripheral countries are also greater the greater the extent of economic integration. For example, one distinction between a common market and a free trade area is that in the former resources are free to migrate, which poses the additional threat for peripheral regions of resource deprivation. Similarly in a monetary union, the threats faced by less competitive countries are even greater than those existing in a common market, since they are not free to devalue in order to restore their competitiveness, thus making adjustment more painful.

All this implies that once one starts on the road towards economic integration, it is better for poorer countries in particular if the process reaches its logical conclusion. This would entail total economic and perhaps even political union in which fiscal responsibility accompanies the harmonisation of monetary and commercial policies. A necessary counter balance to the increased authority of Community institutions would be the development of strengthened regional structures, such as the creation of regional authorities as recommended in the Hume Report to the EC (1987)[6] These authorities would have a vital role to play in developing the indigenous potential of regions and in implementing Community programmes.

---

6. John Hume, *Report on the Regional Problems of Ireland*, European Parliament, 1982-88.

Pluralism and Community

FRANK BARRY

An awareness of other cultures and of how they organise themselves
should encourage reflection on the value of our own heritage and
offer new ideas on potential directions of development for our
society. This has not been happening to any great extent in Ireland
however. Debate here certainly reflects, or reacts to, developments
in British society but the positions adopted are frequently skewed
by the complex historical relationship that exists between the two
countries.

On occasion there emerges from the residue of historical
antagonism an instinctive rejection of the pattern of evolution of
British society; at the same time, however, a social and cultural
dependence that arises naturally from close proximity to a major
economic power has come to be internalised in our consciousness as
a 'backwardness complex'. From this stems the tendency to accept
unquestioningly many other socio-cultural developments emerging
from across the water. The complex is accentuated in our case by a
surprisingly-consensual British view of Irish society, in which the
Right's disdain for the 'barbaric' Ulster working class echoes the
Left's caricature of the 'primitiveness' of the Republic in its failure
to sanction abortion and divorce.

The impact that these instinctive attitudes of ours have had on
how we react to developments abroad has hindered the search for,
and articulation of, a set of social goals capable of motivating the
country and of mapping out a long-term strategy for government.
An openness to social and intellectual developments taking place in
countries with which we have less complicated ties may present us
with a broader perspective from which to engage in a critique of our
own society. Over time, I believe, this will come to be seen as one
of the major advantages of our slowly-strengthening relationship
with continental Europe.

One of the unfortunate results of the 'backwardness complex' to
which we are subject is the failure of the modernising/pluralist camp
to recognise that elements of the traditionalist perspective may be
worth contemplating. With both sides talking past each other in
recent debates, there has been little room for development of either
position. A study of the effects of modernisation in other countries

137

should alert us to the fact that there are dangers involved; these dangers must be confronted, and some type of social action capable of defusing them suggested, if the pluralist vision is to be fully coherent.

Any such sociological analysis will also reveal however that traditionalists cannot hope to keep at bay forever the kinds of changes in attitudes and behaviour that have accompanied the process of economic modernisation – industrialisation and urbanisation – as it has occurred elsewhere. In their mistaken belief that such changes can be prevented by legislation they have been led to reject all forms of pluralism.

It has not been widely recognised however that several strands of pluralist thought can be identified. I will argue here that the libertarian position of the Irish 'New Right', which is one of the dominant elements in the pluralist coalition, is susceptible to the very charges that traditionalists have wrongly levelled against pluralism in general – i.e. that a society based on its precepts will exhibit massive alienation and serious social problems. The alternative strand to be explored in this essay, what we might call a communitarian as opposed to a libertarian pluralism, would respond to the changes wrought by modernisation by seeking to protect the sense of belonging that is of fundamental value in the traditionalist perspective, whilst promoting the greater freedom of choice that modern society affords and demands.

The major part of this essay is concerned then with developing a sociologically-based critique of both libertarianism and traditionalism; some practical implications of the communitarian pluralist vision will also be discussed, with the focus resting on the areas of social and cultural policy and on how the Republic might contribute to the lessening of tension in Northern Ireland.

I want to begin with the ideology of libertarianism, because a critique of its position will introduce us to the sociological perspective from which the foundations of traditionalism can later be explored.

Citizens in all societies are unconsciously socialised into a dominant ideology that determines the parameters of debate about the role of government and the rights and responsibilities of the individual. The ideology upon which British and American society is based is that of liberal individualism. (Irish society is not, at least as yet.) This philosophy, which had its origins in the works of seventeenth- and eighteenth-century British thinkers such as John Locke and Adam Smith, emerged from a concern to limit the arbitrary powers of the state; in this it clearly served a progressive function. According to the view it proposes, society is simply the collection of individuals who bind themselves to each other by freely-entered social contracts; rights are accordingly defined in terms of the limitations of state or societal power over the activities and property of the individual, and the role of government is primarily to defend these rights against other individuals.

This 'free market' theory, which precludes a role for government in guiding, nurturing, or encouraging, is known in its extreme form as libertarianism. Though eclipsed by the rise of the welfare state in the aftermath of the Great Depression, it has come into its own again in more recent times, with the philosophical contributions of writers from Milton Friedman (1962) to Robert Nozick (1974) influencing the administrations of Mrs. Thatcher and President Reagan.

This whole theory of society rests on an over-simplified view of man, however; one which ignores the fact that psychological orientation and behaviour are profoundly affected by socio-economic structure. In this way it is led to overlook one of the basic premises of modern sociology – that community bonds, which involve deep personal feelings as well as quasi-economic 'social contracts', can be seriously ruptured by the forces of unregulated economic modernisation.

In attempting to illustrate the interconnections between societal structure and individual attitudes in an earlier paper, I noted the fact that observers acquainted with life in both the United States and Ireland tended to agree in their descriptions of the differences that manifested themselves. 'Relatively speaking', I wrote, 'American life is pictured as dynamic; the feeling of controlling one's own destiny and the freedom from social constraints there are contrasted with a moralistic and economically-stagnant environment in Ireland. Ireland's advantages, though, are said to include the warmth of its social and communal life, the strength of its family bonds, and the less oppressive level of serious crime. The U.S. emerges as a personally liberating but somewhat alienated society; Ireland as friendly but stultifying. Life in America is painted as fast, furious and exciting; hard work is rewarded, but required. Ireland is relaxed.'

Only by overlooking the sociological commonplace illustrated above – that the views and behaviour of individuals are themselves, through socialisation, products of the community, the culture, and the socio-economic structure – can the philosophy of liberal individualism portray society as a set of contracts between antecedent self-sufficient individuals.

The major practical danger of this individualist perspective is its implication that acute social problems, which should serve as an indictment of social structure, are instead to be seen simply as the result of individual malice. Recognising that behaviour is conditioned by social structure is the key to understanding the connection between the severe social problems of many poorly-planned urban environments, for example, and the alienated individualism of what may hopefully be superseded as 'modern society'. We are forced to recognise in this way that modernisation presents dangers as well as opportunities, and that the concept of modernity promoted by libertarians errs in discounting the social benefits stemming from certain traditional aspects of Irish life.

That we have reason to believe that there may be something of lasting value in traditional social forms becomes clearer once we shift our gaze from the British consensus that forms the background to Irish debate and glance instead at the opinions of modern 'communitarian' thinkers from other countries. Look at the *Irish Journal* of Heinrich Böll (1967) for example, the eminence grise of the German Greens, or the comments on this country made by American radical Paul Goodman, author of *Communitas* and *Growing Up Absurd*, in his lecture on 'Objective Values' in *The Dialectics of Liberation* (1968). While recognising that traditionalism ('the priests, the mothers and the sexual repression') restricts personal freedom, especially of women, ('a lively girl is certainly right to get out') he argues that this is one of 'the good societies in the world at present'.

If we have indeed reached the 'post-modern' phase of intellectual evolution, in which elements of the traditional are coming to be recognised as valuable and as complementary to the modern, then we must ask whether social planning and social action may be able to protect what is of lasting value in traditional patterns, and defuse thereby some of the problems associated with the encroachment of modernity.

According to the sociological mainstream which we have seen to reject the foundations of libertarianism, the fundamental benefit of the traditional community – be it a small country village or inner-city Dublin prior to its destruction – is the sense of belonging that it affords its members. It provides a rootedness, an identity, a stable base in early life; it fosters a bond between oneself and others that keeps at bay the alienated existentialism of the modern world. This bond of loyalty, obligation and identification, arises when people live in close proximity to each other and interact throughout the course of their lives. As historian Eric Hobsbawm writes, in discussing the impact of the industrial revolution on social life: 'The proletarian whose only link with his employer is a cash-nexus must be distinguished from the . . . pre-industrial dependent who has a much more complex human and social relationship with his master, and one which implies duties on both sides, though very unequal ones.' Economic modernisation affects more than the relationship between social classes, of course; bonds between neighbours, and within one's own extended family, are weakened by locational and occupational mobility as well as by the diminished overlap between those with whom one spends one's worktime and one's social life.

Some weakening of shared norms and of community bonds must therefore be accepted as an inevitable consequence of the transition to an urbanised industrial society. By assuming that the overall outcome of unregulated modernisation is simply the sum of outcomes bargained for by individuals engaging in a rational cost/benefit calculus, however, libertarians, as I have already argued, are prevented from realising that something widely recognised to be of lasting value may be lost in the process. Irish traditionalists, though, are equally short-sighted in failing to comprehend that the demand for an acceptance of diversity goes hand in hand with the process of economic modernisation; thus Bishop Newman (1987), for example, writes that pluralism has the effect of 'preventing any one religion from being a source of meaning for all.'

The confusion of cause and effect in Bishop Newman's analysis is unfortunately indicative of a widespread failure to recognise that pluralism and democracy are synonymous in a non-homogeneous society, and it stems from an underlying flaw in the traditionalist perspective, i.e. the assumption that changes in attitudes can be prevented by legislation.

Pluralism represents the democratic response to a diversity of beliefs, a diversity which is frequently brought on by economic modernisation. Enforced conformity to the will of the majority cannot nurture any sense of belonging amongst a community that is growing more heterogeneous. A sense of belonging must embrace the entire community, and it is the wellbeing of this entity, minorities as well as majorities, that becomes the transcendent point of reference for government policy and the framing of law in a pluralist society. This communitarian conception of democracy can be seen to embrace elements of the traditionalist perspective, however, and to be more far reaching than libertarianism, in its implication that the freedom to pursue individual self-interest is strictly bounded by the impact such actions have on community welfare.

When the issues are presented in this light it appears that the ideological differences separating communitarians and libertarians are more fundamental than those that arise in the 'trad/mod' debate. Included alongside traditionalists in the communitarian camp are those who have come under the influence of the various movements which arose in the wake of the radical debates of the 1960s: movements concerned with the environment, the arms race, the position of women in society. This regrouping of ideological camps will emerge, I would suggest, as the Irish Catholic Church shifts its focus over time from the issues of private morality which continue to exercise an anachronistic hold on its attention, and moves towards the conscientious social stance adopted by its counterparts in North and South America for example.

While such a realignment cannot be expected to take place on the issues of divorce, contraception and abortion which have dominated national debate in recent times, some Catholic thinkers have begun to explore lines of thought within which a genuine communitarian discussion could take place. Bishop Donal Murray (1986), for example, in an article which defends the result of the divorce referendum, writes that 'a group has a civil right to be allowed to follow its convictions unless this factor is outweighed by the requirements of social well-being . . . . (However), the supreme aim of society is not simply to be tolerant. It is to build the kind of community in which human beings may flourish and develop their potential to the full. Tolerance is an important value in that process; so too, surely, are concern to strengthen family life and to protect those who would suffer if it were weakened.'

This representation of the traditionalist position, alongside a reiteration of the fact that 'the bishops have repeatedly said that legal questions should be decided on the basis of what is best for society; the fact that something is taught by the Church is not a reason for enshrining it in civil law', offers scope for dialogue and progress. Communitarian pluralists can respond to this position – whether on divorce, contraception or abortion – both with empirical argument, and with the question as to why it is women who have traditionally been left to carry the burden of maintaining communitarianism.

The libertarian response, on the other hand, that 'individuals have aims, society does not, and tolerance is therefore the only issue', offers no room for further dialogue. Neither does Bishop Newman's (1987) confrontational argument, directed against them, that without the authoritative moral referents that institutionalised religion proposes 'there is no moral appeal beyond the individualistic pursuit of interests' and no coherent foundations, therefore, upon which society can be based. Bishop Murray's statement indicates an acceptance of the communitarian middle-ground that the wellbeing of the entire community is indeed capable of serving this function of point of reference for the articulation of social goals.

It is crucial for traditionalists themselves to recognise the extent to which their fundamental insights are preserved within the communitarian strand of pluralist thought. Otherwise, as attitudes and behaviour continue to deviate from traditional patterns, and as the legal endorsement of traditionalist values loses its support base, the libertarian strand, which is ultimately hostile to the whole concept of community, may come to dominate.

The extent to which this is already occurring is indicated by the terminology adopted during the recent abortion debates in which the 'right to life' was juxtaposed with the 'right to choose'. Language imported from the U.S. was employed by both sides, and it reflected libertarian values from which most of the participants would recoil. For traditionalists, as psychiatrist Anthony Clare (1983) noted in discussing divorce, 'personal autonomy is not emphasised . . . Irish society is much more willing to sacrifice the individual to the greater good'. The latter part of this statement of Clare's, however, is precisely the charge that traditionalists level against 'pro-choice' feminists! Viewed in this way the crucial difference between the two sides can clearly be seen to lie in their competing conceptions of 'the greater good'. The adoption of individualist language by all sides shifts the argument away from the fundamental issue of what type of society is desired, and deposits us in the philosophical jungle of conflicting rights.

This tendency for individualist terminology to be imported from more economically-advanced countries and employed in a completely different social climate has been identified in another context by political scientist C. B. MacPherson (1985), who writes that Third World countries 'are closer to the pre-capitalist idea that one's humanity was more a matter of one's membership in the community than of one's freedom from the community, that the greatest human right was the right of belonging to the community, and the severest deprivation was to be cast out. But what has happened is that the Third World countries in so far as they are struggling against their previous subservience to the West, have had to use Western ideological weapons'.

The issue of conflicting rights that has just been touched upon needs to be taken up in further detail however because, as Attracta Ingram (1988) has argued, to focus entirely on the wellbeing of the community and to consider individuals only as elements of current social entities carries the danger that the interests of some will be completely subordinated to those of others. This is the essence of the feminist critique of traditional communitarianism and it forces us to recognise that alongside the alienating consequences of the demise of traditional communality, as suggested earlier in my comparison of Irish and American life, appears the liberation of the individual from the overpowering necessity to conform.

If discussion of the fundamental nature of traditional society can be structured around the concept of belonging, the equivalent term that emerges in analysing modern society is choice. Modern society offers an expanded opportunity of self-expression, and the possibility of experimentation; these are necessary not only for individual development but also for society itself if it is to adapt to advances in knowledge, communications, and technology. Communitarian pluralists, I suggest, are concerned with fostering both a sense of belonging and a diversity necessary for the freedom of choice; in this they see a role for government in encouraging as well as in protecting. Analogous to the community that exhibits these characteristics is the family that nurtures a sense of identity so as to provide a stable base from which its offspring can come to define themselves through personal experience. Belonging defines community, choice implies diversity; together they comprise the communitarian pluralist vision of 'a diversity of communities' or 'a community of communities'.

Before going on to elaborate some of the practical implications of this vision I want to take a brief detour to consider how the analysis of community presented here relates to others based on the structure of power relations within society. Although only infrequently encountered in public discussion in Ireland, the Marxist voice has been responsible for a sustained and penetrating critique of the cultural and political assumptions underlying mainstream intellectual opinion, which it accuses of sidestepping this issue; for a 'random sample' of analyses that work along these lines see e.g. B&ICO (1972) and McCormack (1986). The present paper, in endeavouring to locate itself within parameters comprehensible to the mainstream, by no means seeks to negate the need for studies of society and culture based on power relationships; these analyses I view as complementary.

A hardline Marxist approach that portrays community bonds as simply a camouflage for class domination, however, fails to recognise the implications of the psychological tendency to define ourselves alongside others in a shared culture; those who adopt such a position exclude themselves from the discussion of how Irish culture may, through a process of self-criticism, open itself up to those whom it currently excludes.

A more promising perspective is suggested by revisionists such as Herbert Marcuse (1978) who hold that cultures contain within them a store of knowledge of what people have come to learn about themselves. When this wisdom, through critical analysis, can be disinterred from the other elements of which it is comprised, each culture has a positive contribution to make to the dialectic of human development.

This notion of development occurring through interaction between the diversity of cultures and communities provides an added dynamic to the communitarian pluralist vision.

I now want to discuss some concrete proposals suggested by the theory developed here. These are considered in three sections, the first of which deals with the 'meta-unity' that can emerge when diversity is accepted and harmonised through dialogue, the second with the importance of regional identity in a world of strong homogenising forces, and the third with the implications of the theory for how we are to view social problems and the welfare state.

1   Diversity and Dialogue

Individuals, I have argued, feel a need for community. It is clear however, particularly in the Irish case, that social problems can arise not only from the alienation of the modern society that neither caters for nor recognises this need, but also from the insecurity generated when the culture with which one identifies perceives itself to be under threat of annihilation by another. The cultural problem that accentuates inter-community hostility in Northern Ireland is clearly the siege mentality that has developed amongst both communities, each of which has had and continues to have, good reason to feel itself under threat.

The failure of the historically-dominant Unionist community to accord the rights of recognition and survival to the culture and aspirations of Northern nationalists mirrors exactly the monolithic and uni-dimensional 'official mythology' adopted by the Southern state.

Even if the institutional issue of Northern administration can be overcome, as I believe, within the context of an integrated European Community that would take upon itself the burden of 'contested' areas such as Gibraltar, and ultimately Cyprus, the problem of defusing culture-bound hostility will remain. The question posed here is: what contribution can we in the Republic make towards allowing all the people of this island share a sense of belonging?

The approach I suggest is that we take seriously the responsibility imposed on us jointly by our constitutional claim to Northern Ireland and by our promise 'to cherish all the children of the nation equally'. If there is validity in the traditionalist notion that culture is a crucial constituent of one's identity, then we are bound by these traditional claims and vows to respect the value of Unionist culture and tradition. This requires constructing and embracing a new 'official mythology' that recognises the quality of character demonstrated by the Unionist people on many occasions throughout their history – the courage of the defenders of Derry during the Siege, the victory of liberalism over authoritarianism at the Boyne, the selflessness of the Somme, 'the talents and genius that gave eleven Presidents to the United States of America', as John Hume (1986) writes in another context, ' . . . the constitutional innovation in a people whose forebears wrote the American Declaration of Independence and fashioned the pluralism of the American Constitution'. Barely beginning to recognise the pluralist history of the twenty-six counties and the myth of the monolith, we continue to ignore the contribution of the very group who must be convinced that cultural genocide is not on our agenda. (Instead we find, in the Forum/Anglo-Irish Agreement process, the Southern government identifying itself as a guarantor of the rights and aspirations of nationalists only.)

A far-reaching pluralism would recognise that the 26-county state is itself the product of divisions between Irish people. Carson as much as de Valera is a founding father of this state, as historian Michael Laffan (1984) has suggested. Is it too early to explore the possibility that elements of nobility and courage may have motivated all our founding fathers?

It cannot be too early to recognise the value of inter-cultural openness in our own history, since the Irish folk culture with which our urbanised population comes in contact through education, and comes to regard as its own, has been refracted through the prism of an Anglo-Irish consciousness that recognised its value and the possibility of its imminent demise. If we in the Republic share Hume's view that the Unionist siege mentality hinders the exploration, dissection and reconstruction of the progressive elements of their culture, we could follow the example set us by Yeats, Hyde, Synge, and the rest of our pantheon of cultural heroes, and assist in this renewal. One possibility would be to fund an Institute of Ulster Studies to bring Unionist intellectuals, writers and researchers down to Dublin and to foster a two-way flow of ideas. Trinity College, with its well-established links with that community, would seem an ideal location.

The defence of diverse cultural identities suggested here has numerous other applications. As Terence Brown (1985) points out, cultural pluralism supports the preservation of the Irish language, demonstrating again that traditionalists must align themselves with the communitarian strand of pluralist thought if all the elements of culture which they value are not to be lost to 'the homogeneity of a consumer society'.

Finally, the anti-homogenising thrust of the argument has implications for how Ireland might respond to the growing diversity of races and ethnic groups which have established communities in this country. Since it suggests a policy more akin to the Canadian 'salad bowl' than the American 'melting pot', our community and business groups and local authorities might give some consideration to instituting the kind of ethnic festivals known as 'Caravans' which contribute greatly to the cultural life of many Canadian cities. In these festivals the various ethnic groups establish premises all across the city in which they parade their cultures – their foods and drinks, and their music and dances. Inter-cultural awareness and co-operative activity is stimulated in this way.

2 Urban and Regional Architectural Identity

One of the themes of this essay has been the importance of maintaining a cultural milieu that fosters a sense of identity and belonging. This has implications for environmental planning, a subject on which Bishop Newman writes at length; recent changes in the urban planning strategy of Dublin Corporation, for example, – with the reconstruction of decaying inner-city communities replacing the previous policy of shifting their populations to suburban housing estates – indicate that such lessons are beginning to be learnt. The sense of identity born of the individual's relationship with the regional, and therefore heterogeneous, man-made environment, itself a cultural artefact, also has implications for environmental planning.

Regional architectural identity has fallen prey to the homogenising thrust of economic modernisation more markedly in Ireland than in many other countries. I suggest that this has come about as a result of the backwardness complex discussed earlier, while government has been hindered from responding to the widely-perceived crisis situation by an adherence to the libertarian conception of the rights of private property.

This thesis challenges the view espoused by Robert Ballagh (1988) and Arthur Gibney (1988), who argue that the destruction of the urban fabric of Dublin since the 1960s has been occurring because it is predominantly provincial people living in the suburbs, and therefore lacking urban sensibilities, who wield power in our society. This hypothesis to my mind smacks of the anti-rural values instilled by our backwardness complex: unwittingly so in Ballagh's case, I would think; perhaps less unwittingly on the part of Gibney who as current President of the Royal Institute of Architects of Ireland must attempt to defend their apparent lack of understanding of the importance of context in their work. This anti-rural bias therefore appears as one aspect of the national inferiority complex, another of which is the belief of the local authorities and the city engineers that 'modernity' implies the subservience of the urban heritage to the requirements of the car. It is a disregard for the artefacts and environment of the past that lies at the root of the destruction.

To see this clearly it is sufficient to note that it is the same 'predominantly provincial people', i.e. the Irish people, who are responsible for the unanalysed 'bungalow blight' that afflicts the rural environment. This is inexplicable in terms of the Ballagh-Gibney hypothesis.

Our failure as individuals to protect the integrity of our historic urban and rural environments is to be understood as the result of the misleading notion of modernity with which we have allowed ourselves be burdened. There are some recent developments, in particular the reclaiming of historic Kilkenny City, which give cause for optimism but concrete walls are still spreading, incredibly, across the Aran Islands.

This deterioration of the environment at the hands of individuals exercising their rights of private property can only be combatted by governmental authorities armed with a philosophy that recognises the environment as community property, and community property rights as more than the sum of individual property rights. Adherence to a libertarian ethic prevents government from responding to the destruction of the historic core of cities, towns and villages, and the littering of the countryside with bungalows which have no contextual relationship with the existing landscape, even though these actions damage community property and lower the quality of life in this country. The libertarian ethic prevents government from imposing penalties on those who hold derelict sites which degrade the environment, and on those who 'allow' protected buildings in their possession fall into such a state of dereliction that they must be demolished; likewise it provides the logic behind the laws which allow property owners claim compensation from local authorities which refuse planning permission.

Even more short-sighted is the failure of the authorities to impose aesthetic requirements on grant-aided buildings, a category which probably includes the vast majority of new constructions. This is the kind of thinking that has allowed the disappearance of the traditional thatched cottage, for example; a nationally-symbolic end to a national symbol!

The spirit of the communitarian philosophy espoused here promotes the preservation of the environment by the stick as well as the carrot, so that Dublin city managers could no longer claim with impunity that the city in their charge cannot be protected because of a lack of public funds.

What form might a pluralist planning policy take? One radical solution to the current crisis would be to section the country into areas characterised by an identifiable historic architectural style; certain categories of new buildings in each area might be required to conform to some elements of local style. The scheme, which I suspect would be required only temporarily, would thus promote a plurality of regional identities; 'dialogue' and development would occur through the natural blending of styles along regional peripheries.

3   Social Policy

The communitarian perspective, as mentioned earlier, causes us to recognise that social problems are the symptoms of defective social structure. 'Law and order' cannot therefore provide an adequate long-term solution; stability can be achieved only by the construction of a society that treats its disadvantaged elements more justly.

This should not be taken as a defence of all the features of the welfare state as it exists at present in Western Europe, of course. Defenders of the welfare state ignore at their peril the ways in which government intervention can inhibit economic growth by distorting the pattern of incentives offered by the 'free market'; social policy must be designed pragmatically if it is to achieve the goals it is set.

The whole philosophy of the welfare state is under attack from the libertarian camp at the moment however, and it is crucial that we recognise how short-sighted these criticisms can be. By defusing social tension, social policy offers a payback even to those who must finance it; the alternative available to them, the advantaged of our society, is to live behind barred windows, as their counterparts in Latin America do, or in the walled-in suburban communities that resemble fortified medieval cities, as they have begun to do in Southern California. Some elements of welfare statism ultimately benefit everyone in society, a point the libertarians fail to recognise.

This paper goes further, however, in suggesting that conventional political debate takes far too narrow a view of 'social welfare'; there can be no rigid distinction between Social and Cultural Policy once it is recognised that the wellbeing of all is linked to that of the disadvantaged, and the wellbeing of the individual to that of the culture.

There are developments within the European Community which indicate that these connections are coming to be recognised; the Regional Development Fund and policies for the protection of minority cultures, for example. A pluralist Europe must be the hope of all of us here in Ireland; a pluralist Ireland is a vision that can inspire us.

References

Ballagh, Robert (1988) 'The Irish couldn't give a fart in their green corduroys about art.' Lecture delivered during Arts Week festival, University College Dublin.

Barry, Frank (1987) 'Between Tradition and Modernity: Cultural Values and the Problems of Irish Society.' *The Irish Review*, no 2.

Böll, Heinrich (1967) *Irish Journal* (New York: McGraw Hill).

British and Irish Communist Organisation (1972) *The Economics of Partition* (Belfast: BICO)

Brown, Terence (1985) *Ireland: A Social and Cultural History 1922-1985* (London: Fontana Press).

Clare, Anthony (1983) Psychiatry and Irish Culture (interview by Clodagh O'Reilly). *The Crane Bag*, vol 7, no 2.

Friedman, Milton (1962) *Capitalism and Freedom* (Chicago: University of Chicago Press).

Gibney, Arthur (1988) 'Architecture and the Politics of the Ideal City.' Inaugural address to the Royal Institute of Architects of Ireland.

Goodman, Paul (1968) 'Objective Values,' in David Cooper (ed.) *The Dialectics of Liberation* (Penguin Books).

Hobsbawm, Eric (1968) *Industry and Empire: an economic history of Britain since 1750* (London: Weidenfeld and Nicolson).

Hume, John (1986) 'A New Ireland: The Acceptance of Diversity,' *Studies*, vol 75, no 300.

Ingram, Attracta (1988) 'Autonomy, Feminism and Community.' Working Paper (forthcoming), Women's Studies Forum, University College Dublin.

Laffan, Michael (1984) 'Two Irish States', *The Crane Bag*, vol 8, no 1.

Marcuse, Herbert (1978) *The Aesthetic Dimension* (Boston: Beacon Press).

MacCormack, W. J. (1986) *The Battle of the Books: Two Decades of Irish Cultural Debate* (Mullingar: Lilliput Press).

MacPherson, C. B., (1985) 'Problems of Human Rights in the Late Twentieth Century,' in *The Rise and Fall of Economic Justice* (Oxford University Press).

Murray, Donal (1986) 'How Pluralist are Pluralists?' *Studies*, vol 75, no 300.

Newman, Jeremiah (1987) *Return to the Sacred: A Socio-Religious Analysis* (Dublin: Four Courts Press).

Nozick, Robert (1974) *Anarchy, State and Utopia* (Oxford: Blackwell).

A Granular Society

IVOR BROWNE

In 1992 we are told that Europe will be taking a further step towards political and economic integration. There will be free movement throughout the community with the abolition of customs and national borders. This is to be welcomed and is simply part of a wider and very gradual movement on the surface of our planet (at times an almost imperceptible movement) towards the creation of one single, global society. This movement can be discerned in a number of areas; the rock music culture has become virtually international and it has become increasingly hard to tell the place of origin of the songs, music, accents, dress and appearance of groups, etc.; the growth and expansion of transnational companies which neither know nor respect any national boundaries and which have set up technological, transport and telecommunications systems which are increasingly world-wide. Here too we see the global linking up of diasporas, of scientific research right across the world, of intellectual endeavour of many kinds and the growth of a world literature. These are but a few examples of an increasingly manifest global world culture.

If this movement towards a united states of Europe and, on a wider scale, towards a global world culture, however much it is to be welcomed from one point of view, is not to be very destructive in other ways to our fundamental nature as living human beings, then it implies and indeed demands an equally imperceptible and penetrating movement, in the opposite direction, towards decentralization and the emergence of strong, much more autonomous regional and local structures.

If I were asked why I see such a reverse development as a necessary balancing evolution, I would point to our inherent biological nature. In the end of all we are living creatures, still retain our animal nature and, although human beings are perhaps the most adaptable of all living species, we are nevertheless not capable of adapting to simply any kind of circumstances. The human being is a living system, like all other living creatures, and what is more, like many other species we are intensely social animals. We begin life in relationship and, just as we require essential nutritional ingredients, if we are to remain healthy we need to be embedded in intimate and personal social relationships throughout our lifetime, otherwise we become mad.

So, if this process of centralization towards a united states of Europe, and ultimately towards a global society, is to go ahead without any counter-balancing movement towards decentralization, then a point will be reached (as is already evident in the USA) where there is nothing between the isolated human individual and enormous conglomerations of literally millions of people. This inevitably leads to the feelings of alienation and anhomie already so prevalent among the young in contemporary society, where so many of them experience a sense of isolation and pointlessness; have no sense of future or purpose in living. What every day becomes more urgently necessary then, is the emergence of a counterbalancing process of decentralization across society. And this is particularly necessary at the regional and local level.

The Nation State: Before and After

For some hundreds of years now European society has experienced an undue emphasis on the nation state, defined by geographical borders. This has manifested itself in the cult of nationalism with all its attendant wars, bloodshed and intolerance of the rights of other nations. It might be argued that it was always so, but this is not true. In earliler tribal cultures such as (to take but two examples) the Ba mButi in the rain forests of the Congo, or the ancient Celtic civilization which spread right across Europe, there was no clear nationhood or fixed geographical borders. But this did not simply mean a group of disconnected warring tribes. In societies such as these there was a clearly unified culture, with a common language, religion, laws and crafts and artifacts; so that an individual pigmy, for example, could be taken from his own local tribal group and moved perhaps 1,000 miles to another tribal cluster where he would rapidly feel completely at home, recognising everything and able to communicate freely with his neighbours. The same was largely true in Celtic society, where a bard or a lawyer could travel freely from one end of Ireland to the other and right through Scotland, from one distinct tribal kingdom to another, but always finding himself in a continuous, understandable culture, language, system of law, etc.

The fairly recent development of the nation state in Europe and elsewhere therefore, has been damaging not only to the possibility of a wider union of peoples (such as a united Europe) but has also led, since the industrial revolution, to the dismemberment and virtual disappearance of regional and local societal-structures. I am thinking of the loss of autonomy and vibrant life of provinces (to be able to recognise the difference between a person from Connaught, and someone from Leinster or Dublin), local towns or city states such as Venice or Genoa in Italy, villages, tribal clusters and extended families, in which the individual was ultimately embedded and could recognise and know him or herself. All of these smaller societal entities have withered, indeed have virtually disappeared in recent times, losing all the richness of difference or diversity, colour and intimate personal relationship characteristic of local life. It is out of such local autonomy and relationship that person-hood with all its loving, hating intimacy and creativity emerges. Without this the essence of what is to be human will wither and die.

This is not to say that such a counter-development of decentralization (allowing for appropriate centralilzation even up to the global level) should mean the disappearance of nationalism or the nation-state altogether, but rather that this level should diminish and lessen in influence so as to bring the hierarchy of societal structures or living systems into harmony, so that no one dimension of society cannibalises or expresses itself to the detriment and proper life and autonomy of the levels below or above it. What is valuable about national identity or the notion of nationhood is really a cultural statement, defined by language, music and other cultural characteristics as well as by geographical location. And indeed to be Irish, French or Italian can extend beyond geographical boundaries so that one can think of, for example, the greater Irish nation perhaps encompassing as many as 70 million people, able to link themselves in one way or another to a common ethnic culture, while the Irish nation state is only a small island with less than 5 million people.

To look to the emergence of such a process of decentralization is not simply a hopeless dream or harking back to a sentimental past. On the contrary, there is an increasing awareness and evidence of such a movement in a number of European countries at the present time. In countries such as Italy, Germany or Switzerland such a healthy regional and local emphasis has always remained strong and now, in France, Spain and here in Ireland, a renewed awareness of the importance of such decentralization is clearly discernible. Within the past year several Irish members of the European Parliament – John Hume, Eileen Lemass, Mary Banotti and others – have put forward and have had accepted plans for regional development and new growth of local structures. Such movements are still weak when compared to the overweaning forces of centralization, but there is no doubt about the growing awareness in Europe of the need for such a development.

All over the European countries communities are stirring and, although this movement remains incipient, the voice of ordinary people looking once again to have a personal responsibility and control over their lives is beginning to be heard. Nor are such movements purely local or isolated: there is frequently an awareness and even an intercommunication with similar movements in other parts of the world. For example, in Ireland we see the conscious application of liberation theology, which had its origins in South America, now becoming a driving force here in projects with the unemployed, the travelling people and other disadvantaged groups in our society. What is emerging ever more clearly from community projects and movements which are beginning in the alienated ghettoes of the inner cities across Europe, is that there can be no hope for the individual person who is marginalized to gain a foothold in society, to learn the skills they need if they are to have a decent life and if they are to have any self respect or personal autonomy, unless they can feel themselves part of a bounded community of human size, where personal relationships are possible.

Community Projects
To take a concrete example from my own professional experience: A fundamental principle of the democratic psychiatric reform which is under way in Italy and which has also been clear to some of us in Ireland for a number of years, is that any training that will enable the disadvantaged young person of our inner cities who is demotivated and alienated to learn what he/she needs to know to find a place in society, will fail unless such training is part of a social contract to the community; unless the activity through which the skills are being acquired is also providing a service or fulfilling a useful function for the community in which that person lives.

This is what has been happening, for instance, in the inner city project in Derry which has been under way now for nearly ten years and where upwards of five hundred unemployed young people who dropped out of school are revitalizing the old inner city: rebuilding old, derelict buildings, setting up small craft industries and undertaking a range of useful community services, so that what was a dead, bombed-out city following the troubles, is now throbbing with life and enterprise. A similar project is now getting under way in the North-West quadrant of the inner city of Dublin which has been run down and virtually derelict for many years. Out of a community of approximately twenty thousand there are some five thousand unemployed, many of whom are at risk for social or psychiatric breakdown. The whole area is in urgent need of major urban renewal. The local Stoneybatter community have already produced an excellent development plan, to chart the way forward, but on their own have little hope of fully realising this potential. What is proposed now under the heading of the 'Brendan Project' is a joint effort between rehabilitation and mental health professionals on the one hand, working with the community on the other.

The idea is to create, in this quadrant of central Dublin, a living city for the future but one which is designed to help the local community to break out of the poverty trap. The project will be primarily a cultural undertaking; the creation of a living city, celebrating the arts, music, drama and sporting activities of all kinds, with some economic and commercial underpinning to create a rounded development. It will be an urban development for the next century, built by the disadvantaged and unemployed *for* the disadvantaged and unemployed. It will be for the people, by the people and of the people – for those who live in it and for those who will come to enjoy it from other parts of the greater Dublin area. There seems little doubt that such a development would attract major international interest among architects, social planners and socially minded industrialists. There is also little doubt that it would merit substantial funding from the European regional fund and other international financial sources.

What will make this project unique, should it get under way, and an interesting example of the concept of devolution being put forward in this paper, is that while it will be a truly local communal endeavour on the one hand, it will at the same time be linked with a wider European perspective. For it is also proposed that it will participate in a 'Greater European Project' which is soon to commence, and will be centred on the concept of 'habilitation' and skills for living, these to be applied both to the disadvantaged unemployed and at risk population and to new chronic psychiatric patients, who are now the central problem facing community psychiatry. This 'GEP' is to include projects from Italy, Germany and possibly Northern Greece, and Ireland (through the Brendan Project) has been invited to become an active participant. Thus we have here an example of a movement which on the one hand is truly local in character, centered on personal communal development, but at the same time is part of an integrated European-wide endeavour involving similar local projects in a number of member states.

Interconnections

These are but some examples, among many, which I feel illustrate well both the opportunity and the difficulty inherent in any attempt to bring about human change. Whether we are talking about change in a human individual or in society the question which must be asked is – how can this change begin? During this century fundamental changes have been taking place in our scientific understanding of the world and our view of the nature of reality. Fritzof Capra describes this change in our scientific world view in the following way: 'The material world, according to contemporary physics, is not a mechanical system of separate objects but rather appears as a complex web of relationships. Sub-atomic particles cannot be understood as isolated, separate entities but have to be seen as interconnections, or correlations, in a network of events. *The notion of separate objects is an idealisation which is often very useful but has no fundamental validity.* All such objects are patterns in an inseparable cosmic process and these patterns are intrinsically dynamic. Sub-atomic particles are not made of any material substance. They have a certain mass but this mass is a form of energy. Energy, however, is always associated with processes, with activity: it is a measure of activity. Sub-atomic particles, then, are bundles of energy or patterns of activity . . . . The world view of modern physics is holistic and ecological. It emphasises the fundamental inter-relatedness and interdependence of all phenomena and also the intrinsically dynamic nature of the physical reality. To extend this view to the description of living organisms we have to go beyond physics.'

The more we understand of the nature of reality and of ourselves as human beings, the clearer it becomes that everything is interconnected; that there is no such thing as a separate human individual or community. If we apply this view to society then it inevitably follows that what is taking place in one part of society, as for example joyriding, gang rape, vandalism, or vicious attacks on old people around the countryside, must be ultimately related and interconnected with what is happening in other sectors which we ordinarily think of as normal healthy society – the apparently genteel life which goes on in better off middle class suburbs. If there is any merit in such a view then we must all have a share in the responsibility for the vicious and sordid activities which are daily going on in some of the more deprived and disadvantaged sections of our society. We have to ask the question how far all of us are dumping the negative aspects of ourselves into others and using certain persons or groups in society as scapegoats. This should in no way be interpreted to mean that these people have not their own proper share of responsibility for what they are doing or that there are not some very vicious human beings around. But nevertheless we still have to ask in what way have we all, society, contributed to this viciousness. How do we maintain it? I will resist the question 'Why?'.

Herein lies the dilemma. If we take this statement seriously, and so often we see this work out in practice, for one human individual to really change would involve the family and community in which she/he is embedded also changing fundamentally, and for this change to really take root would imply a similar change in the wider society, indeed in human society as a whole. But reciprocally the whole of human society cannot change unless real change takes place in the heart of each individual who makes it up. This is the human merry-go-round on which we appear to have been stuck for thousands of years. On the one hand we have appeals from the various religions to each of us to change our ways but if you examine this proposition honestly it becomes quite clear that one cannot really change as an individual unless the society out of which we emerge changes also. On the other hand we have political reformers and revolutionaries who have perennially attempted to create a more humane society by introducing a new political system or different ideology but this always founders on the bedrock that the individuals who have to operate this new system haven't really changed and hence everything goes back once again to where it was.

It may seem a trifle far-fetched to put the problem in this way but if one looks around the world at all the attempts over the last half-century to bring about real change in human society we will see how often what looked like hopeful and enthusiastic experiments withered away after a time and merged back eventually into the same old status quo. This lesson has been repeated but not learned over and over again. So, looking at the situation from this aspect, brings one back relentlessly to the conclusion that real human change is impossible. No part can change unless the whole changes and the whole cannot change unless there is change in the parts. Is there any way out of this impasse?

The Human Group in Systems Theory
Each of us is conceived and born already in the context of relationship and, from the very beginning, each of us emerges out of some form of primary human group; at the very least a nuclear family. In fact, almost always some form of wider communal setting is also present within which the family rests. That is, we are already embedded in a society, in a culture, and in fact this primary group culture, if we think about it, extends back in some form unbroken to the very dawn of human history. While the life of the human individual is finite and represents only a transitory moment in the evolutionary time-scale, the human group, in whatever form this may take at a given time, is not finite and has had an unbroken continuous existence stretching back over two to five million years since the very first appearance of homo sapiens on this planet. Indeed it now seems very likely that what passed across from the pre-human to the human species was not some remarkable individual mutation but rather the crossing over of a group of hominids to finally achieve fully conscious human status. So, as far as we can discern through the mists of the dawn of human history, at no point do we find first the individual and then the emergence of the group or community, but rather always the human group, some form of primitive society in which the individual is embedded. Indeed the emergence of the highly sophisticated, conscious, individual human person out of the primary human group has been a long and painful process and represents a crowning achievement

of only fairly recent times.

So we arrive at a position where it must be accepted that there is no such thing as a separate human individual; first and last, we find the individual person embedded in some form of primary social unit. The fundamental question which faces us then is 'what is the nature of the human group?' Is it simply a collection of individuals or is it some form of 'separate being' which has an existence in its own right, distinct from the individuals who make it up? Which ever way we answer this question will alter the very basis of our thinking about ourselves. Fortunately we are not simply shooting in the dark, for the work of a number of scientists in recent years is helping to illuminate our understanding of this and a number of related questions. Most of this work falls within the sphere of what has loosely been called General Systems Theory.

A system may be defined as an integrated whole which derives its essential properties from the inter-relationship between its parts. A system, therefore, cannot be understood by analysing the parts of which it is made up but rather by focusing upon the dynamic inter-relations and inter-dependencies between its parts. All throughout nature we find examples of systems both in the living and the non-living world but our concern here is with living systems.

The basic principle of a living system is what the Nobel Prize scientist Illya Prigogene, refers to as 'self-organisation'. The work of Maturana and Varela is also of fundamental importance here; they have termed this principle 'autopoeisis'. By a penetrating analysis, they have shown that the essential characteristics of anything which is alive is that it is self-regulating and self-producing, the term they coin for this is 'autopoiesis' – 'auto' meaning self and 'poiesis' (from the Greek root *poinine*) meaning to produce, i.e. self-producing. According to this view then, the essence of something which is living is that it actively maintains and produces itself, that its first priority is to maintain itself in existence. Thus, a living organism, as Fritsof Capra says, is a self-organising system, which means that its order in structure and function is not imposed by the environment but is established and maintained by the system itself. This theory maintains, then, that any subject of study can be held to be 'alive' to be 'living', to be an organism if, and only if, it fulfils the following conditions:

(a)   It contains a number of elements.

(b)   These elements are involved in a dynamic process of inter-relationship.

(c)   It is separated from its environment by a boundary of its own elements such that it permits transactions of import and export across the boundary, i.e., it is an open (not closed) system surrounded by a semi-permeable membrane.

(d) It maintains and renews (regenerates) its own elements by its own internal processes. Living organisms continually renew themselves, cells breaking down and building up structures, tissues and organs replacing their cells in continual cycles, and so on. Nevertheless the living system maintains its overall structure and appearance. Its components are continually renewed and recycled, but its being – the pattern of organisation – remains relatively stable.

(e) Finally, living systems show a tendency to transcend themselves, as Capra says, 'to reach out creatively beyond their boundaries and limitations to generate new structures and new forms of organisation. This principle of self-transcendence manifests itself in the process of learning, development and evolution.' Thus, living systems not only tend to change and adapt, but also reproduce themselves and thus ensure survival and evolution of the species.[1]

---

1. So much then for the definition of a living system. But if these are the essential characteristics which describe what it is to be alive, then they must apply to every living being – whether plant or animal, a single-celled organism, a dog, a monkey, or a human being. But there is something important to be noted here, and indeed this is the essential aspect which I wish most to emphasise, for it relates specifically to the central theme of this paper; this is the interesting characteristic of living systems that they tend to form a hierarchical order of one living system within another. Thus the basic living system making up all supra-ordinate systems is the cell. The most common form of life on this planet is still the uni-cellular organism or amoeba but, over the long course of evolution, nature has found ways for cells to combine to form new multicellular living systems such as a bee, an ant, a baboon, or a human being but, here and there in the multitude of forms which life takes, we find a third order of living systems coming into being. The most highly organised examples are to be found among the social insects – the termite mound or ant heap, the beehive – and this is hardly an accident for, in terms of evolutionary history, these organisms are many millions of years older than say, the mammalian group to which we belong. The important thing to note here is that these third order systems fulfil the definition of a living system just as completely as do the individual bees or ants of which they are composed and it is therefore increasingly being realised by entomologists that, for example, a beehive or termite mound must truly be classed as a living creature in its own right.

   In a similar way, although the process has not as yet developed so highly, various birds, fishes and mammalian groups must also be recognised as forming third order systems such as a colony of baboons. Where we find this happening, as in the case of the cell within our own bodies, or where a third order is involved – the cell within the body of a bee and the bee within the body of a beehive – we find the supra-ordinate system is in a position to influence over the primary or secondary systems of which it is constituted. Each system retains its proper integrity as a living system at its own level but nevertheless its autopoiesis is depressed and transmission and exchange across its boundary is increased and to a significant degree under the influence of the supra-ordinate system.

   Beyond this further supra-ordinate living systems can be discerned ecosystems

Questions of Minorities

Like many in the 1960s, I had idealistic hopes of society breaking up and reconstituting itself in a granular form, creating an enlightened, loving form of society. These idealistic visions of a transformed society have not come to pass. Transformation has indeed been taking place and high order human systems have mushroomed and spread throughout most of the world, growing more enormous and powerful with each passing day. But they are huge, mindless, bureaucratic systems, composed of human beings but not in any sense embodying enlightened or loving human values – transnational corporations, state departments, insurance empires, international banks and others – all impersonal, all anti-human and destructive of the total environment of the planet.

From this point of view, the Irish and Irish society may be seen to have some special characteristics. It will be clear from what has been said so far that, given human nature as it is, the existence of minority groups will tend to be an universal problem within any society. But for two main reasons, arising from its historical context, I believe Irish society is likely to have special difficulty in relation to tolerance of minority groups within it. Centuries of colonial domination here have left a cultural legacy where, even after sixty years of partial freedom, Irish society will tend to see authority (the locus of control) as located outside itself: that is, to experience itself as *'other directed'*. The other reason why this is so lies in the special position of the Roman Catholic Church in this country. Presumably because of its long years of persecution, when it represented the only life line of the people, the church holds a very intimate and central position in Irish society. When the British granted Catholic emancipation in the early years of the nineteenth century, they in fact made available to themselves a more powerful means of colonial domination over the hearts and minds of the people than they had ever wielded up to that time. For the church, however intimately it may be built into

---

such as the coral reef where many species of both plant and animal life live in a balanced co-existence or symbiotic relationship; another example would be the teeming life of the African plains and finally there is, of course, the living envelope covering the surface of the entire planet – the biosphere, maintaining itself, until recently at any rate, as a delicately balanced, self-referential, living system. One point should be clarified here in speaking of supra-ordinate human living systems. The fact that a higher order of living system may exist and that as a human individual I may be under the influence of a supra-ordinate group system, should not in any way be taken to mean that the supra-ordinate system is necessarily more complex or more highly developed than the individual living systems of which it is constituted. On the contrary, all the evidence would suggest that the individual human person is by far the most complex and most highly developed form of life of which we have any knowledge on this planet. Most human third order living systems are by comparison primitive, largely unconscious and simple in their behaviours: nevertheless they do have a powerful supra-ordinate influence on the human individual within them.

the fabric of Irish society, drawing its priests from the people, takes its ultimate authority from outside the country. This has been used in collusion with British colonialism over and over again in the last two hundred years to frustrate any attempt towards the growth of a full national identity which would draw together Irish people of various religious denominations. We have had an upsetting and painful example of this some years ago in the visit of the Papal emissary to a hunger striker in Long Kesh to try to persuade him to give up his fast. There was no equivalent visit from Rome to the British Government to try to persuade them to change their frozen colonial attitude which has remained obdurately unchanged for over sixty years.

There is nevertheless some evidence in recent years of a change on the part of the Irish clergy and Bishops to free themselves from this authoritarian relationship to Irish society. Strangely enough it is Irish society rather than the Church itself which tends to keep forcing us back into the same 'other directed' relationship. I believe this is because of our fear and unwillingness as individuals and as a society to take on our own personal authority; to make the conscious break with the old institutionalised colonial relationships. There are signs however that the third generation since the revolution, and the young people coming on, may be free enough and conscious enough within themselves to accomplish what the idealists of 1916 were unable to grasp fully and what the maimed country town shopkeeper generation, clinging meanly to survival during the '30s and '50s, lost sight of altogether. It may be hoped that the new generation, better educated and more conscious, now emerging into a European context, may be finally able to free themselves enough to take on their own self-direction and to create a fuller more human identity which is able to accept within itself all the streams and minorities which make up Irish society today.

Exchange Entropy: Towards an Open System
What, you may well ask, is the relevance of all this to human change and development? Well, as already stressed, this must necessarily involve bringing about change within society. The question is how can this be achieved when education and human development are always taking place within the context of the present society and within the group culture which is already there. This, if we think about it, always inevitably produces more of the same. There have been over the past thirty years many attempts to introduce innovative education and community development projects in many parts of the world. Our experience has been similar to that of many others. Somehow the efforts to bring about change seemed to be dissipated out into an ever-widening circle, so that while for a time there may be enthusiastic endeavour for change within the experi-

mental project, this dribbles away into the wider community and it becomes painfully clear that if the experiment were to take and have an enduring effect, this would involve bringing about a change in the whole society; what happens, in fact, is that the effort for change simply disappears into the ever-widening pool of society and everything goes back to where it started.

A second outcome which we have often seen is where a group withdraws from the community and an attempt is made to create the perfect alternative society – a commune or closed-off artificial community is established which breaks all connection or interchange with the rest of society. While perfection and peace may appear to reign for a short time, inevitably the closed society begins to stagnate and decline, the activity dries up and eventually the whole thing withers and dies, as happened with Synanon in California and, all too horribly, in the Jim Jones experiment ending in mass suicide in Guyana.

It is here that the illuminating insights of Teilhard de Chardin and the more recent pioneering and meticulous work of Prigogene et al. on self-organising, non-linear systems help us to understand more clearly why these innovative attempts to bring about real social change and human development have had so little long term success up to the present and why, in spite of so much idealistic endeavour, everything seems relentlessly to drift back to square one.

The second law of thermodynamics states that every physical process will result in a net decrease in the amount of order (hence a net increase in the amount of disorder) in the universe as a whole. Entropy (from the Greek 'entropian' meaning evolution) is that quantity which indexes the amount of disorder in a system at any given time. The second law thus implies that every physical process will result in an irreversible increase in the amount of entropy in the universe as a whole, over time. Entropy has, therefore, sometimes been referred to as 'time's arrow'. Since its formulation, this law has appeared to most physicists to be one of the greatest achievements of theoretical physics, one of the cornerstones of our understanding of the physical world. It was thus thought to be universal in its application.

It seemed evident then that in our immediate physical environment on this planet the second law of thermodynamicsw was relentlessly at work – the planet was running down; natural resources being gobbled up at an accelerating rate and, with each reaction, entropy was increasing. Then de Chardin drew attention to a strange paradox which, although it was not appreciated at the time, fundamentally altered this whole concept of the universe. He pointed out that in the midst of this dissipative view of the world, biological life has appeared and has been growing continually, becoming ever more complex, alive and conscious and concentrating more energy unto itself. He referred again and again to this in the last years of his life:

> On the one hand, we have in physics a matter which slides irresistibly, following the line of least resistance, in the direction of the most probable forms of distribution. And on the other hand, we have in biology the same matter drifting (no less irresistibly but in this case in a sort of 'greater effort' for survival) towards ever more improbable, because ever more complex, forms of arrangement.

In another essay, written shortly before his death, he returned to this question:

> However, it may well be, perhaps, that this contradiction is a warning to our minds that we must completely reverse the way in which we see things. We still persist in regarding the physical as constituting the 'true' phenomenon in the universe, and the psychic as a sort of epiphenomenon . . . . If we really wish to unify the real, we should completely reverse the values – that is, we should consider the whole of thermodynamics as an unstable and ephemeral bi-effect of the concentration on itself of what we call 'consciousness' or 'spirit' . . . . In other words, there is no longer just one type of energy in the world: there are two different energies, one axial, increasing, and irreversible, and the other peripheral or tangential, constant, reversible. And these two energies are linked together in 'arrangement', but without, nevertheless, being able either to form a compound or directly to be transformed into one another, because they operate at different levels.

From this point of view if we take a fresh look at the world the startling fact emerges that the whole stuff of the universe appears to be built up of units – 'wholes'; these combine to form at each level a genuine synthesis, a new pattern of organisation creating a larger and more complex 'whole'. This remarkable design seems to run right through from the quark to the galaxy in outer space. In *The Phenomenon of Man* Teilhard had this to say:

> After allowing itself to be captivated by the charms of analysis to the extent of falling into illusion, modern thought is at last getting used once more to the idea of the creative value of synthesis in evolution. It is beginning to see that there is definitely more in the molecule than in the atom, more in the cell than the molecule, more in society than in the individual, and more in mathematical construction than in calculations

and theorems. We are now inclined to admit that at each further degree of combinations something which is irreducible to isolated elements emerges in a new order. With this admission, consciousness, life and thought, are on the threshold of acquiring a right to existence in terms of science.

In the same chapter he makes an important qualification of this emphasis, which is very much to the point in our consideration here of the question of a 'granular' society, when he says:

In any domain – whether it be the cells of the body, the members of a society, or the elements of a spiritual synthesis – union differentiates. In every organised whole, the parts perfect themselves and fulfil themselves. Through neglect of this universal rule, many a system of pantheism has led us astray to the cult of a great 'All' in which individuals were supposed to be merged like a drop in the ocean, or like a dissolving grain of salt. Applied to the case of the summation of consciousness, the law of union rids us of this perilous and recurrent illusion. No, following the confluent orbits of their centres, the grains of consciousness do not tend to lose outlines and blend but, on the contrary, to accentuate the depth and incommunicability of their *egos*. The more 'other' they become in conjunction, the more they find themselves as 'self'.

Illya Prigogene in his work on the characteristics of self-organising systems (what he calls irreversible non-linear transformations under conditions far from equilibrium), has dealt with this much more systematically and in far more detail. He points out that a thermodynamically isolated system is one which neither energy nor mass can enter or leave. In actual practice the only truly isolated system possible is the universe as a whole. The thermodynamically closed system is one which energy can enter and leave but matter cannot. A well-sealed steamboiler, whose water can be heated or cooled but cannot escape, is an example of such a closed system. It was specifically to explain certain properties of such 'steam engines' that the second law was first devised. Most biological, psychological and social systems, however, are neither isolated nor closed. They are, instead, thermo-dynamically open systems. An open system is one which is capable of exchanging both energy and matter with its environment. Such open systems have always been viewed as anomalous from the point of view of classical thermo-dynamics. However, when the principles underlying the second law are extended to these systems, a new set of properties emerge which were not formerly apparent. These new properties include capacity for 'self-organisation' – i.e. for a 'spontaneous' shift from a lower to a higher level of organisational complexity. Prigogene has named such self-organisating systems 'dissipative structures' and says they are capable of 'exchange entropy', since they can maintain their organisational complexity only by continually dissipating the positive entropy which they produce, back into the environment. We can say that each such locally developing system achieves an increase in structural order and complexity only by 'ingesting', 'digesting', and 'assimilating' the negative entophy (i.e. the orderliness) previously possessed by the structures in its surrounding environment, and by 'excreting' back into that environment 'waste products' which are higher in positive entropy (i.e. disorderliness) than those which it initially ingested.

Towards a Self-Organising System

Taking this basic work on self-organising systems and applying it now to the question of human development, that is to the question of how we can bring about change at the level of society; and, taking maturana and Varela's concept of autopoiesis into consideration, a quite different approach to the problem begins to become apparent.

It appears to me inescapable that if we are to hope to educate for real human development, to bring about real human change, this will only be possible if we find ways to create bounded human systems. But these must be open systems with semi-permeable boundedness so that exchange with the surrounding environment (i.e. society) can be managed and controlled sufficiently to allow self-organisation, growth and development to go on within the system and not to allow this to be simply dissipated into the surrounding society.

My position is that there is a vast reservoir of untapped energy, ability and creative potential in any human individual but most of this potential usually lies dormant and is not available to the person. There is always untapped potential. If however this human potential is to be realised then two fundamental issues have to be faced and tackled.

The first is personal authority. Most human beings, particularly in this post-colonial country, fail to establish any reasonable degree of personal authority. By this I mean that they have little awareness as to whom or what they are and that most of the decisions concerning their lives are being taken by authorities outside of themselves – their family, state or corporate organisations, many of whose centres of power are operating from outside the country altogether.

Many of our school-leavers, particularly those coming from socially deprived areas, are almost devoid of self-direction. Throughout their school days rote knowledge has been fed into them. They may have become literate or have developed some specific skills, but all of this is derived from outside of themselves and they can seldom make a statement as to whom or what they are or ask questions of the world in which they live.

The hypothesis presented then is that unless the centre of control is discovered by each of us within ourselves, there's no possibility of the emergence of creativity, of the realization of the potential within us, of taking a fresh look at the world so that we can create new forms of work and activity.

This is a crucial question for any person or society, the question of personal authority and self-direction. Human beings are intended to take responsibility for all that is within them. Direction from outside is a sick symptom for the person or society, a symptom of lost autonomy, lost power. This is mainly a function of the boundary of a living system (whether this be an individual or a group) in the management of the interaction between what is inside or outside the system. The crucial question is where this 'authority' or 'control' lies: to be self-directing, or self-motivating, lies at the very heart of what it is to be alive, to be human.

The second essential principle is that the person begins to understand and take responsibility for the role each of us has to play as part of a group, a member of society. The essential thing that has to be learned here is that within society, in the families and groups within which we live, each of us tends to be given a role with an expected set of attitudes and behaviours which are often quite different from the way we see ourselves as individuals.

People are often only dimly aware of being made to behave in this way, of the role they are given by the group, such as peace-maker, rebel, leader, follower, the talker or the silent one, etc. One has the unpleasant feeling of being forced to be someone one does not wish to be, over and over again, in the various groups we participate in as we go through life. The crucial learning here, which again can only take place within the space of a managed bounded human system, is to become aware of the characteristic ways in which we participate and relate with others and to start to take responsibility for this.

In contemporary Western society, this element is almost invariably seen in competitive terms, a world of winners and losers. More and more in our society, we see the few who struggle their way to the top, who find a comfortable place for themselves, and the many for whom society has no place.

The learning of our involvement with groups within which we live, is absolutely crucial if people are ever to change to a more co-operative way of functioning. To me, it is quite clear now that any alternative strategy of work and living will have to emerge from such a co-operative base, and will only be possible with human beings who have some understanding of these realities.

It should now be clearer why it is necessary to establish a bounded living system, a 'human oasis' where the group is managed so as to provide a space for its many parts. This removes the outside controls which are normally present in society, so that a young person is left face to face with his or her own behaviour. If they have not, up to this time, learned any skills in managing themselves, usually a good deal of confusion and uncertainty will result. The setting has to be managed so as to provide, within the limits of tolerance, sufficient emotional space and freedom for individuals to experience themselves and their behaviour.

Not having the resources within themselves for self-direction and self-management, they may become highly anxious. This may manifest itself in destructive, anti-social or other forms of acting-out behaviour. But, providing that the group setting as a whole can be managed, the natural tendency in all of us towards self-management and creative expression will come to the surface.

A change towards the personal, by very definition, cannot take place across society en masse, for this would only result in denial of the very personal dimension we are trying to enhance. If there is to be any hope of change in this direction, fundamental to it must be the creation of some nucleus within which it can happen, some basic unit of society where these personalised processes can take root.

The Granular Society
This time the synthesis must be at the human level, a human module which will form the basic unit of a 'granular' society. Because this will represent a genuinely new synthesis at the human level, the forces holding it together, and energising principle organising and maintaining it in being, must also be of a quite different order. The atom, the molecule, the living cell, each is maintained in existence by a pattern of forces, by energy in a form appropriate to its own level. When we come to a synthesis at the human level it must be asked what form will the organisational forces now take, where will we turn to find an energising principle which will maintain and vitalise our human module. It is true that in the human being the earlier electro-chemical forms of energy are still at work in the atoms, molecules and cells which go to make us up. But to bind one human to another, to create a true communion of human beings, some new principle must be introduced.

To find the answer, I believe we must turn once again to the personal dimension and look at the kinds of bonds which operate in basic human structures already in existence. Here we find the power of love and conscious understanding, psychological and emotional forces operating at the level of consciousness as between one human person and another. However, as is found in lower forms of synthesis, for example with the atom or the molecule, the forces operating are not simply those of attraction. On the contrary the individual components of, say, an atom maintain a dynamic relationship always striving towards a stable arrangement – a state of balance between the forces of attraction and repulsion. So too, at the human level, the need for intimacy, closeness and love is always balanced by the need to keep a measure of distance and separateness between oneself and the loved ones – the need at times for privacy, to separate and be purely oneself. I think if we are to make any progress with human relationships in society it is as vital to understand this need for separateness, distinctness and uniqueness and personal development, as the need for love and intimate relationship.

This living human system then must have a surrounding membrane providing a clear separation or boundary between itself and the rest of society. This would be partly geographical and spatial but because, as already explained, the organisational forces operating are at the level of consciousness, of human love and understanding, the boundary membrane must be mainly of a psychological nature, which would provide a protective mechanism, a semipermeable membrane, to filter uncontrolled sensory bombardment and mass communication from outside.

Just as the achievement of the cell membrane constituted a great leap forward with the emergence of the first living substance and allowed the heightening intensity of various chemical processes to take place within the living cell and not to be lost by diffusion into the surrounding milieu, so the surrounding psychological membrane would allow an intensification of internal communication and human relationship, heightening the intensity of human processes of love and ideas within.

At the same time, this bounded system must be an open system, allowing the free exit and entrance of individuals to go or to come from other human modules. In other words, it would be the structure as a whole and the patterns of forces/bonds and relationships within it which would remain stable but, as is the case with atoms and ions moving in and out of the living cell, any given individual could leave, being replaced by another from outside, without disturbing the overall arrangement.

What I now see is the possibility, difficult though it may be, and however much the scales are tilted against it, of setting up islands, human systems, bounded both spatially and psychically, where a truly human education can begin and where real personal growth and development can take place in a context of personal relationships. Much of the knowledge and understanding necessary to set up such bounded human systems is now available as never before. But this time we must learn from nature and from what biological systems have to teach us: through the slow painful process of evolution, stretching back over millions of years. We must learn what the living cell and other living systems had to learn – that a boundary must be created, but one which allows and manages appropriate exchange with the environment and is neither too open nor too closed. We must not make the mistake of the communes of the '60s, which shut themselves off from the world to create the perfect society and then withered and died.

If these 'human islands' are to achieve anything they must involve the whole person and the whole life cycle from the cradle to the grave. Both male and female dimensions of sexuality must find their expressions in each person, and both women and men must be able to participate fully and equally and each make their full contribution to the whole. They must be places where all can come to 'live' and to 'learn'; to 'work' and to 'play'; and more important, simply to 'be'.

It is quite clear now that no partial concept of education, such as our own present school system, can ever really achieve anything different; it can only further reinforce the schizophrenic splitting process which is more and more affecting all aspects of our society. New curricula, smaller classes and all the other current slogans for progress, all mean nothing and will achieve nothing. If the bounded human system which I am proposing is to have success as a 'human island' where real change and growth can take place in the midst of a fragmenting and deteriorating society, then all these issues will have to be faced and worked at unflinchingly.

This growing voice calling for decentralization and devolution, coming from many parts of the world, should not be misunderstood as a regression to parochialism or some form of primitive tribal culture. There can be no question of humanity turning backwards; on the contrary, the growth of consciousness, education, and understanding; the vastly increased potential for personal relationship, have all become possible with the growth of modern technology and communications. What is required is a further development of technology and even more advanced systems of communication, but a technology utilised economically with careful management of scarce energy resources, subjugated to serve the genuine needs of human beings. This would allow further automation of heavy technology thus permitting human beings greater freedom to develop the primary infrastructure of society. Were such an infrastructure of personalised human modules (basically self-running neighbourhoods and communities) to be built up then central functions could look very different. While it is impossible at this stage to say exactly what form these would take, they should be able to take on more of a co-ordinating role, guiding and influencing the basically self-running local structures, planning for the future and supervising central technology. The present top heavy civil service and government departments, and multistate bureaucracies such as that in the EEC headquarters in Brussels, could thus be vastly trimmed down and hopefully replaced, to a greater extent, by impermanent working parties, task groups and planning think tanks. These could come together to do a job and then break up. Human beings could thus preserve much more of their individual and group energies for the primary human structures of society concerned with ordinary living.

This groping for a different way is appearing in various countries and under the guise of differing ideologies, but I think a much deeper logic than any of the present political or philosophical systems is at work. A deeper logic which is coming from the sheer necessity for human beings to resolve their relationship to the world and to each other, if they are to survive. Humans who, for almost the total period since they first appeared on this planet, have been struggling with nature, are now – as the pressure of the human layer covering the surface of the earth increases – coming face to face with themselves. This is the crux of the human question which has totally altered within the last hundred years. It is one on which our health and sanity, and unless we can solve it, the continued existence of human life on this planet depends.

The Role of the European Community's Structural Funds in the 1990s

ALAN MATTHEWS

Introduction

During the debate leading up to the referendum on the Single European Act in May 1987, much attention focused on the implications for Irish neutrality and foreign policy of institutionalising the system of European Political Co-operation. The economic consequences were, for once, underplayed. Subsequently, more has been heard of the Community's programme to complete the internal market by 1992. Many of the provisions of the Single Act were designed to expedite the necessary decision-making towards that end. From an Irish perspective, however, particular importance attaches to those provisions in the Single Act which provided for a new section on Economic and Social Cohesion to be added to the Treaty of Rome which Ireland signed in 1973.

Economic and social cohesion is Euro-speak for reducing regional disparities within the EC and ensuring that the economically weaker member states, such as Ireland, are helped to keep up with economic and social developments in the richer Community countries. According to the Single Act, this objective is to be pursued in three ways: (a) through the conduct and coordination of the national economic policies of the member states; (b) by being taken into account in the implementation of the internal market programme and in other common policies; and (c) by deliberate Community action through the Community's structural funds and the other Community financial instruments.

The Community has three structural funds: the Guidance Section of FEOGA (the Agricultural Fund), the Social Fund and the Regional Fund. The FEOGA Guidance Section was provided for in Article 40 of the Rome Treaty in order to attain the objectives of the common agricultural policy, in particular, increased productivity through the modernisation of agricultural structures, marketing and processing activities. The European Social Fund was also set up by the Treaty of Rome to improve employment opportunities for workers in the common market through vocational training measures and aid to increase their geographical and occupational mobility within the Community. The third of the structural funds, the Regional Fund, was not established until 1975, seventeen years after the creation of the Community, and it had to wait until the Single Act to be given a specific basis in the EC Treaty. It awards grants to public and private organisations in depressed or underdeveloped regions for industrial or infrastructural investment.

In 1985, these three structural funds were joined by the integrated Mediterranean Programmes under which additional resources are directed to underdeveloped regions in southern Europe which face increased competition from the further enlargement of the Community in 1986 to include Spain and Portugal. In addition to the structural funds, the Community has a number of financial instruments which can be used for structural purposes. The most important of these is the European Investment Bank whose brief is specifically to lend to projects in the less developed Community regions in order to contribute to the balanced and steady development of the common market.

The Single Act required the European Commission to review the operations of the structural funds and to submit a comprehensive proposal on what amendments were necessary to enable them to better contribute to the objective of economic and social cohesion, to increase their efficiency and to co-ordinate their activities both with each other and with the operations of the Community's financial instruments.

The Commission responded to this invitation by putting forward what it called a framework regulation in August 1987. This framework regulation was an ambitious attempt to fundamentally change the way in which the structural funds would operate. Among its major proposals was a plan to double the resources available to the structural funds by 1992. It also called for the concentration of the activities of the funds on specific objectives, for a new method of operation based on principles of complementarity, partnership and programming, and for simplified procedures and improved coordination between the funds.

The proposals in themselves were not new. From as far back as 1977 the Commission has attempted to bring about greater coordination between the activities of the various funds. For many years it has campaigned vigorously for a greater Community say in the disbursement of Community funds, for the greater involvement of regional and local bodies in formulating Community programmes, and for the adoption of an integrated, programming approach. These objectives have been viewed with suspicion by the member states, who have objected to the ceding of greater authority to the Commission in the allocation and distribution of funds, on the one hand, and to the potential competition from local and regional bodies, on the other.

Not surprisingly, the August 1987 proposal also proved controversial. However, at the meeting of the European Council on February 13, 1988 the Commission won a considerable victory when the Council adopted its major elements. The framework regulation was finally approved by the Council of Ministers in June 1988.

In July 1988 the Commission submitted a further package of four regulations to the Council. Three of these propose specific reforms in the three major structural funds, while the fourth, called a 'horizontal' regulation, lays down amended provisions common to all the funds and sets down procedures to coordinate their activities with each other and with the European Investment Bank. The intention is that these additional regulations should be adopted before the end of 1988, so that the activities of the funds, from 1 January 1989 on, will be based on the new guidelines which emerge. Provision is made for transitional arrangements to cover the period before the new arrangements become fully effective.

This chapter discusses the likely significance of these changes in the structural funds for Ireland in the 1990s. The most obvious issue is their impact on the expected flow of resources from the EC over the next few years. Here the increase in the size of the structural funds must be set against the increased competition for these funds from the other poorer EC member states, in particular, Greece, Spain and Portugal. The adverse impact of the ongoing reforms in the common agricultural policy on the likely size of transfers from that source must also be taken into account.

But the volume of overall transfers is only one element in assessing whether the new arrangements for the structural funds will sufficiently assist Ireland to keep up with developments in the rest of the Community; of equal importance are the ways in which these funds will be spent. Here the Commission's new proposals for the operation of the funds will have a major impact. The kinds of eligible investments, the emphasis on integrated programmes and the way in which local and regional bodies are involved will decisively influence the productivity of the funds which are obtained.

Finally, the changes in the structural funds are a further step on the way to a more integrated, and possibly more united, Europe. At least implicitly, they tell us something more about the principles which presently underlie this development, and reveal a little more about the nature of the Community to which we are committed. Understanding these principles, and the conflicting pressures which give rise to them, should enable us to better focus our energies to move the Community in directions we might like.

The Volume of Transfers through the Structural Funds
The likely impact on the increased resources available for the structural funds can best be understood in the context of previous experi-

ence. Because the EC budget allows for multiannual programming, two series are available for the amount of transfers to Ireland through the structural funds in the past, called commitment appropriations and payment appropriations respectively. Commitment appropriations in any year relate to multiannual programmes which are financed in that and subsequent years. Payment appropriations made in any year relate to commitments entered into in that year and in previous years. Commitments represent money promised, payments represent money handed over. Actual receipts on a payments basis are shown in Table 1, while for comparison annual commitments are given in the Appendix.

Table 1 shows that there has been a steady increase in the size of payments made through the structural funds, although when inflation is taken into account the increase is less impressive. Between 1980 and 1986 the value of money depreciated by 85 per cent, so although payments in the later year were double those in 1980, the real increase was quite small. The most striking feature of the table, however, is that structural fund payments are dwarfed by payments received through the EC's Agricultural Fund to support farm prices. Of total Irish receipts from the EC over the period 1973 to 1986, structural fund spending amounted to just 22 per cent (NESC 1988).

Table 1.   Ireland's receipts from the EC structural funds, £m.

Year	Regional Fund	Social Fund	FEOGA Guidance	Total Structural	FEOGA Guarantee
1977	8.5	8.2	7.4	24.1	245.1
1978	11.1	19.3	9.7	40.1	365.6
1979	25.5	28.8	18.5	72.8	396.5
1980	46.4	46.7	31.8	124.9	381.1
1981	54.6	45.3	41.9	141.8	304.6
1982	66.1	73.2	59.6	198.9	344.3
1983	58.2	92.7	63.7	214.6	441.7
1984	65.2	84.3	49.3	198.8	644.6
1985	76.0	141.3	55.8	273.1	836.6
1986	77.1	124.5	46.6	248.8	884.0
1987	87.0	193.0	67.9	347.9	739.6

Source: *The Single European Act*, Stationery Office, May 1987; latest years from the relevant Departments.

The distribution of payments between the funds is also interesting. In absolute terms the Social Fund has been most important (9.6 per cent of total EC transfers over the period 1973-86). The Regional Fund (7.1 per cent of all transfers) has barely kept up with inflation throughout the 1980s and was only just more important as a source of receipts than the FEOGA Guidance Section (5.5 per cent of the total). In recent years agricultural and related off-farm investment has fallen off and this is reflected in the levelling off in receipts from this fund in the mid-1980s, even in nominal terms.

The amount of money which Ireland receives from the structural funds is a function of the total resources committed to these funds in the EC budget and Ireland's share of these totals. Ireland's shares of the three funds in the 1980s are shown in Table 2 for both commitment and payment appropriations. It can be seen that for some years Ireland's share of total EC commitments was greater than its share of total EC payments while in other years this is reversed. The differences are accounted for by variations in the timing of the start-up of major commitments both in Ireland and abroad, as well as by the speed with which projects which have been promised money are actually implemented on the ground.

A sharp fall in the percentage received from all three funds is evident after 1985, arising from the accession of Spain and Portugal. This was partially compensated by an increase in the total size of funds, so that Ireland's receipts in absolute terms were less affected. Historically, Ireland has been most successful with respect to the Social Fund, obtaining in one year (1983) over 15 per cent of the payments made in that year. In this the country was aided by its status as a 'superpriority' region for Social Fund purposes. Ireland has also done well from the FEOGA Guidance Section, obtaining on average around 10 per cent of all funds available. The country has been least successful with respect to the Regional Fund, obtaining only just over 6 per cent on a commitments basis although rather more in actual payments terms. Unlike the other funds, the distribution of Regional Fund monies was controlled throughout the period, first by fixed quota allocations and subsequently by a somewhat more flexible system of indicative ranges.

Table 2. **Ireland's share of the EC structural funds, per cent**

		1982	1983 EUR 10	1984	1985	1986 EUR 12	1987
FEOGA Guidance	CA	11.4	10.6	9.0	9.7	8.4	8.6
Section	PA	13.2	11.7	9.9	10.6	8.8	9.3
Social Fund	CA	9.5	9.7	11.8	12.3	9.3	7.8
	PA	12.7	15.1	8.2	12.1	8.7	9.8
Regional Fund	CA	6.2	5.0	6.8	6.3	3.8	4.8
	PA	9.6	7.5	7.7	7.3	3.2	4.5
Total	CA	8.4	7.8	9.0	9.2	6.4	6.5
	PA	11.6	10.9	8.3	9.7	6.3	7.5

NOTES:
CA = committment appropriations
PA = payment appropriations
Source: Court of Auditors' reports: own estimates for 1987

Ireland's expected receipts from the structural funds in future will also be determined jointly by the overall size of the funds and the share which the country succeeds in obtaining. In the framework regulation of June 1988 it was agreed to increase the commitment appropriations for the structural funds (7,700 million ECU in 1988) by 1,300 million ECU a year (in 1988 prices) over the period 1989-92 to 12,900 million ECU in 1992, and that the effort would be continued to ensure that in 1993 the figure would be double the 1987 level.

Ireland's share of these funds will be influenced by three other commitments contained in the framework regulation. The first is that structural fund contributions to a defined list of priority regions should be doubled by 1992. These regions, which include both Ireland and Northern Ireland, generally have a per capita GDP less than 75 per cent of the Community average. There is a further commitment to make 'a particular effort' to assist the least/prosperous regions within this priority list. Finally, the Commission will try to ensure that up to 80 per cent of Regional Fund commitments may be directed towards the priority regions.

These commitments are not as generous as they sound. Although the priority regions are to receive the bulk of Regional Fund monies, there is no commitment to the overall size of this Fund. The only binding commitment with respect to transfer volumes is that the total flows from all funds to the priority regions will double by 1992. As the overall objective is to double the structural funds by 1993, then doubling the funds received by the priority regions by 1992 hardly represents a breakthrough to focus more selectively on the Community's more disadvantaged regions. A more robust objective would have been to seek to double the *proportion* of funds going to the priority regions rather than just the absolute amounts. Given this timid move in the direction of greater targeting on the priority regions, Ireland's share will depend on its ranking within this group. Here the Irish negotiators at the European Council achieved a significant commitment from the Commission that Ireland will be included in the list of least prosperous regions for which a special effort is to be made. There is a further commitment that the resources received by the least developed regions as a group will be doubled, and it is understood the Government is satisfied that this commitment also applies to Ireland within this group.

If we assume that commitment appropriations are doubled by 1992, and that Ireland's relative position within the group of priority regions remains unchanged from that in 1987, then total structural fund commitments to Ireland could increase by £350 million (see Appendix 1). A somewhat higher figure, up to £400 million, might reasonably be envisaged if the commitment obtained at the European Council to give even higher priority to the least developed regions, including Ireland, has practical effect. Given the absence of fixed national quotas Ireland's receipts will depend on the quality and acceptability of the operational programmes and other schemes submitted to Brussels for support, and the speed with which projects can be implemented on the ground. Generally actual payments lag behind commitments, and because payments to Ireland were unusually high relative to commitments in 1987, the expected increase in Irish receipts between 1987 and 1992 will be lower than the above figures, perhaps in the range £250 – £300 million (this estimate is based on the assumption that payments will work out at 85 per cent of commitments in 1992). While a welcome boost to the flow of funds into the country, it is likely that FEOGA Guarantee expenditure for agricultural price support will still be a more important source of transfers in that year.

Disbursement of Structural Fund Assistance
It is not only the volume of transfers which will be affected by the new structural fund arrangements. The projects eligible for support, the rates of assistance and the way in which applications for support will be made are also affected by the new directives. Some of the major changes are highlighted below.

Objectives
The new framework regulation has for the first time identified a limited number of priority objectives designed to strengthen the Community's economic and social cohesion. Future funding from the structural funds must be justified in terms of at least one of these objectives. They are:

1. promoting the development and structural adjustment of the regions whose development is lagging behind;
2. converting the regions, frontier regions or parts of regions (including employment areas and urban communities) seriously affected by industrial decline;
3. combating long-term unemployment;
4. facilitating the occupational integration of young people;
5. with a view to reform of the common agricultural policy: (a) speeding up the adjustment of agricultural structures, and (b) promoting the development of rural areas.

In turn, each structural fund has a specific set of tasks which underpins one or more of these objectives. The Regional Fund, for example, has the essential task of providing support for Objectives 1 and 2 above, as well as participating in operations towards Objective 5 (b). It can do this by providing support for productive investment and infrastructure investment, as well as for measures which exploit the potential for internally generated development in the regions concerned. The Social Fund will contribute primarily towards Objectives 3 and 4, although it can also support measures for Objectives 1, 2, and 5 (b), by providing support throughout the Community for vocational training measures and aids for employment and for the creation of self-employed activities. The pursuit of Objective 5 is primarily the function of FEOGA Guidance Section, although the other two funds can be called upon for measures designed to promote Objective 5 (b).

Because each fund is geared to supporting particular activities, the balance between the funds has important implications for the ways EC resources can be used. For example, a larger Social Fund at the Community level will make it easier to obtain funds for training and employment schemes relative to funds for road projects or technological infrastructure development which must be funded from the Regional Fund. Ireland will welcome the greater emphasis on Regional Fund spending in the total package for the priority regions, as there must be limits to the extent to which we can profitably absorb continuing increases in Social Fund spending. One possible difficulty to increasing Regional Fund spending – the need for the Irish government to put up its share of the cost – has been alleviated now that Community assistance has been increased to a maximum of 75 per cent of the total cost and at least 50 per cent of public expenditure in priority regions. In practice, the norm may be rather less, between 65 and 70 per cent, depending on the outcome of the negotiations now taking place on the follow-up regulations. Further, private sector projects accepted as part of a government programme will be eligible for support without the Government being required to make any contribution at all.

The Programming Approach

The framework regulation introduces an important change in the management of EC transfers by emphasising a programming approach. This has two main elements. For each Objective for which funding is sought the Government must submit by March 1989 an overall plan setting out its priorities in the area, how it proposes to tackle these problems, and an indication of the use to be made of assistance available under the funds or from the European Investment Bank. For Objective 1 regions such as Ireland, for example, a national development plan for the country will be submitted, setting out the development priorities selected and the corresponding operations under each objective (recall that Ireland as a whole is treated as a single region for EC structural fund purposes). While development plans have been required for

Regional Fund assistance in the past the requirement has never been taken that seriously. The Commission clearly intends that in future they should play a greater role.

The second element is that applications for assistance will mainly be grouped in the form of operational programmes. An operational programme is defined as consisting of a series of multiannual measures implemented through recourse to one or more funds or the European Investment Bank. Some operational programmes will be sectoral in nature, covering the whole country, while others will be sub-national covering specific geographical regions. In August the Government announced the composition of seven regions for which sub-national programmes will be drawn up.

The Commission will then examine the proposed plans and operations to determine whether they are consistent with the objectives of the framework regulation. On the basis of this examination it will establish the 'Community support framework' for Community structural operations. This framework will include, among other things, a multiannual financing plan, with details of the amount of assistance and which funding sources will be used.

This will be a critical negotiation, for on its outcome will depend the flow of EC resources over the medium term. The sequence of the negotiations is likely to give rise to certain problems, because programmes must be drawn up in the absence of firm figures on what resources will likely be available. The Commission has promised that, to facilitate planning of assistance in priority regions, 85 per cent of regional fund appropriations will be allocated on a quota basis between member states, this allocation to be based on various socio-economic criteria, but Ireland's share has not yet been determined. The difficulty is exacerbated at sub-national level where programmes have to be drawn up without any clear idea of the share-out of possible funds between the seven regions and between sub-national programmes and sectoral programmes. The Government has appointed a team of consultants to draw up the programme of funding for the Greater Dublin region, which is one of the seven sub-national regions, and it intends that work on the other sub-national programmes will proceed in parallel, so that as many programmes as possible can be submitted by March 1989 along with the national development plan. Some criticism of the delay in getting the preparation of programmes underway may be warranted. While the final agreement was not reached until June 1988, the outline was available since August 1987. There must be a fear that the hurried attempts to draw up operational programmes now may have an adverse effect on the quality of the programmes submitted.

Partnership

Programming is one element in what the Commission calls an 'integrated approach' to structural fund expenditure. In principle, it should enable the resources of the different funds to be harnessed within the framework of a multiannual programme to achieve stated objectives. The other element the Commission calls 'partnership'. This means that the activities and responsibilities of the different levels of government involved in an operational programme – the Commission itself, the member state and the competent authorities designated by the latter at national, regional, local or other level – are clearly defined within the framework of the overall agreement. Partnership is intended to cover the preparation, financing, monitoring and assessment of operations.

The Commission's hope for this integrated approach is that it will help to achieve synergy between the different measures and ensure the organised convergence of the efforts of different partners with different backgrounds and different responsibilities. To this end each operational programme will be supervised by a monitoring committee consisting of representatives of the interested parties. By drawing local authorities into the preparation and implementation of programmes, the Commission hopes to draw on their local knowledge and experience to improve the quality and efficiency of the projects undertaken.

In the case of the Greater Dublin Area regional programme, which was the first to be established, the Government opted for a monitoring committee dominated by public officials, with minimal private sector representation and with no democratic involvement. It was subsequently announced that a two-tier management structure for the sub-national programmes would be established with an inner core of central and local government officials together with Commission representatives, and an advisory committee composed of local representatives, interest groups and private individuals. Given the time constraint, however, the process of drawing up development programmes and negotiating the Community support framework with Brussels will inevitably be a centralised affair. The impact which the advisory committees can make is as yet unclear.

Complementarity

What the Commission calls complementarity can be translated into the requirements of 'additionality' and 'conditionality'. Additionality is, or should be, a non-issue which yet manages to generate a lot of heat in discussions of the structural funds. Additionality is usually taken to mean that the availability of structural fund finance should induce additional investment, not simply provide additional finance to existing investments. The hope is expressed that, because structural fund financing is available, more infrastructure investment, or more training, will be undertaken than would be the case in the absence of this money. A strong case can be made, for example, that the Social Fund has played an incentive role with regard to training in Ireland, and that the state's capability to provide training both in general, and with regard to specific groups such as itinerants and women, has been increased (Hart and Laffan, 1983). Conditionality underlines the Commission's view that funds are not simply handed over to member states to do with them what they will, but are to be used within the framework of Community policies and programmes.

The significance of complementarity depends on whose viewpoint is being considered. The Commission is interested in complementarity because it rejects the notion of simply being a clearing house for financial transfers between the member states. It wishes to have an active role in determining priorities and influencing structural interventions. Complementarity is therefore part of the Commission's own agenda to maximise its power and status.

Within Ireland, additionality has had a separate meaning. Controversy has arisen because the less-favoured regions argue that Department of Finance procedures with respect to Regional Fund monies have not led to additional spending on regional development activities within Ireland. Generally what happens is that the Department of Finance submits a list of projects from the Public Capital Programme for co-financing to Brussels, projects which it would probably have been prepared to finance in any case. The evidence supports the view that the bulk of Regional Fund expenditure which can be assigned to particular regions has benefited those which are better-off.

From a national viewpoint, we should not be overly concerned with ensuring additionality. Although the Commission wishes to see the structural funds providing an incentive to increased capital spending in the weaker regions, it is worth undertaking capital expenditure only up to the point where it can yield a return sufficient to meet the cost of borrowing. Because the size of Community transfers is more or less fixed, it does not make sense to undertake investments with a lower rate of return if Community funds can be obtained by submitting the more profitable projects in any case.

The criticism of the lack of additionality with respect to regional spending within the country may now be alleviated by the development of sub-national programmes, and by ensuring that local and regional authorities have a greater input than at present into how development funds in their areas might be spent.

Conclusions
The reform of the structural funds initiated by the Single European Act was designed to complement the measures taken to complete

the single market by 1992. It is argued that the initial impact of market completion and greater mobility of capital and labour within the Community could be to concentrate production and resources in the richer Community regions. The reform of the structural funds was designed to provide these funds with adequate resources to deal with the problems arising, to concentrate their activities on a limited number of priority objectives, to cement a new method of operation based on programming and partnership, and to generally simplify the procedures and improve the coordination of the funds themselves.

For Ireland, a doubling of structural fund receipts by 1992 will provide a welcome, if modest, addition to Exchequer resources, particularly in the context of limited growth in FEOGA Guarantee expenditures forseeable in the next few years.

The Commission's attempts to insist on reformed procedures for the disbursement of funds, based on the ideas of programming and partnership, are in themselves desirable. Certain points of tension are already evident, however. The haste with which operational programmes at both the sub-national and sectoral levels must be prepared in order to make an early submission to the Commission may adversely affect the quality of projects included. The recent announcement of new management structures for the sub-national programmes goes some way to alleviating fears that the Government appeared to be taking a very bureaucratic and centralised approach to the preparation of the Irish submission. The Government may well feel that there are dangers in raising expectations about Brussels largesse which cannot be satisifed, and indeed there have been indications of this with respect to the Greater Dublin programme. Nonetheless, the decisions to be taken go to the heart of Irish development strategy in the 1990s, and it is to be hoped that more popular debate on the content of this strategy will be encouraged.

A further danger is that the increased rates of Community assistance provided for in the structural fund reforms – up to possibly 75 per cent of project expenditures – may create the impression that less attention need be paid to project costs, and that projects will be submitted simply to avail of Community funding despite a low rate of return overall. Because Community funds used in one project are not available for another, there is as great a need for careful calculation as ever.

On a wider canvas, the structural funds agreement struck at the February 1988 European Council in Brussels can be evaluated in terms both of its implications for the evolution of the Community itself and for Irish relationships with that Community. The resources involved, as a proportion of the total Community budget, and even more in relation to overall Community GDP, are pitiably small in relation to the objectives set. Structural fund spending of 14 billion ECU in today's prices in 1992 would represent less than 0.3 per cent of Community GDP, or 10 per cent of the present gross capital formation of the poorest regions covering 30 per cent of the Community's population. In mature federal systems, a much higher proportion of GDP is redistributed through the various equalisation mechanisms of the federal budget.

The present level of funding is essentially a compromise between those member states likely to be net claimants on the funds, and countries such as Germany and Britain which, given the ideological complexion of their present governments, tend to play down the importance of intergovernmental transfers in the maintenance of cohesion. For these governments the best guarantee of economic convergence between the weaker and stronger member states is the pursuit of what they would see as sensible macro-economic policies in the weaker countries. They prefer to emphasise the role of private sector financial flows through the banking system in overcoming regional disequilibria. Although a country like Germany, as the single largest net contributor to the structural funds, might be expected to downplay the importance of inter-governmental redistribution, its resistance is strengthened by this neo-liberal ideological climate. From an Irish viewpoint, it is impor-tant to stress that what happens to the size of the structural funds after 1992 will depend on the political coalitions which can be built in the next few years.

Even a small structural funds budget can have a high redistribu-tive impact if it is targeted on the most disadvantaged regions. Here the Commission's attempts to focus the funds more selectively should be welcomed, but as argued above, its degree of success has been limited to date, and there must be fears that Community aid will tend to diffuse over larger and larger areas over time.

We also noted the Commission's determination that structural fund expenditure should reflect Community priorities and not simply be a means of reimbursing national governments for expen-diture they undertake. This is achieved by offering Community assistance in the form of matching grants for specific objectives and programmes. Of course, it is up to national governments to submit programmes and projects for financing in the first instance, and the remit of the funds has been drawn widely enough to mean that meeting Community criteria has not been an onerous constraint in the past. Over time, however, the existence of Community incen-tives to expand certain programmes at the expense of others will play an increasing role in determining the allocation of investment priorities.

Finally, it will be of interest to see whether the formulation of sub-national programmes and the requirement to submit an Irish regional development plan to Brussels will breathe new life into regional policy in this country, as recommended in the Hume Report (1987). The situation in which each of the seven regions have nothing to lose in pressing their claims on a common Brussels pool is an extremely unhealthy one, and will put enormous pressure on central government to reconcile competing claims. The precedent of the Health Boards, also in a situation of power but no responsibility, may serve as a warning of what to expect. It may be that the tensions generated will provide the impetus to a more thorough-going reform of local and regional structures.

References
Hart, J., and Laffan, B. (1983), 'Consequences of the Community's Regional and Social Policies', in Coombes, D., ed., *Ireland and the European Communities*, Dublin, Gill and MacMillan.

National Economic and Social Council (in association with the Northern Ireland Economic Council) (1988), *Economic Implications for Northern Ireland and the Republic of Ireland of Recent Developments in the European Community*, Dublin.

APPENDIX

Structural funds approved for Ireland (commitment appropriations), £m

Year	Regional Fund	Social Fund	FEOGA Guidance Section	Total Funds	FEOGA Guarantee Section	Total (1)
1977	12.6	19.7	16.6	48.9	244.5	294.6
1978	23.6	29.8	27.5	80.9	366.1	447.1
1979	41.4	38.5	28.0	107.9	397.9	550.2
1980	52.6	53.5	40.7	146.8	377.4	572.2
1981	67.7	73.0	54.8	195.5	305.0	551.2
1982	79.0	97.0	60.9	236.9	344.3	634.5
1983	77.4	134.3	75.7	287.4	436.7	769.5
1984	114.0	158.0	53.0	325.0	644.6	974.0
1985	113.0	193.0	56.0	362.0	835.0	1208.3
1986	96.0	170.7	46.6	313.3	883.7	1205.7
1987	125.0	157.8	68.2	351.0	739.6	1099.8

Note (1): Includes other transfers not separately identified.
Source: European Commission Office, Dublin.

— PART III —
CULTURAL PERSPECTIVES

Migrant Minds

Dove that ventured outside, flying from the dovecote;
housed and protected again, one with the day, the night,
knows what serenity is, for she has felt her wings
pass through all distance and fear in the course of her wanderings . . .

Being arches itself over the vast abyss.
Ah the ball that we dared, that we hurled into infinite space,
doesn't it fill our hands differently with its return:
heavier by the weight of where it has been.

Rainer Maria Rilke

Introductory Note
The following statements by Bono, Durcan and Jordan are edited versions of a lengthy conversation which we conducted together on an afternoon in May 1988. The contribution by Ballagh, who could not be present at the original session, was written as a response and subsequently inserted. Each of the participants represents a different art form – Bono (music), Durcan (poetry), Jordan (cinema) and Ballagh (painting). But despite their different media, there are some telling convergences of mind.

We're talking about a new generation which grew up in the Ireland of the sixties and seventies – a changing culture where television, cinema and popular music exercised a more formative influence than the traditional pieties of revivalist Ireland. This was the 'blank generation' of revolt and experimentation: a new breed of urbanized and internationalized youth determined to wipe the slate clean, to start again from scratch. Sons busy burying their fathers. Daughters desperate to escape the mothers of memory.

There is much said about journeying. Each posits the virtue of a migrant mind tired of the old ideologies and hungry for some 'other place', some utopia where they could meet strangers who would let them be, be themselves. But this post-sixties model of cultural migration differs from the inherited patterns of Irish emigration in that it affirms the option, or at least the possibility, of return. The journey is a two-way ticket. And its virtue lies in the fact that on returning home you know that you will never be totally at home. The old ideologies of fixed national identity or insular salvation can never suffice again. Once bitten by the tooth of exile, the migrant mind recognizes that 'homecoming' is an imaginative quest, not a literal event.

The discovery that one is always something of an outsider or misfit – at home as well as abroad – grants a certain liberty to rediscover and recreate what is most valuable in one's own tradition. Having taken one's distance from the 'homeland', physically or mentally, you can return to it and find there something of immense and lasting value. Traditions of myth and music can be explored again with a new-found and non-fanatical freedom.

This is where modernity's obsession with absolute novelty and rupture – its frequent repudiation of historical memory – is perhaps tempered by a post-modern awareness that we cannot afford to *not* know our past. Rupture is complemented by remembrance. Creation *ex nihilo* gives way to the more playful practice of re-creation. We are more ready to acknowledge that the waters are muddied; that the established ideologies of purity and identity have often proved demeaning or destructive; that the future is not guaranteed by some ineluctable destiny; that history is a healthy confluence of tenses – past traditions mingling fruitfully with present crises and future aspirations. The postmodern mind also resists the modernist contempt for the so-called mass media; it democratically celebrates the confounding of distinctions between 'high' art and 'popular' culture. Thus, in the conversations which follow, we find that Bono, one of the most popular singers of this decade, invokes the poetic exemplars of Heaney and Kavanagh. While the poet, Durcan, invokes the popular exemplars of Dylan, the Stones, Duke Ellington and Van Morrison. Jordan blends a literary admiration for Yeats and Joyce with a fascination for the electronic media of cinema, TV and video, in which he now works. While Ballagh produces visual art which mingles themes drawn from the great classical traditions with motifs taken from the popular contemporary techniques of comic strip, poster portrait and newsreel documentary.

Disillusioned with the 'hard ideologies' which have defined us according to a single, unadulterated 'identity' (Nationalist, Unionist, Catholic or Protestant), this new generation of Irish artists affirms the positive value of confusion, uncertainty, homelessness, migrancy, questioning, questing for 'another place'. This does not amount, in any sense, to a repudiation of their Irish culture, or indeed to a denial of a specifically 'Irish thing' about their work. On the contrary, each acknowledges a fundamental sense of belonging and fidelity to a 'native place'. It is, to be sure, not the Nation-State in any official sense. It is a place more local than the nation, more personally and communally experienced – one not circumscribed by abstract statutes or boundaries. A place where the old antagonism between the native and the alternative ceases to apply. A place of recreation only disclosed when one has ventured out in search of the no-place (*u-topos*) which is always elsewhere. Here we understand that we can be Irish *and* citizens of the world without contradiction.

The Irish thing surfaces, almost in spite of oneself, when the obsession with a unique identity is abandoned. The reason we could not find it was perhaps that we were looking too hard, too self-consciously, too fanatically. Now, as we are rediscovering ourselves through our encounter with others, reclaiming our voice in our migrations through other cultures and continents – Europe, Britain, North America – we are beginning to realize that the Irish thing was always there. We could not recognize it for as long as we assumed we were at home with ourselves, sufficient unto ourselves, slaves to the illusion that we were masters on our island, Robinson Crusoes of a land apart. It takes the migrant mind to know that the island is without frontiers, that the seas are waterways connecting us with others, that the journey to the other place harbours the truth of homecoming to our own place.

Richard Kearney,
June 1988

— BONO: THE WHITE NIGGER —
PAUL HEWSON

How does the music of U2 relate to our being Irish? I come to this question as someone who does not know who he is. There are people out there who know who they are . . . I like to meet these people . . . But I am not one of them. When I was growing up I didn't know where I came from . . . I didn't know if I was middle class, working class, Catholic, Protestant . . . I knew I was from Ballymun, Dublin but I didn't know what that meant. I didn't know I was Irish until I went to America. I never actually thought about it. One of the reasons I want to contribute to this discussion now is that I've become interested in these questions lately. But I come to it with no set point of view.

It is curious that U2 are seen as this 'Irish' thing. So much emphasis is placed on it. And we ourselves emphasize it. But if you look at the surface level of music – its obvious contents – there's maybe nothing very Irish about it. It comes from a suburban blank generation culture which I grew up in, watching cartoons on TV, Thunderbirds and Hanna Barbera and designer violence. That was the real world, concrete, grey, kicking footballs and admiring English football stars. That's the culture I came from, and that's what our music reflects, on the surface at least. It is very 'un-Irish' in the accepted sense.

However, I now realise that beneath the surface there are certain Irish characteristics to the music . . . even the choice of words. Our producer, Brian Eno, said that he thought that I was a better poet than a songwriter . . . what I think he meant by that was the sound, rhythm and colour of the words seem at times as important as the meaning. The love of language *for its own sake* and not just as a vehicle to comment on or describe events, seems to me to be very Irish – you grow up reading Joyce for God's sake or Beckett, and they seem to abuse and therefore use the English language in new and interesting ways.

With U2, people often point to a song like 'Sunday, Bloody Sunday' as an example of our Irishness, but for me it's not, and in retrospect it didn't succeed in making its point. We had this highfalutin' idea to contrast or make the connection between the blood of the crucifixion on Easter Sunday and the blood of the victims in Derry on Bloody Sunday. The idea of Jesus dying to save us from death is a painful irony to both Catholic and Protestant in the light of the troubles. Anyway, now when I look at the words, all I see is a description of that day as a tragedy in the tradition of Peggy Seeger or American folk: 'And the battle's yet begun / There's many lost but tell me who has won / The trenches dug within our hearts / Mothers, children, brothers, sisters torn apart'.

To me the sound and colour of the language in a song like 'A Sort of Homecoming' is more Irish: 'The wind will crack in wintertime / A lightning bomblast waltz / No spoken words . . . just a scream . . . / See the sky the burning rain, she will die and live again / Tonight, we'll build a bridge across the sea and land'. This is not American folk or blues. The words are much more influenced by poets like Heaney or Kavanagh . . . than say, Woodie Guthrie.

I used to think U2 came out of a void, a black hole; we seemed completely rootless. Though we had many influences, our version of Rock 'n' Roll didn't sound like anyone else's in the present or in the past. In 85 I met Bob Dylan for the first time backstage at Slane Castle 85. He sat there talking about the McPeeke Family . . . this Irish group I'd never even heard of . . . and how he used to hang around backstage at Makem & Clancy concerts – yeah I said, I remember they used to be on the Late Late Show! . . . and then I began to listen more carefully to the bold and bald sound of Irish Folk singers . . . I recall listening to Paul Brady kick up more of a storm with an acoustic guitar than most people could do with a rock band. I told Dylan and Van Morrison who was there at the time, that I felt we didn't belong to any tradition, it was like we were lost in space, floating over many traditions but not belonging to any one of them. It then struck us that there was a journey to be undertaken. There was something to be discovered.

We started looking back into American music, Gospel, Blues, the likes of Robert Johnson . . . John Lee Hooker. Old songs of fear and faith. As I said when we first started the band, we felt like outsiders to Rock Music but these themes were very much inside U2, they were also very Irish so even though there isn't an obvious Irishness in a song like 'Bullet The Blue Sky' (a U2 song about military interference in El Salvador), there is something Irish about the subject of oppression and also, I think, about the language I used to paint the picture: 'In the howling wind comes a stinging rain / See them driving nails into souls on the tree of pain / You plant a demon seed, you raise a flower of fire / See them burning crosses see the flames higher and higher'. I feel there is a strong link between American and Irish traditional music. So you see we found the 'Irish Thing' through the American: Gospel, Blues, Robert Johnson, Bob Dylan, these became passports home.

Though we had grown up on it, for some reason we also felt outsiders to the English Rock 'n' Roll scene. At the time it all seemed surface with nothing behind the surface. We were up there scruffy, soaked in sweat, unpoised – not concealing but revealing ourselves, what was on our minds and in our hearts. I began to realise how alien this was to the white, stiff upper lip syndrome which I still find in UK music criticism . . . . They seemed to find any kind of passion hard to take, they prefer a mask of *cool* . . . unless you're black. Which is interesting, because though this passion is to me an Irish characteristic, in American blacks it's called *soul*. I was called a 'White Nigger' once by a black musician, and I took it as he meant it, as a compliment. The Irish, like the blacks, feel like outsiders. There's a feeling of being homeless, migrant, but I suppose that's what all art is – a search for identity. The images of our songs are confused, classical, biblical, American, Irish, English, but not in a negative sense. The fight, the struggle for a synthesis is what's interesting about them. The idea of an incomplete, questioning, even abandoned identity is very attractive to me.

Our journey to America eventually turned us back to where we came from. It brought up musical questions and also political questions. During Bobby Sands' hunger strike – we had money thrown onto the stage because we were Irish . . . you couldn't but be moved by the courage and conviction of this man . . . yet we struggled with the question, is this the right way? Is violence inevitable? Is it the only answer to partition in Northern Ireland? Again there was a parallel between the Irish and the blacks. In the 60s the 'Black Civil Rights Movement' led by Martin Luther King had resisted a bloody upsurge. I've read Dr King's *Strength to Love* and was inspired by his movement of aggressive but non-violent resistance. Here was a man who believed enough in his cause to give his life, but would never take a life . . . an 'armed struggle' seems cowardly in comparison. I know it's not that simple, but we must get beyond confrontation, beyond a revolution where ideas matter more than people . . . surely we are coming out of that period where we believed that just one bang of the door and it would swing open . . . it's just not like that. I mean, I'm from the South and relatively uneducated about the situation, but if war in Northern Ireland is what it means to be Irish then we must redefine Irishness. There was a time when Political thinkers could tolerate violence as a way forward, but this is a different time . . . the old ideologies of the Right and the Left – as promising a final solution – are redundant. This is the late 80s, we are only a decade away from the year 2000 – the micro-chip will dwarf the machine in its impact on our lives; multinational corporations don't need people in their workforce anymore – just people to sell to . . . we have a new problem, we need a new solution.

Even in music and art there's a changing of the guard; it's the end of the 'cold wave' and hopefully of the hardness associated with modernism, where chaos is not challenged just reflected . . . like a mirror.

There's a warmth and humanity in Irish music that I don't see in the big city music of London or New York. What kind of music will people be listening to in the 1990s? Machine music? Sophisticated noise of a New York dance club? I don't think so. I feel the music that people will be holding under their arms like holy books or treasures will be much more traditional, be it Irish, American, soul, reggae, cajun – these musics may be reinterpreted by the new technology but as we are more dehumanised, urbanised, corralled into confusion, surely we will turn to simplicity, to 'the pure drop' of Seamus Ennis, the voice of Van Morrison. The anger of U2 is not cold or cynical; I hope an ambition to 'kick the darkness till it bleeds daylight' will have its place.

Maybe we Irish are misfits, travellers, never really at home, but always talking about it. I met a fisherman who told me we were like salmon: it's upriver all the time, against the odds, the river doesn't want us . . . yet we want a way home . . . but there is no home. Religious minds tell us *exile is what having eaten the apple means*, that 'home' is a spiritual condition. We in Ireland already know this, not because we've been exiles, but because hardships, be they economic or political, have forced us to be less material . . . I don't swallow the Church's idea of 'pie in the sky' when we die either! That's the worst of religion . . . accept the crap now, we'll have diamonds later. I much prefer the notion of 'Thy Kingdom Come on Earth as it is in Heaven'. Some Heaven on earth right now would be nice – they should preach that! I mean we get some glimpses of it in music, painting, the West of Ireland, Donegal, people, sex, conversation . . . a few pints, a glass of whiskey. Even if it's been a cause of bitterness and has on occasion been warped by organised religion, our Christianity, our sense of the spirit, is valuable, especially right now when a hard, empirical approach to things is beginning to give way to a more open metaphysical questioning. Belief in God does not necessarily imply a lack of belief in men.

I don't know, maybe Romantic Ireland is dead and gone. If the America I love only exists in my imagination, maybe the Ireland I love is the same. Dublin, I mean, everybody gives out about Dublin and there's lots of things to give out about . . . unemployment, what the planners have done to the people of Tallaght and Ballymun, the architects who have defaced what was a beautiful city, these are the real vandals . . . but still we love the city . . . .

I met a U2 fan in Switzerland recently who said to me: 'Jazus Bono, I can't wait to get home and throw some litter on the ground!' – I think I know what he meant.

— PASSAGE TO UTOPIA —
PAUL DURCAN

When Bono began by saying he doesn't know who he is – well that's exactly how I feel. I want to approach the question about a future Ireland without frontiers in terms of a journey. I want to talk about the experience of energy received from moving about. The journey moves between two main poles – opposite poles – violence and utopia. But I will return to this.

Here I am on the 22 May 1988, thinking self-consciously about myself. A thing I don't normally do. Looking back on my life as a practising artist I see it as a journey, or a series of journeys. My work as a poet has always been a searching for the *other place*. The notion of 'utopia' is fundamental to something about myself, and I think, about human nature. It is a theme which has cropped up again and again in my recent readings of Primo Levi, the Italian Jew whose books bear witness to his time in a Nazi concentration camp, Leonardo Boff, the Latin American theologian of liberation, and Richard Kearney. Utopia, for me as for them, does not mean harking back to a 'lost Eden'. All my life I have been looking for a Mont Sainte Victoire. And it is no accident that most of my books have the names of places in them. I see Cézanne sitting there looking over at this mountain. And one way or another I think that all of us who are artists are doing this.

Some eighteen years ago, I wrote a poem called 'O Westport in the Light of Asia Minor' and more recently I wrote a poem called 'Going Home to Russia'. What I would like to do here is to read the journey between these two poems in search of an 'other place' in terms of a travel diary. I use the term journey both in the sense of a poetic composition and in the more literal sense of moving about between harbours and airports and railways. The whole thing is a matter of connections. And these connections, with all their strange accidents and coincidences, are in turn a matter of metamorphosis.

I want to concentrate here on one particular journey – a journey to Italy and back which I made a month ago. I was participating in a conference in Turin on the question of Celtic identity. I was especially struck by a seminar there conducted by the Italian 'postmodern' philosopher, Gianni Vattimo. It was a revelation to me. Vattimo spoke humorously and with energy of the strength to be gained from a recognition of the 'feebleness of one's identity' and of the 'casual role of the self'. These phrases, heard in a foreign place, connected with things Patrick Kavanagh had been saying twenty or thirty years ago – and that I've been mulling over for years. In particular, I think of his celebration of what he called the art of 'complete casualness'.

Turin was also very important for me as the city of Primo Levi. This survivor of the violence of Auschwitz who endured so much violence, survived to tell the tale and finally committed suicide just a year ago. I was deeply aware of his presence in this place of his birth. I did a reading of 'Going Home to Russia' at the conference; and after it a woman came up to me and said: 'I feel very sorry for you. We Italians and Continentals have been through that journey ourselves'. This was not an isolated view. Some days later in Rome I met a doctor who is a committed member of the Italian Communist Party and he spoke to me of Pier Paolo Pasolini and his disillusionment with the 1968 movement. Pasolini was, of course, also a committed communist but he caused great controversy when he published an essay denouncing the hatred he had seen in the eyes of fanatical students in the student revolution of the sixties. He contrasted the violence of the students to the beleaguered and bewildered faces of the policemen from the country, concluding that he had no doubt with whom he identified.

At the Turin conference on Celtic Identity there was a Scottish poet, George MacBeth and a Welsh poet, Danny Abse. Though the participants in the conference were ostensibly in search of some kind of common identity, what struck me most was the crucial differences which distinguished their childhood memories and mine. They both read poems about their experiences of the Second World War – of roofs tumbling in during a bombing raid, of the family in fear and the threat of invasion. And I thought, by contrast, of our cosy insularity in Ireland. Then and now. And I recalled Primo Levi's warning that it could happen again. At that moment I saw my own country not as a neutral defender of peace unaffected by the 'outside' world, but as harbouring its own fascism with its own brand of violence.

After Turin and Rome, I visited Assisi. I can still see the painting of St Francis – a man of peace – by Cimabue. And I recall looking across the valley at Assisi from Perugia one evening – and seeing the town hanging there in the sky. And again the image of Mont Sainte Victoire came back to me. The other place. Utopia. The home away from home.

After the reading that evening in Perugia I was asked by a TV interviewer whether it was possible to be a poet in a world of mass-media? I replied that it was precisely because it was a mass-media society that it was more possible than ever to be a poet. He was surprised. But I believe it. The old division between art and popular culture is happily disappearing. And as I thought more about it a number of instances came to mind. I thought of Christy Moore singing Jimmy McCarthy's 'Ride On' in the National Stadium in Dublin – an occasion and a place which for me were full of the aroma of poetry. I thought of the Russian poet, Bulat Okudjhava's phrase that 'poetry is a way of giving us back to ourselves'. I thought of the marvellous audience that I had during the first day of the Belfast Workers Festival this year – without that kind of audience hungry for music and poetry there can be no work of art, either factually or metaphysically. And I thought of Trafalgar Square – one of the most crowded and democratic places in the world – and a visit I made to the National Gallery to see the floor mosaic by the Russian emigré, Boris Anrep. It is called 'Compassion' and features the poet, Anna Akmatova, lying naked with angels guarding her against the demons of war. The painting is inspired by David's 'The Death of Marat' (the 14 year-old boy shot dead for shouting 'Vive le Roi'). And finally, I thought of two films which I saw with my daughter, Sarah, during a recent visit to Paris – *Down by Law* by Jim Jarmusch (about solidarity and humour between prisoners in the U.S.) and *Sacrifice* by Tarkovsky (about an act of love which saves the world from a nuclear holocaust). Thinking of all these examples of art expressing itself through popular and democratic media, struggling with the horrors of violence, I was reminded of the power of music and poetry. A power greater than the power of armies and scaffolds and bombs.

It's not that I'm an optimist. I agree with Primo Levi when he says that we must keep on remembering what happened. So that it can never happen again. I believe that violence is at the end of every question. That it is not confined to the Nazis but can happen in any society, in our own society. When I see a photograph or a TV image of a body on the side of a road in Northern Ireland with a head hanging out of it covered in blood and full of bullets, I find it so difficult to cope with this terrifying reality. But there are no less dramatic things about our day to day living here which frighten me. The way some of our legal and medical professionals speak in a way that dehumanizes the people they are dealing with. The use of terms like 'access to children' after the breakdown of a marriage, the manner in which divorce is regarded as a moral evil thereby ignoring the suffering that certain couples are actually living through. Violence can be sensed in the very way words can be used to deny the fact that people are human beings. For me the most obvious examples of this in Ireland are the ways in which people tend to speak of war and nationalism (be it republican or loyalist). As a child, I fed myself on comics about the war between the Nazis and the British. I even had recurring nightmares about being chased by the Gestapo and being agonized by whether I would talk or not. But I now know that the violence can happen here too. It is not confined to the Nazis. I often worry about what Ireland will be like for our children in the 1990s.

One of the things I brought back with me from Turin was

Vattimo's injunction to rejoice in the 'feebleness of our indentity'. This is his motto for the new postmodern era, his hope for an end to ideological war and violence. Sometimes I am accused of betraying the nation because I don't support the traditional sense of nationalist identity. The very word nationalism sometimes fills me with disgust. This does not mean that I reject the local place of origin. I respect Kavanagh's statement that it takes a lifetime to get to know the corner of a field, that there is a valid pride of place – what he called the 'parish' rather than the 'province'. When Bono speaks of his generation coming from the 'void', I feel like quoting Angelo Roncali after he was made Patriarch of Venice in the 1950s – 'like any other man I come from a particular family and a particular place'. This feeling about place is very important. As far back as I can remember, journeys to places were powerful experiences. Travelling to Mayo or Portrane. There was a sense that there were no fences, no boundaries, each step along the way was a kingdom, with its own story.

I don't want to debunk 19th-century nationalism. But for my generation things have changed a lot. I recall an incident in 1966 when a British journalist in a pub asked me what 1916 meant to me. I told him quite honestly that it was very remote for me. That I was more interested in what Patrick Kavanagh was saying at this time. Patrick Kavanagh and I shared a common interest in Jack Kerouac, the Rolling Stones and Bob Dylan. (I even wrote out all the words of Dylan's 'Desolation Row' for Kavanagh – all 200 of them). The British journalist just couldn't understand this; he felt I was betraying the Irish cause.

If only I could imagine people being as moved by utopia as by what they believe nationalism to be! Duke Ellington means more to me as an exemplar than William Butler Yeats. I have this image of him travelling around the world in a dressing gown composing these beautiful numbers. And this is what I find so attractive about Bono's idea of the Irish blackman. I can just picture him – a great jazzman or saxophonist wandering around Europe. He wouldn't be a 'bucklepper', a stage Irishman jumping up on counters and fitting into the revivalist image. Kavanagh denounced this cliché as a 'pure-bred English lie'. The whole business of Kavanagh's life was not to have an identity. His was a philosophy of 'not caring'. For him the 'incompleteness of the self' was a virtue. He called for a sense of repose, beyond the obsession with identity, of being open to the world of the now. 'To look on is enough in the business of love', he once put it. How difficult it is, this way of dispossession, getting out of oneself and listening. Even when one goes to see a play or a film sometimes one realizes how easy it is to be caught up inside oneself. That's why Kavanagh's favourite words were 'abandon', 'gay', 'explosive'. You can imagine what an extraordinary revelation it was for me to come across a postmodern philosopher in Turin, called Vattimo, saying the same thing as Kavanagh was saying in the sixties – advocating that we abandon the obsession with identity. And surely Vattimo is close to Kavanagh when he claims that it is in poetry rather than in politics that we can find a free, non-fanatical, postmodern attitude to our myths.

I feel very divided on the question of home. On the one hand I yearn for some kind of home, some place where emotion can be recollected in tranquillity, where I can rest. On the other, I think of the protagonist of the new testament – the acceptance of loss and death, the refusal to take out insurance policies, the challenge to all of us to leave home, to go on journeys.

At the end of every question, there is the problem of violence. Art is one way of responding to this. The end of art is peace – to take a quote from Heaney's poem 'The Harvest Bow'. The reason Primo Levi took his own life one year after the publication of his last book, *The Drowned and the Saved*, was that he felt it was all going to happen again. One must keep on giving witness all the time. This is what my journey to Italy taught me. And also my journey to Russia. Violence is not an alternative in personal, national or international behaviour. The lesson of all my journeys has been that utopia is peace. And that pacifism is not an option but a necessity. To believe in utopia is to believe that there is some kind of homecoming in the 'other place'. Asia Minor. Russia. Turin. The quest for the 'other place' – whether it take the image of Mont Sainte Victoire or the village of Assisi hanging in the sky – enables us to be freer, no longer captive to our island. It also encourages us to struggle for peace in our first and literal home. You see things when you return from the journey that you had not seen before. You are filled with new outrages, new dreams.

— IMAGINING OTHERWISE —
NEIL JORDAN

When I started writing I felt very pressured by the question: How do I cope with the notion of Irishness? It meant almost nothing to me. I was, of course, profoundly moved by the Irish literature I encountered as a student – Yeats and Joyce. But how was I to write about the experience I knew, as someone born in Sligo and growing up in the suburban streets of Dublin in the sixties? The great books of Anglo-Irish literature had very little to do with this, they had no real resonance at this level. My most acute dilemma was – how to write stories about contemporary urban life in Ireland without being swamped in the language and mythology of Joyce. Indeed I recall the contemptuous response of one of my professors in UCD when I suggested we have a course on contemporary Irish writing: 'How dare you presume that your experience measures up to that of our great literary tradition'. The first real story I wrote was about an Irish labourer who cut his wrists in a London baths. Almost every work of fiction I've indulged in has been an escape to an alternative landscape – to a space or time not associated with the traditional themes of great Irish literature. (And it *is* great – whatever one might think of the Young Ireland movement, revivalist nationalism or Joyce's obsession with his homeland). The primary questions for me were: Who am I? What do my experiences mean? What am I – a person here and now who puts pen to paper to express himself – in relation to the huge pressure of tradition?

The only identity, at a cultural level, that I could forge was one that came from the worlds of television, popular music and cinema which I was experiencing daily. Applied to literature this seemed strangely disembodied. It didn't have the surety of something handed down by tradition or my parents. It was with this problem in mind that I wrote a novel called *The Past*. The narrator is someone trying to retrace the life of his parents, to find out what lay behind the great mythological mystery which shrouded their past. And there were analogies with de Valera and the heroes and heroines of Irish nationalism. This held a fascination for me whose experience seemed so suburban and mundane – great in its own way, but not graced by any of these senses of belonging.

For me, to make films was to escape from these questions, these hankerings. In the world of cinema, none of these questions existed; there had never been an 'Irish' cinema. My mother and my sisters are painters. And I share with them the sense that the visual is free from the constraints and pressures of our literary tradition. The Irish question is – how to get rid of it. There are more interesting questions than the crippling one about 'Irish identity'. The encounter with other worlds – be it the world of cinema or painting which have no past for us – delivers a different sense of oneself. Once one succeeds in shaking off the paralysing question of self-conscious identity, one discovers that there are certain specifically Irish features to your imagination. It's a funny journey. I had a strange experience when I first went to America. It was with the Sheridan brothers and a theatre company we had just formed. We were struck by the fact that almost all the little artefacts of landscape we came across – highways, skyscrapers, desert scenes etc.- were even more familiar to us, thanks to the media of popular culture, than the typical landscape associated with Ireland – a crumbling castle, a green hill, a village church. The American landscape was what we were looking at every day of the week in TV serials and

Hollywood movies. And I said to myself: Wouldn't it be wonderful to make your own landscape as resonant and familiar to other people as this landscape was to me. That's why I used shots of the Sally Gap and Bray beach in *Angel* and a ruined old manor in *High Spirits*.

What I found most liberating when I first started working in cinema was that there was no set of assumptions and associations specifically related to being an Irish director. But having worked in it now for several years, I find the Irish thing is emerging. When I go to Italy or France or the States and I'm asked what I feel about belonging to the new movement in British cinema, I reply rather weakly, 'Well, I'm not British, you know'. I find myself resisting being defined in terms that have nothing to do with me. The importance I give to the emotional articulation of my world and work is not something typical in British cinema. The attempt to imagine another state of living, another way of being, is I believe very Irish. It's difficult to say what exactly underlies this or why it should be so. It's something to do with the quest for another place, another manner of thinking. It's a dissatisfaction with the accepted and scientifically approved explanations of the world.

Lucien Freud's paintings are typically British. They are perfect expressions of his class and society – easeful, graceful, comfortable. By contrast, the very inarticulacy with which the Irish explain their world is actually a virtue in a strange way. There's a sense that the reality is too large, that it doesn't fit the language. And this awareness of the inadequacy of language is perhaps why we are so fascinated by it, so good at reworking it in new and original ways. I think this is what Friel meant in *Translations* when he has one of his characters say that 'confusion is not an ignoble condition'. He is also talking about a certain nobility of failure. The failure of Hugh Mór to get to Glenties and stick his pike into a British soldier. In one way, failure can be a great liberator, can't it? If we could only begin from the recognition that we are 'failed'. If we could only see the virtue of this. The great stupidity of Irish history has been the pretence to be a self-enclosed and unconfused nation.

Ireland is confused. But at least the confusion is a reality. My recent film, *High Spirits*, is basically about a man (Peter O'Toole) who runs an unworkable enterprise, who inherits an ungovernable fact – a hotel which nobody will come to. This is an experience which everybody in Ireland has experienced: living in an unworkable society, a state which never quite became a state, which feels itself to be the drab sister of other nation states. The hotel owner just can't make it work. But then he gets this idea – he will make the break by pretending his ruined castle is haunted and thus attract people. People come to the hotel, but it's a disaster. And then, in spite of himself, it happens. The magic happens. The disaster becomes a triumph. There is something of the Oscar Wilde comedy about it.

Our mistake was to assume that we could be at home in a single nation. We fed ourselves on ideologies of violence and instant salvation, the illusion that history is a continuum moving forward to its perfect destiny. We thus forgot that we can never be at home anywhere. Perhaps it is one of the functions of writers and artists to remind the nation of this. To expose the old ideologies. To feel in exile abroad and also when one returns home. To remain faithful to the no-place (*u-topos*) in us all. As a film maker I feel bereft in Ireland – like a shoemaker without his leather – and yet I always remain something of an 'outsider' in other countries. I think it is only when you accept the condition of being a transient, when you realize that home is impossible, that you find a certain peace.

— RESPONDING —

BOBBY BALLAGH

Richard Kearney speaks of a convergence of minds between the invited participants yet I must confess to feeling slightly at variance with some of the stated views. In trying to flesh out this divergence my gaze settled on his phrase 'all speak of the critical experience of growing up in the new Ireland of the sixties and seventies'. Since my own formative years were spent in the fifties perhaps this accounts for some difference, after all the passage from the fifties to the sixties in Ireland was marked by changes more radical and perhaps more contradictory than others felt since the foundation of the state. In the Ireland that I grew up in cultural life was dominated by a vision of Ireland that was narrow, exclusive and deeply conserva-

'Homage to Dürer', 1984. Collection Albrecht Dürer House, Nuremberg.

'In the heart of the Hibernian Metropolis', 1988. Reproduced with the permission of New Artists, Amsterdam.

'Page from an Irish Manuscript'. 1981 collection House of Humour and Satire, Gabrovo, Bulgaria.

tive. The 'true' Ireland was viewed as being gaelic, rural and catholic, explicitly defined in De Valera's gospel of 'frugal self-sufficiency'. Education for the majority was both authoritarian, in that it was dominated by a rigid bigoted Roman Catholic orthodoxy and brutal, since corporal punishment was still an integral part of the system. Today it is difficult to imagine that, in the fifties, the Catholic Archbishop of Dublin stated publicly it was a sin to watch Yugoslavia, a communist country, playing football, yet this did happen. It was against this reactionary background that most of my ideas and attitudes were formed.

However, instead of articulating an opposition in exile like so many others I decided to stay in Ireland, to attempt not only to build a career as an artist but also to try to participate in efforts to change Irish attitudes. In fact others, far more influential than I, were beginning to accept that De Valera's dream of a rural arcadia based on protecting the native entrepreneur could not sustain the nation. A way of life that had once been extolled as the authentic base upon which the nation securely rested was no longer considered viable. In 1959 De Valera was replaced by Sean Lemass and new economic policies were set in train which opened up the country to international capital, beginning a process of dependency that continues to this day. This remarkable 'volte-face' by the Fianna Fáil government was achieved with the intellectual integrity of the 'with one bound he was free' solution to the dilemma of the doomed hero at the end of each serial or 'follier-up' that we as kids, eagerly watched each week in the local flea-pit. Also this action was made possible by the total absence of any serious ideological basis to Irish political life. Just as nature abhors a vacuum so too any ideological vacuum in society will be quickly filled. Consequently, I am convinced that our present difficulties cannot be resolved through the abandonment of so-called 'hard' ideologies. The real task is to oppose conservative attitudes with radical progressive ideas.

The kind of society set in train in the early sixties and reinforced in the seventies by our accession to the EC has created a situation of dependence. We seem to have become totally reliant on others to provide the answers to our many problems. Our own institutions appear to have failed us completely. Someone once wrote 'the shape of Irish society (and institutions) fits the Irish people like a badly tailored suit, we do not acknowledge the suit as our own, we do not feel at home in it, but we tolerate it as we have always tolerated everything'. There is a real irony in the way James Molyneaux so easily rerouted C. J. Haughey's oft repeated barb about the North being a 'failed political entity' in a more southerly direction. In this context I await, with interest, Neil Jordan's new film and its analogy between Peter O'Toole's unworkable hotel and Ireland's failed condition as a modern state. It seems to me that in the present

'The Conversation' 1977. Private collection, on loan Butler Gallery, Kilkenny.

'No. 3', 1977. Hugh Lane Municipal Gallery, Dublin.

debilitated situation where Yeats' feared 'greasy till' rules the roost and where Irish political life is devoid of vision, our artists can play a significant role. Brian Friel, the playwright, noted 'that you've got to produce documents, sounds and images in order to make yourself distinctive' and that 'if there's a sense of decline about how the country is, it's because we can't readily produce these identification marks'. So the problem is one of identity, after all 'documents, sounds and images' abound in Ireland today, yet how many are like the aforementioned ill-fitting suit– fashioned by others, for others and then adopted, second hand, by us. Therefore, the creation of documents, sounds and images that relate to our experience becomes much more than simply an aesthetic issue, it becomes a political imperative. Unfortunately it remains a vexed question as to the exact nature of what we are prepared to accept as an Irish cultural identity. When I began to work as an artist I remember being infuriated by criticisms which suggested that I was 'un-Irish', that I was importing an alien culture into Ireland. I was angry because I felt that my work was an honest response to my own urban background, formed from many influences including the movies, comic books and popular music. Of course many urban people in western society share a similar background and consequently a common visual language, yet I felt that there was something essentially different in my work to that produced by other artists from other countries.

It was in 1975 that the nature of this difference became apparent to me. At the time I was commissioned to paint some pictures for a restaurant in Clonmel, Co. Tipperary, with the proviso that they be of local interest. After searching to find a suitable theme I finally settled on the 18th-century author Laurence Sterne, who was born in Clonmel in 1713; afterwards he lived in Carrickfergus, Mullingar, Dublin and Annamoe until he left for schooling in Halifax and further education in Cambridge. I read his famous book 'The Life and Opinions of Tristram Shandy, Gentleman' for the first time in 1975 and was immediately struck by what I felt to be a common sensibility even though we were separated in time by over two centuries. I first felt that we simply shared a common artistic purpose but slowly it occurred to me that the book was steeped in, what I can only call, an Irish sensibility. The conversational style of the writing, the sense of humour and irony, the use of parody and the 'frisky digressions' all go to create a book, that however un-Irish it may appear on the surface and however much Sterne may be categorised as an English writer, has at its core, uncontestably, a real Irishness. In my opinion, Laurence Sterne quite naturally absorbed these characteristics during his formative years in Ireland. I now sensed that an Irish identity is not something that can be superficially imposed on a work of art, for example through the application of Celtic ornament, but rather that it is something that goes much deeper and is, in essence, difficult to define. It could be summarised possibly as an attitude to life or more accurately a way of dealing with life, consisting of, perhaps, a preponderance to irony, satire or metaphor, a sense of humour (often dark), an enjoyment of parody and above all a healthy scepticism. These attributes are not uniquely Irish, but nonetheless the Irish do possess them in abundance. And there are sound reasons as to why this should be the case. After all Irish history, being a history of colonialism, oppression and marginalisation, has meant that whenever subversive ideas were to be communicated it became necessary to employ some sort of disguise – for example, poets frequently used metaphor to communicate their feelings when a direct statement would have been considered treasonable. Over the years this predeliction for subverting dialogue has become second nature to the Irish. A problem however is that since these attributes are indeed second nature to the Irish, often we can fail to take full notice of them. Frequently it can be an outsider who draws our attention to these 'Irish' characteristics.

To sum up, I believe that earnestly questing for an Irish cultural identity can be counter-productive. I am certain that a distinctive identity will surface quite naturally if the artist speaks with his/her own voice about his/her own experience and environment. I remain convinced that filling empty modernist vessels with 'Irish' contents or enscribing Celtic decoration on modern art objects or the slavish adoption of international styles can only substitute a specious counterfeit for the 'real' thing.

Coming out of Hibernation? The Myth of Modernity in Irish Culture

LUKE GIBBONS

History has stopped, one is in a kind of post-history which is without meaning.
Jean Baudrillard

1

There is a well known story which relates how de Valera was captured during the Civil War while making a speech at Ennis. A year later he returned to the same spot, cleared his throat, and began: 'As I was saying before I was interrupted . . . .' A week may be a long time in English politics but in Ireland a year is merely a pause for breath in the middle of a sentence.

The historian Oliver MacDonagh has argued that the 'contemporaneity of the past', the tendency to collapse the past into an ever receding present, is one of the distinguishing features of Irish political culture.[1] 'The memory of the dead' certainly played a key role in the nationalist call to arms, and more than one commentator has pointed out how the opening paragraph of the 1916 proclamation looks to the past rather than the present for its political mandate: 'Irishmen and Irishwomen: In the name of God and of the dead generations from which she receives her old tradition of nationhood, Ireland, through us, summons her children to her flag and strikes for her freedom'. As nationhood belonged to the cultural as much as to the political domain, what Frank O'Connor referred to as 'the backward look' also fixed literature and the arts within its controlling vision. While T. S. Eliot was trying earnestly to renew contact with a literary heritage in his famous essay 'Tradition and the Individual Talent', Irish writers such as James Joyce and Sean Ó Faoláin were attempting to escape the nightmare of history.

It is generally accepted that Irish society had to await the end of the de Valera era to awake from its nostalgic slumbers. With revisionist hindsight, 1959 is taken as the *annus mirabilis* of modern Ireland, the year in which God said 'Let Lemass be!' – and there was light, dispelling the mists of traditionalism which had obscured the path to progress and industrialization. The appointment of Sean Lemass as Taoiseach paved the way for the First Programme for

---

1. Oliver MacDonagh *States of Mind*, London: Allen and Unwin 1983, ch. 1.

Economic Expansion, a major initiative inspired by a senior civil servant, T. K. Whittaker, which broke with the protectionist policies of the previous generation and extended an open welcome to foreign investment and multi-national capital. The subsequent exposure of Irish society to the ways of the world on the crest of a post-world War II boom is familiar to students of recent Irish history. In 1961 Ireland applied for membership of the EEC and finally gained admittance in 1973. In 1962, it took its place in the global village of mass communications with the opening of Telefís Éireann. In the same year, the hardened arteries of Irish Catholicism were revitalized by the Second Vatican Council (1962-65) which brought an infusion of new ideas and values in the rigourist moral regime of the post-Famine era. This change was echoed in the educational arena by the publication of the 1965 Report *Investment in Education*, which set out to remove the school from the sacristy, and place it in line with the need for greater technological change in Irish society. These developments took place against a wider economic backdrop which saw a shift from agriculture to industry as the mainstay of the Irish economy: in the period 1961 to 1980, employment in the agricultural sector fell from one-third to one-fifth of the work force, while those working in industry increased from 16 to 30 per cent.

In political circles, it was widely expected that the new sweeping changes would break the old moulds, and bring an end to civil war politics. The historic meeting in 1965 between Sean Lemass and Terence O'Neill, the recently appointed Prime Minister of Northern Ireland, was considered an important breakthrough in this regard, as was the Anglo-Irish free-trade pact agreed at the end of the same year. Many on the left had equal cause to welcome the demise of nationalism. Writing in 1980, Paul Bew, Peter Gibbon and Henry Patterson could state confidently that 'urbanization and industrialization have relegated the national question to the margin of Irish politics',[2] thus clearing the way for a realignment in politics along class lines, or on a left/right division, as in other advanced European countries. Nationalism, it seemed, was obsolete in the new international order. Much was made of the fact that half of the population was not only under the age of twenty-five but, as the Industrial Development Authority (IDA) billboards proudly proclaimed, was not merely young but European as well. The land of eternal youth had turned out to be a land without frontiers.

The screening of the award-winning drama *The Ballroom of Romance* in 1982 provided a focus for the reassuring belief that the fifties were no longer with us. Here was a world that seemed as

---

2. Paul Bew, Peter Gibbon and Henry Patterson, 'Some Aspects of Nationalism and Socialism in Ireland: 1968-1978', in Austen Morgan and Bob Purdie (eds.), *Ireland: Divided Nation, Divided Class*, London: Ink Links, 1980, p. 160.

remote from contemporary Ireland as did Brideshead from the England of the 1980s. Viewers could confront the harsh realities of poverty, emigration, sexual repression and the enforced domestication of women, secure in the knowledge that 'The factory was coming to town' – a recurrent topic in conversations between characters in the play – which would make all these features of the old social order redundant. Such optimism, however, seems strangely at odds with the Irish experience in the late 1980s. The chronic unemployment, the Granard tragedy, the Kerry babies controversy, the demoralization in the aftermath of the abortion and divorce referenda, the dismantling of the welfare services, the reappearance of full-scale emigration, the new censorship mentality and, above all, the moving statues, constituted a return of the repressed for those intent on bringing Ireland into the modern world. If a Rip Van Winkle fell asleep in the 1950s and woke up in 1988, he could be forgiven for thinking that nothing had changed in between. Even the Brylcreem look and baggy trousers were back in vogue, thanks to the influence of 'retro-chic' fashion. In the political arena, the resurgence of nationalism following the hunger strikes in 1981 was a stark reminder to those revisionist critics, whether on the right or left, who had written it off as a historical anachronism. The equation of urbanization and industrial development with enlightenment values of progress, secularization and cosmopolitanism proved no longer viable in the austere cultural climate of the 1980s.

2

For some commentators, the collapse of the social and economic policies of the 1960s and 70s was sufficient to throw into question the whole project of modernization as it applied to a newly industrialized country such as Ireland. Others, however, preferred a different explanation, concentrating on what they perceived to be the native obstacles to progress and development, rather than as the inherent deficiencies in the modernization process itself. Primary among these was the persistence of *tradition*, the tenacity of rural values in the face of social change. 'For all our urbanization', wrote John Healy, 'we are still a people of the land with the old value system of the land'.[3] The argument that the dead weight of tradition was never really dislodged in Irish society, and that rural values were the main factor retarding the forces of progress, was thrown into bold relief in a newspaper headline, following the abortion referendum in 1983: 'TWO NATIONS!' proclaimed *The Irish Independent*, as if henceforth the main division in Irish society was

3. John Healy, 'Why Charlie Controls the 25th Dáil', *In Dublin: Election '87* (special issue), 7 February, 1987, p. 15.

not between the North and the South, or even labour and capital, but that which existed between the country and the city.

In this new version of the battle between the ancients and the moderns, it is not as if the urban/rural divide is so pronounced that the city is left to its own devices as an agency of modernization, while the countryside languishes in what Marx called 'the idiocy of rural life'. Part of the animus against the enduring influence of traditional values is that they are not simply confined to the rural hinterland but have distorted and indeed have prevented the development of a genuine urban identity in Irish cities. An Irish sociologist was once quoted as saying that Dublin was the largest village in the world, with Belfast coming a close second. In a vigorous polemic against sentimentalists who advocate a return to rural values as a panacea for Ireland's social problems, Declan Kiberd has argued that the social problems themselves derive from the lingering malaise of rural ideology. The corrosive effects of urban crime, inner city decay, inept planning, and the educational fallout of the dole-queues, is attributed by Kiberd to the fact that decision makers have invariably come from a rural background. Pointing out that it was a Donegal man, Neil Blaney, who planned and promoted the tower blocks of Ballymun, Kiberd goes on to quote a leading architect, John Meagher, on the reasons for the destruction of the social fabric of the city: 'This city is run by road engineers who are all first generation country people and have no idea how cities should be designed.'[4] Contrary to Brendan Behan's wisecrack, the culchies no longer end where the tram tracks begin. The city in Ireland is simply the country at one remove.

The problem with this analysis is that it assumes that the rural ideology which presided over the national revival was a genuine expression of country life, as if the plain people of Ireland had only to look into their hearts to see what de Valera was thinking. It ignores the extent to which idealizations of rural existence, the longing for community and primitive simplicity, are the product of an urban sensibility, and are cultural fictions imposed on the lives of those they purport to represent. In the United States, for example, it was not cowboys who sang the praises of the Old West but rather writers and intellectuals from the East, intent on establishing a mythology of the last frontier. By the same token, it was urban based writers, intellectuals and political leaders who created romantic Ireland, and perpetrated the myth that the further west you go, the more you come into contact with the real Ireland.

In a recent article on the abiding influence of rural ideology on Irish literature, Fintan O'Toole takes account of the fact that 'the notion of the peasant and of the country which the peasant

4. Declan Kiberd, 'The Moral Superiority of Rural Villages', *The Irish Times*, 9 December 1986.

embodied was not a reflection of Irish reality but an artificial literary creation, largely made in Dublin, for Dubliners'. However, he manages to exonerate the metropolitan centre from ultimate responsibility for this imaginary Ireland by arguing that the appeal of 'the myth of the West' for the Dublin audience derived largely from the fact that they were of rural extraction, and since they were 'often no more than a generation removed from the countryside a visit to the Abbey was a travelogue into its collective past'.[5] The hankering for a return to nature and the simple life therefore is a form of nostalgia for a world which was lost, and is simply an attempt to restore to the countryside an ideology which was taken from it in the first place. This view of rural nostalgia accords with Raymond Williams' definition of 'residual ideology', that is, a value system which outlives its own era and survives in a new social order.[6]

The difficulty with this argument lies in its assumption that the rural myths cultivated during the revival conformed in an earlier period to the actual experience of life in the countryside: an assumption which O'Toole appears to reject above and which, in any case, is clearly at odds with the harsh realities of agrarian society in nineteenth-century Ireland. There would in fact have been no need to leave the countryside and go further afield if life was an idyllic affair of cosy homesteads and comely maidens dancing on the village green. As Kerby Miller has pointed out in his study of Irish emigration, the backward look towards a peasant arcadia does not represent a form of *continuity* with the rural past of the emigrant, but a *break* with it. The shock of the city and the new world resulted in a dislocation rather than a continuation of the emigrant's previous rural experience. The precipitating factor in the construction of romantic Ireland, then, was the metropolitan centre, and by extension the social upheavals wrought by the modernization process. As Miller puts it: 'those very innovations, so pregnant with social disruption and demoralization, themselves encouraged greater popular reliance on traditional outlooks and 'explanations' which could relieve the tensions consequent on rapid transition'.[7]

It is often forgotten that what are now taken as traditional values – myths of community, the sanctity of the family, devotion to faith and fatherland – are not a residue from an old Gaelic order but are of quite recent vintage, dating in fact from what Emmet Larkin has called 'the devotional revolution' in post-Famine Ireland. As such

5. Fintan O'Toole, 'Going West: The country versus the city in Irish writing', *The Crane Bag*, vol. 9, no. 2, 1985, pp. 112-13.
6. See Raymond Williams, *Marxism and Literature*, Oxford: Oxford University Press, 1977, pp. 121-28. It is important to note that Williams 'careful elaboration of the concept of residual ideology' would challenge the view that it could function as a *dominant* ideology'.
7. Kerby Miller, 'Emigration, ideology and identity in post-famine Ireland', *Studies*, vol. 75, no. 300, Winter 1986, p. 517.

they were part of the first phase of modernization rather than an obstacle to it. The 'traditionalism' and religious conservatism associated with the west of Ireland, for example, so evident in the results of the abortion and divorce referenda, is a comparatively late development, given that in the early nineteenth century Connacht was the region with the least, not the highest, Mass attendance, with figures in some places falling as low as 20%. What happened in between to alter this situation? The centralization of church control under Cardinal Cullen in the post-Famine era brought the more refractory forms of popular belief – 'genuine' traditional practices, if you like – into line with mainstream Roman Catholicism. This devotional revolution was part of an overall modernizing thrust which included the resolution of the land question and the national revival, all of which were a response to the pressures placed on Irish society by its gradual, direct integration into the capitalist world economy. As Miller again expresses it, those 'in the forefront of capitalist development . . . found it most expedient and essential to explain or justify their innovations and consequent dominance in traditional categories which could inhibit resentment and resistance from those who were or felt disadvantaged by the resultant discontinuities'.[8] Tradition, therefore, unlike Topsy, did not just grow and grow: it was imposed on the rural hinterland by the metropolitan centre.

3

In an interview in 1980, the artist Robert Ballagh suggested that those who judge Ireland by its promotional images abroad must risk a certain cultural schizophrenia: 'You have the IDA out in the US selling Ireland as a modern progressive go-ahead capitalist society. Invest in Ireland and make a profit. And you have Bord Fáilte eulogizing roads where you won't see a car from one end of the day to the other: it's almost as if they're advertising a country nobody lives in'.[9] The implication here is that the dynamic image of Ireland as a high-tech paradise projected by the IDA is somehow incompatible with the image of Ireland as an unspoiled romantic wilderness promoted by Bord Fáilte. Certainly tourist literature is not known for its emphasis on the economic realities of Ireland – the dole queues, the multinational corporations, the fact that more people are employed in industry than agriculture, the rise of agribusiness and the extinction of the small farmer. To this extent, the dream Ireland of Bord Fáilte obscures the technocratic world of the IDA. But the exclusion is not mutual. The most striking feature of IDA

8. Ibid., p. 518.
9. 'Getting away from outworn shibboleths of Irishness', *Sunday Independent*, 9 November 1980.

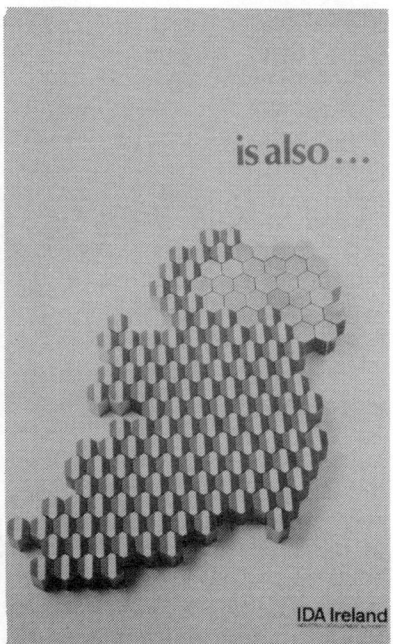

FIG. I   FIG. 2

promotional material is that it does not simply acknowledge but actively perpetuates the myth of romantic Ireland, incorporating both modernity and tradition within its frame of reference. The shamrock not only acquires a new biochemical identity (*Fig. 1*) but the great antinomies of romantic ideology, nature and industry, landscape and technology, are magically reconciled within the terms of the formula (*Figs. 2 and 3*). As the IDA brochure from which this cover is taken expresses it:

> A relative latecomer to industrialization, Ireland has been able to avoid the excesses of the original industrial revolution. The factories and the bustling towns and cities exist in harmony with the Ireland the tourists flock to see, a land of unsurpassed natural beauty

The location of advanced technological factories in remote, often spectacular settings was motivated, not by a love of the picturesque as the IDA's own copy would have us believe, but by the more prosaic imperatives of a regional policy which guided the IDA's industrial strategy until the early 1980s. This policy could be described as industrialization without urbanization. Part of the attraction of outlying rural areas for industrial investment was that they lacked the strong traditions of trade union militancy which are

FIG. 3

FIG. 4

FIG. 5

characteristic of the urban working class. By the end of the 1970s, only one quarter of new industrial employment was generated in the east of the country: the west and midlands were the main target areas of the new industrial policy, with the north-west receiving particular attention. To this extent, then, the images of the old and the new co-existing side by side which feature in more perceptive representations of Ireland make sense (*Figs. 4 and 5*) and it was perhaps this phenomenon which renewed interest in the 'residual ideology' thesis, reinforcing the argument that traditional rural values were displacing urbanization as the underlying rationale of economic development.

Yet, while recognising the failure of modernization, these accounts of arrested development convey the impression that the pull of the past is due solely to the traditional sector, as if the metropolitan centre, by contrast, could only impel a society towards the future. What is not investigated is the possibility that it is the modernization process itself, or rather the mutant which passes for modernization in Ireland, which is the source of the social and cultural 'backlash' of the 1980s. In 1983, the IDA undertook a fundamental reappraisal of its industrial strategy, shifting the emphasis from employment towards *wealth* creation. Given the inexorable flow of wealth from the periphery towards the centre, this reformulation of policy in effect consigned the outlying regions to economic stagnation.[10] We might expect then that having been freed from the obligation to accommodate itself to tradition, a more clear-cut emphasis on progress and cosmopolitanism – the cultural dynamic conventionally associated with the centre – would ensue. In fact, the opposite happened. The invocation of the past grew even more pronounced in IDA promotional literature, as the subject matter of the images retreated in time towards the 16th century (*Fig. 6*), to the island of saints and scholars (*Fig. 7*) and eventually towards remote antiquity (*Fig. 8*). The more intangible the connection with the present, the more likely it was to appear in an image. Newgrange surfaced not only in IDA brochures but also in the Bank of Ireland's publicity material (*Fig. 9*). Dolmens proved particularly attractive to the new pre- (or rather post-) history, appearing in advertisements for Guinness, Digital computers (*Fig. 10*) and, again, the Bank of Ireland (*Fig. 11*). The appeal of remote antiquity to today's filofax generation is spelled out in the copy accompanying the Bank of Ireland's celebration of the dolmen in its calendar for 1987:

Our modern world owes much to our remote ancestors, unknown men and women who were no less intelligent and

---

10. See T. A. Boylan and M. P. Cuddy, 'Regional industrial policy: performance and challenge', *Administration*, vol. 32, no. 3, 1984.

School of Engineering, Trinity College, Dublin

IN A 16TH CENTURY IRISH UNIVERSITY: 21ST CENTURY KNOWLEDGE.

The Irish.
The Irish have always had a hunger and respect for education. Today, over 40% of our college students choose science and technology.
Ireland.
A member of the European Common Market. Noted for its favorable government attitudes towards business. The most profitable industrial location in Europe for US manufacturers.
Ireland. Home of the Irish. The young Europeans.

IDA Ireland ♣
INDUSTRIAL DEVELOPMENT AUTHORITY
IDA Ireland has offices in New York (212) 972 1000, Chicago (312) 644 7474, Cleveland (216) 861 0365/6, Los Angeles (213) 629 0081, Menlo Park (415) 854 1800, Houston (713) 966 0000, Boston (617) 367 8025, Fort Lauderdale (305) 785 9430, Atlanta (404) 351 8474

REPUBLIC OF IRELAND

"WE'RE THE YOUNG EUROPEANS."

FIG. 6

inventive than the scientists and technologists of our times. We thought that, in plotting your course through 1987, you might draw encouragement and inspiration from these twelve illustrations of prehistoric planning.

This is not a reassertion of vestigal ideology, as if 'prehistoric planning' was part of an ancient cultural legacy which survived into the contemporary world. It is instead an invented tradition, a recourse to the past which exceeds even the most imaginative flights of nationalist history in its desire to confer an aura of permanence on the new information order. The facility with which distant aeons are collapsed into the present has more in common with the ersatz history of American wax museums than with the lingering traces of rural values.[11] Traditionalism looks to history for continuity: neo-traditionalism abolishes not only continuity but history itself.

4

It is no coincidence that neo-traditionalism, a fabricated relationship to the past, appears in conjunction with the new information technologies. Part of the driving force of the Industrial Revolution in its western capitalist phase was that it acted as an engine of the Enlightenment, carrying liberal ideals of reason, progress and universal values in its train. This is the blueprint which dominated theories of modernization as late as the 1960s, and it advocated full integration into the 'free world' economy as a means of breaking down the 'Chinese walls' of obscurantism which impeded develop- ment in traditional societies. With the emergence of transnational corporations and a new international division of labour in the after- math of the second world war, it became clear that modernization, in this sense, had less to do with development than with *under*de- velopment, i.e. with systematically increasing the dependency of peripheral countries on the economic power of the metropolitan centre. When rapid industrialization did take place, moreover, as in the Far East and particularly Japan, it did not follow the western route but appeared to negotiate its own distinctive path to develop- ment. A heavy emphasis on micro-electronics and computer indus- tries is partly responsible for the sudden elevation of these economic regions to the ranks of advanced capitalist economies. What is more interesting for our present purposes is that industrial policies based on the new information technologies need no longer replace tradi- tion, but may actively refashion and intensify its grip on society. Instead of retarding economic growth, Chinese walls, or their national equivalents, may often accelerate it.

The Japanese case is particularly instructive, given the tendency

11. Umberto Eco, *Travels in Hyper reality*, London: Picador, 1987, ch. 1.

FIG. 7   FIG. 8

FIG. 9   FIG. 10

of recent initiatives at a policy level in Ireland to circumvent the Anglo-American axis and look to Japan as a model for economic development.[12] Many commentators have drawn attention to the manner in which pre-industrial values of familialism, group loyalty, deference to authority and, indeed, weak trade union organization, have presided over the Japanese economic miracle, instead of the individualism and liberal humanism associated with modernization in the west. It is as if in an eastern setting, Adam Smith's invisible hand had brought about a mysterious fusion of tradition and modernity rather than a convergence between private and public interests. While nativist apologists within Japan have been eager to proclaim this as a vindication of the Japanese way of life, and its veneration of the past, a more accurate appraisal would see it not as a conservation but as a *reactivation* of tradition from a distinctively contemporary standpoint. As Johann Arnason has written of the 'Janus-faced' nature of Japanese modernization: 'it combined an exceptionally thorough effort to assimilate the achievements of a more advanced civilization . . . with the reappropriation and revalorization of a tradition that had previously been marginalized or at least divorced from the real centres of power for a long time'.[13] There is no genuine recrudescence of traditional values: rather 'traditions' are manipulated and selected from the past according as they lend themselves to the dictates of the present. The clock may be turned back at a cultural or even social level, but industrialization proceeds apace. Hence the phenomenon of 'regressive modernization', a form of advanced industrial development which, unlike the initial Industrial Revolution, has no commitment to social, political or cultural modernization. It is from this perspective that we should view the IDA's slogan: 'Missing the Industrial Revolution was the best thing that ever happened to the Irish' (*Fig. 12*).

This is saying, in effect, that an industrial revolution in an electronic age need no longer be encumbered by a vision of social progress. Applied to Ireland in the 1980s, this means that the 'conservative backlash', or the reversion to traditional values of family, faith and fatherland, may not be an aberration but may even be a logical extension of the modernization policies pursued by successive governments and development agencies. In 1979 almost one million PAYE workers took to the streets of Dublin in a protest

---

12. See Eoin O'Malley, 'Reflections on Ireland's economic identity', *Studies*, vol. 75, no. 300, Winter 1986, p. 485.

13. Johann Arnason, 'The modern constellation and the Japanese enigma: Part 1', *Thesis Eleven*, no. 17, 1987. See also Robert J. Smith's smiliar observation on the alleged survival of pre-industrial values into the modern era: 'This phenomenon is not a simple transfer into modern corporatism of an established tradition . . . it too is a new device that meets new needs of industrial society as the Japanese perceive it'. (*Japanese Society: Tradition, Self and the Social Order*, Cambridge University Press, 1983, p. 66.)

FIG. 11

FIG. 12

march against the punitive tax regime in the Republic. This was seen by many contemporary observers as the coming of age of the Irish working class, the culmination of the modernization process. Within a few months, a million people had again gathered in Dublin, but this time it was in the Phoenix Park to greet Pope John Paul II. This was taken by the same commentators as a throwback to a previous era, but in fact it was this gathering, rather than the PAYE march, which was a portent of things to come. The Phoenix Park was an appropriate setting for traditional Ireland to emerge from the ashes.

The idea that modernization is helping Ireland to 'catch up' with its advanced industrial neighbours is no longer tenable. If there is any convergence between European nations in the run up to 1992, it is at the level of regressive social policies. As Edward Said has pointed out, those who equate fundamentalism and revivalism with pre-modern societies such as Iran often forget that the heartlands of fundamentalism are in the West, in the 'Victorian values' of Thatcherite Britain or in Ronald Reagan's call for a 'return to the range' in the United States.[14] The bogey of traditionalism and rural values can no longer be used in Ireland as a scapegoat for a regressive politics that emanates from the metropolitan centre. As Declan O'Connell has acutely observed: 'The romantic idealist ideology that dominated Irish political debate for so long and (is) traced to western small farmers' 'remote economic situation' and 'shelter from worldly pressures' might also be understood more fully as a consequence of capitalist underdevelopment'.[15] The IDA image of Ireland as the silicon valley of Europe may not be so far removed after all from the valley of the squinting windows.

14. Edward Said 'Orientalism Reconsidered', in F. Barker et al. *Literature, Politics and Theory*, London: Methuen, 1986, p. 218.
15. Declan O'Connell, 'Sociological Theory & Irish Political Research' in *Power, Conflict & Inequaltiy* (eds. Kelly, O'Dowd, Wickham). Dublin, 1982, p. 196.

Ireland Without Frontiers? The Challenge of the Communications Revolution

DESMOND BELL

Capital by its very nature drives beyond every spatial barrier. Thus the creation of the physical conditions of exchange – of the means of communication and transport – of the annihilation of space by time becomes an extraordinary necessity for it . . . .   Karl Marx, 1857

We live, so the media gurus tell us, in a global village. The exponential growth in electronic communications– telephonic, audio-visual and computer data interchanges – have, as Marx put it over a hundred years ago reflecting on the introduction of telegraph, facilitated the 'annihilation of space by time'. The world has shrunk.

At first appearance this revolution in communications seems like a good thing from an Irish perspective. As our revisionist intellectuals keep telling us, we Irish have been too insular and culturally introspective as a nation. A rigid cultural nationalism remains our dominant regional aesthetic. Despite its radical roots, this speculative investment in 'tradition' soon ossified into a rigidly conservative ethos hostile to both European modernist currents *and* popular culture. Both were seen as subject to invidious 'foreign influences'. Perhaps this sclerosis was inevitable given the imperatives of nation building in the context of post-partitionist politics.

The communications revolution, some predict, will end this isolation. It is hoped that Ireland's integration into the emerging world information order will facilitate a more open, pluralistic and 'post-nationalist' cultural reconstruction. In the future, tradition and modernity may productively interact. Irish culture will become characterized by a 'creative pluralism'. To quote Richard Kearney, for the first time we might be able, 'to construe the question of cultural identity as a frontierless tooing and froing between national and international perspectives'.[1] The technological optimists argue that the coming 'information society' will provide us with new communicational resources to enhance cultural exchange with other countries and regions. In turn national communication and media structures will be decentralised. Overall our culture will be

---

1. Richard Kearney, 'Our Evolving Culture Without Frontiers', in *The Irish Times*, 29 Dec 1987.

greatly enriched as it emerges under the banner of a vibrant 'radical electicism'.[2]

The Emerging World Information Order

Over the last ten years there has been an intense debate about the global distribution of communication resources. The publication of the Report of the MacBride Commission,[3] has fuelled expectations about the emergence of a more democratic communication order. Within the envisaged, more equitable, new world information order, it is hoped that 'the mass media can make a substantial contribution towards . . . the strengthening of peace, international security, and the lessening of international tensions . . . . ' (MacBride, 1980) Ireland with its experience of colonialism, political neutrality and intermediate location on the development scale between the 'third world' and the advanced capitalist economies, is in a privileged position it is argued to facilitate communication between East and West, between North and South. As Kearney asks[4]

> Availing of our privileged access to the major First World information centres – for example the European space satellites agency – could we not be simultaneously establishing contact with other small and post-colonial societies in the Second and Third Worlds?

In addition the new electronic networking possibilities and interactive capabilities of contemporary telecommunication technology, some argue,[5] provide the material means to effect a decentralisation of our national political and administrative structures. Ireland already has a sophisticated micro-wave telecommunications network criss-crossing the entire country. We are a highly cabled country, with over 300,000 households now receiving cable TV services. An additional MMDS system ('cable over the air') is being planned to provide multi-channel TV outside the already cabled urban areas. Ireland, as a 'wired society' has, the futurists predict, the opportunity to become truly a country 'without frontiers', a state of dispersed power and authority.

---

2. Kenneth Frampton, the US architectural theorist, prefers the term 'critical regionalism' which he defines as an aesthetic strategy which seeks, 'to mediate the impact of universal civilization with elements derived INDIRECTLY from the peculiarities of a particular place.' (Towards a Critical Regionalism, in Hal Foster (edit) *PostModern Culture*, Pluto Press, 1985.

3. The MacBride Commission: *Many Voices, One World*, Report by International Commission for the Study of Communication Problems, Unesco, Paris 1980.

4. Kearney, *op cit.*

5. Richard Pine: 'After MacBride: Ireland and the New World Communication Order', *Crane Bag*, Vol. 8 No. 2, Media and Popular Culture, 1984.

Undoubtedly the last few years have seen the emergence of a radically new phase in the development of the electronic media. Data transmission systems are increasingly interactive in character and with the primacy of the microcomputer need no longer be vertically integrated. Similarly within the audio-visual field the new media technologies, particularly video and cable, have a technical capacity to encourage 'narrowcasting' forms of signal distribution to specialist user groups. Some argue we are witnessing the end of the broadcasting era and the centralized and hierarchical organization of mass communication which characterized this.[6] The information society, it is argued, will be one of decentered mass communications (the term MASS media, with its late nineteenth century imagery of the volatile and manipulable urban crowd, becomes even less appropriate).

As the recent report produced by The Association for Film and Television in the Celtic Countries argues,[7]

> The old arguments about networks being unable to carry extensive programming for linguistic and other minority interests because of the greater claims by the majority on network time will no longer be sustainable. New communication services, whether on satellite, cable or a combination of the two, can now provide improved access to groups of people throughout the (European) Community, in addition to releasing terrestial services for new forms of regional broadcasting.

With the proliferation of cheap and accessible means of cultural production and exchange – video, the microcomputer, reprographic publishing systems, local radio – everyone, we are told, will potentially be a producer as well as a consumer of messages and meanings in the 'global village'. Brecht's dream of a mass media functioning as a real apparatus of communication formulated as he began his constructivist experiments with public radio, would finally be realised. We would have developed a system which knows how, as he put it, 'to receive as well as transmit, how to let the listener speak as well as hear, how to bring him into a relationship with others instead of isolating him'.[8] Can the telematic revolution enable us to align for the first time the economic dynamic of modernization with the untried cultural project of modernism – an aesthetic of radical innovation and democratic participation?

6. *ibid.*
7. The Association for Film and Television in the Celtic Countries: *New Information Technologies and their impact on Peripheral and Sparsely Populated Areas*, Dublin 1984.
8. Bertolt Brecht: Radio as a means of Communication. Trans. Stuart Hood, *Screen* 20, Nos. 3 & 4, Winter 1979-80.

However, perhaps we should be cautious about some of the extravagant claims made for the new media by the theorists of the 'information society' and 'communications culture'. These futurists often naively assume that the information and communication revolution we are now witnessing will necessarily entail a major extension of democratic process and public access. In the computopia they envisage the state will simply wither away. As knowledge becomes the most important factor of production, capitalist avarice will be replaced by informed social responsibility.

However, notwithstanding the technical feasability of decentralising and democratising cultural production, there are significant economic and political barriers to achieving these social objectives in the current period. There always have been under capitalism.

Brecht, wiley materialist that he was, fully realised that the property relations of the capitalist system militated against radical innovations in the structure of our means of communication. The media under capitalist control would continue, he accepted, to be run for profit and to secure bourgeois political hegemony. His proposals for truly interactive media were, he accepted, necessarily utopian and pre-emptive.

> Unrealizable in this social system, realizable in another, these proposals, which are, after all, only the natural consequences of technical development, help towards the propagation and shaping of that OTHER system.[9]

The current pattern of ownership and control of global communication resources remains a major obstacle to the decentralisation and democratization of the global information system.

International Communication and Corporate Capital

Indeed the global communications system remains an adjunct of monopoly capital. Accompanying the transnationalisation of the world's economy, under the aegis of US, Japanese and to a lesser extent European capital, has been the internationalisation of cultural and informational production and distribution. The volume of transborder data-flows, the life-blood of the contemporary multinational firm, dramatically expands each year. Within these dispersed enterprises information and decision-making continues to be concentrated at the metropolitan headquarters of these organisations. The decentralisation of production has been accompanied by the centralisation of strategic control within the new international division of labour. Indeed *the international communications infras-*

---

9.   *Ibid.*

tructure has facilitated this decentralization-centralization dynamic of transnational capital.

In Ireland Bórd Telecom have spent over 1.5 billion pounds – much of it taxpayers money – modernising the country's telecommunications sinced 1982. Given Ireland's degree of economic dependence on US investment, and the malleability of government policy in the face of pressures from the multi-nationals, the process of remoulding the country's domestic media and communications structures to facilitate the marketing and organizational requirements of foreign conglomerates is more advanced here than elsewhere. The public service dimension of our communications and media systems has eroded probably faster than anywhere else.

For example, a central element in the industrial policy plans of the current Fianna Fáil government is the creation of an international financial services centre on a site beside the city's historic Custom House. A key requirement in attracting international finance corporations is the provision of state-of-the-art communication facilities. The de-regulation of financial markets has been accompanied by the new dependency of dealers on a sophisticated telematic infrastructure as the computer has come to reign supreme in this sector. Bórd Telecom are already developing a sophisticated earth station on the Custom House Docks site. This will relay via an ISDN system, the telephonic, computer data, video and facsimile communications of the incoming multi-national customers. These firms will be conducting transactions right across the globe. Ireland may well come to serve as a telematic gateway linking the European mainland to the US, providing customised services to corporate users rather than facilitating international understanding.

The paradox is that these improved facilities for international communication firmly vested as they are in the hands of transnational capital, will make overseas investors even less responsive to the social demands of the Irish state. The black holes in the economy, caused by the transfer pricing and profit repatriation practices of the MNCs, will become deeper and even harder to trace. The ease with which transactions can be conducted with organizations outside the state, by apparatus provided by the state, will encourage many of these manufacturing firms to continue to use Ireland primarily as an offshore assembly centre and access point to EC markets. The fostering of native research and development expertise will be further retarded and the benefit of the state-aided transnational sector to the indigenous industrial sector minimized. The MNCs are set to become even less accountable to the Irish people and their political representatives. The Custom House development may materialise as a fortified high-tech island of privilege surrounded by the sprawling dereliction of impoverished and marginalised inner city Dublin. Such unevenness is a feature of capitalist development. We recall the anthropological insight [10]that,

THERE IS A THIRD WORLD IN EVERY FIRST WORLD
A FIRST WORLD IN EVERY THIRD WORLD

As with the building of the railways in post-famine Ireland, which it was hoped would bring industry and commerce into the impoverished West but which facilitated the wholesale emigration of the population and further peripheralisation of this regional economy, the improved telematic structure, tailored as it is to the needs of transnational capital, may in fact exacerbate the dependent and uneven character of Irish development.

Broadcasting De-Regulation and the Public Interest
Similar ominous developments are happening in audio-visual production. Increasingly the 'footprints' of direct broadcasting satellites in the hands of media magnates and conglomerates spread beyond political boundaries. Cable distribution systems provide additional tendrils enabling the emerging international commercial media system to reach into more and more homes. Cable delivers programming and services most of which originate outside Ireland in the US dominated international media market.

While the bureaucrats in Brussels enthuse about the possibility of 'television without frontiers' within the European Community – the emergence of a common market for media products and services – the reality is that US penetration of the European audio-visual space increases. RTE already has the lowest ratio of home-produced programmes to imported programming in the European Broadcasting Union. Now the national station is facing competition for the attention of audiences and for advertising revenues from not only the four British terrestrial television stations, but also from cable delivered pan-European commercial satellite.[11] With the launching of new British based DBS satellites in conjunction with the arrival of cheaper receiving dishes, a torrent of new channels will be flooding into Ireland.[12]

The old RTE broadcasting monopoly was justified by arguments of spectrum scarcity and by a rhetoric of cultural nationalism. Throughout Europe such public service monopolies over the air waves have collapsed in the face of the new 'narrowcasting'

---

10. Trinh T. Minh-ha: *Discourse*, Fall/Winter 1987.
11. As RTE still owns an 80% controlling share in Cablelink, the largest cable operator in the country, the situation is somewhat perverse, although it has recently announced its intention to sell its shareholding.
12. For a review of media developments in Ireland see Desmond Bell and Niall Meehan: International Telecommunications Deregulation and Ireland's Communication Policy, *Journal of Communication*, 38 (1), 1988.

technologies. With the introduction of these new media technologies, such as VCRs, cable and satellites, the capacity of nation states to regulate the 'free flow' of information and cultural commodities lessens.

In addition the new conservative ideological climate has seen a significant number of western governments espouse neo-liberal economic programmes. These aim to 'roll back the frontiers of the state' and promote market-led media developments. Indeed within the field of communications the decline of the public domain has advanced faster and further than in other areas of economic and social life. For the information economy has become the axis around which industrial restructuring is now occurring and accordingly is seen as a potential new source of profits. Even within government policy deliberations on the media the television viewer and radio listener is increasingly being viewed as a *consumer* rather than as a *citizen* with political and cultural rights in the spheres of education and information.

Increasingly it seems as if Irish government policy in this area is primarily designed to facilitate the interests of private investors rather than to meet the communication needs of its citizens. We can list the sorry catalogue of mismanagement of national resources in the communication field by successive Irish governments; the handing over of effective control of a planned Irish DBS satellite to the Hughes Corporation, a huge US aerospace and communications conglomerate; the introduction of legislation to give commercial operators a free run at developing local radio services for profit rather than to serve community intersts; the systematic harassing of RTE which has been starved of investment capital while at the same time the government actively promotes the introduction of a purely commercial TV channel and relay system; the undermining of the small but exceptionally creative indigenous film industry by abolishing the Irish Film Board which provided invaluable financial assistance to film makers while continuing to aid via the Industrial Development Authority, 'entertainment led', larger and more commercial enterprises in the audio visual area.

The evidence to date from a number of European countries suggests[13] that the deregulation of broadcasting and erosion of public service provision, rather than leading to an explosion of innovative programming, heterogeneity of output, regionalisation of production and services and greater public access to cultural production, has in fact led in many of the countries of Europe to exactly the opposite. Deregulated television is subject to acute commercial pressures to maximise audiences in order to optimise

---

13. See for example, G. Richeri: Television from Service to Business: European Tendencies and the Italian Case, in Drummond (ed) *Television in Transition*, British Film Institute, 1985.

advertising revenues and meet spiralling production costs. This has led to greater homogeneity of programming as channels respond to the increased competition and potential audience fragmentation by going 'down market'. Minority programming, educational, informational and investigative current affairs and documentary programming are all sacrificed for 'pure entertainment' shows. As the 'ratings war' hots up RTE has responded by restructuring its radio and television service and its programme schedules marginalising its public service functions. Does RTE still have an educational service?[14] Is it seriously interested in drama? The stations limited commitment to supporting drama, given the universally recognized strength of Irish theatre, is particularly perverse and only intelligible within the emerging political economy of television.

A Media Debate?

Yet while there has been a widespread political debate, (particularly on the Left) about the erosion of Irish sovereignty as a result of our economic dependence on multi-national investment, and while there is considerable unease about the extension of the legislative and political authority of Brussels, no parallel debate about the evaporation of Ireland's cultural integrity in the wake of our growing communicational dependency, has ensued.

Indeed, it has to be admitted that the Left in Ireland and more generally those committed to a democratic communication order, have found themselves in somewhat of a dilemma with regard to these developments. Broadcasting historically developed in Ireland within a so called public service model. This, although inspired by the BBC's Reithean tradition, was adapted to the nation building needs of the new bourgeois state. The broadcasting service was viewed as an 'instrument of public policy' with which to buttress national sovereignty and defend the cultural integrity of Ireland.[15] There was an almost complete political consensus amongst the political parties in the Dáil up until the sixties that broadcasting should be under state ownership and control. As such the service that developed was both politically and culturally conservative, and hostile to popular culture. In turn, for the Left in Ireland, as elsewhere, the public media came to be regarded, in the words of Louis Althusser, the French Marxist philosopher, as an 'ideological state apparatus' playing a central role in the maintenance of

---

14. It remains a public scandal that RTE, given its technical resources, has been unable or unwilling to launch a national distance learning system on the Open University model.

15. See my 'Proclaiming the Republic: Broadcasting Policy and the Corporate State in Ireland', *West European Politics*, Vol 8, No. 2, April 1985.

capitalist hegemony. The broadcasting system was clearly on the other side of the barricades.

Today as states throughout Europe privatise broadcasting and deregulate media markets, the Left finds itself in the paradoxical position of defending the public service mode of media provision. We rally behind RTE despite our profound reservations about the hierarchical, conservative and non-participative character of the station. The debate about the media in Ireland – as indeed elsewhere – has, as the Right have managed to set the agenda for communication developments, degenerated into sloganising about the relative merits of 'public service' as opposed to 'free market' models of broadcasting.

The current situation from the perspective of those committed to the democratization of communication may seem one of gloom and despondency. Sometimes perhaps we are too ready to look to technology to effect change because little intrinsic movement can be perceived within Irish culture and society itself. Yet while we must remain sceptical about the social claims made by the information society theorists for telematic innovation per se, at the same time we must be ready to exploit the mobilising and emancipatory possibilities inherent in the new means of communication. That, I think, is the historical lesson to be learnt from the modernist experimentation with the mass media in the first two decades of this century with which Brecht was associated. The media remain the site of a political struggle. In the context of the corrosive pessimism of the eighties it may be necessary to return to the critical legacy of the modernist avant garde project in order to move the debate on the media beyond both the sterility of the public service *v* the market argument and the naivety of the technological optimists. Indeed, abandonment of this critical legacy may, as I have argued, in part, have conditioned our chronic crisis of imagination about the mass media. Come back situationalists all is forgiven!

Postmodernism in Ireland
This tack is not without certain difficulties. The sort of social and political engagement entailed in the media practice of the historic avant garde – Rodchenko, Heartfield and Moholy-Nagy's develop-ment of photomontage, Mayakovsky posters and collage, Vertov's Kino Eye, Piscator and Meyerhold's theatre – has gone out of fashion in the cynical eighties. Of course contemporary crisis torn Ireland is not revolutionary Russia or Weimar Germany. Many of the actual media practices of the constructivist avant garde have passed into the sylistic repertoire of today's advertising industry or are endlessly recycled in rock video products and have returned to mock us.

Moreover the critical tradition I invoke is one which appears foreign to us here in Ireland. This is so despite the courageous attempt by an avant garde within RTE in the sixties to draw on the situationalist experience and on the community media movement to open up a debate within Ireland about public access to 'our' media. This group also in its subsequent independent film work concretely interrogated the dominant modes of representation of gender, nation and identity in Irish television.[16]

Ireland, however, was largely untouched by the high tide of European modernism and cultural internationalism. We have passed effortlessly into a post-modern malaise. While successive waves of the modernist avant garde, Cubists, Dada, Constructivists and Surrealists, did manage to storm the citadels of high culture and the academy in much of Europe and the US, Ireland however, was largely immune to this modernist offensive. The historic avant garde with its full-scale attack on bourgeois artistic conventions and mysticism and celebration of mass society, science and the new media, was still-born in post-partition Ireland. Romanticism with its primal longing for community and tradition was historically never really confronted by any coherent and indigenous modernist movement of a socially radical character in Irish society.

Indeed, cultural nationalism was able to present itself unchallenged, in the context of the struggle for national independence, as *the* socially radical aesthetic. Moreover, more recently 'the traditionalist project', albeit in an increasingly ersatz form, has found new allies. Sections of the 'new Left' have in their arcadianism and blanket hostility to the media made common cause with the 'old conservatives'. This popular front against modernity has also tapped into the prevailing intellectual pessimism and nihilism which parades itself under the banner of a certain spurious 'postmodernism'.

The use of this term in an Irish context is not without certain difficulties. It suggests a phase of cultural exhaustion that comes after the implosion of a once dominant modernism. But, as I have argued, Ireland never really experienced a form of socially engaged modernism. 'Modernism', in the sense that Richard Kearney uses it,[17] hit Ireland late, a consequence of the economic *MODERNI-ZATION* of the sixties rather than of the social ferment of early twentieth-century Europe. Modernism as an artistic movement had

---

16. Members of this group include Lelia Doolan, Bob Quinn and Cathal Black. See in particular *Sit Down and be Counted*, Lelia Doolan, Bob Quinn and Jack Dowling, Dublin, Wellington, 1969.

17. See, for example, Richard Kearney's introduction to *Transitions: Narratives in Modern Irish Culture*, Wolfhound Press, Dublin 1987 and Manchester University Press, 1988, and his series of articles on 'Postmodern Ireland' in *The Irish Times* Dec. 28-31, 1987 (reprinted in *The Clash of Ideas*, ed. M. Hederman, Gill & MacMillan, 1988).

by then already run out of steam globally and eschewed its politically radical origins. In 1960s Ireland 'modernism' as pseudo international style and sensibility was championed not by a radical avant garde but by the purveyors of consumer capitalism (as indeed it was elsewhere). In Ireland this modernism degenerated into a shoddy simulation of consumer prosperity in a society undergoing a tawdry and shortlived experience of the global post-war capitalist boom.

That boom is over – the term post-modern in Ireland carries with it images of dereliction and abandonment. Indeed the Irish economy may have great difficulty evolving into an information-led 'post-industrial society' precisely because it has never fully achieved the status of an industrial economy. Similarly without a genuinely modernist movement, post-modernism may be another sterile fad masking a new conservatism. It may not entail the hoped-for 'critical regionalism', i.e. the reconstruction and renewal of critical and adversarial culture aspirations, in and through its engagement with the regionally specific and culturally plural. Rather, we may be experiencing a provincial flight into nostalgia in the face of the ever-present contradictions of modernity. In Ireland a rear guard is already waiting in the wings without Irish society ever having been able to sustain an *indigenous* avant-garde.

Such are the contradictions of Irish modernization that we have prematurely entered the post-modern era. We are experiencing for example – in the sphere of economic ideology, 'monetarism' without a prior social democracy; in politics a 'new right' without an old left, 'post-nationalism' with the national question materially unresolved; at the social level, a return to 'family values' without the advances of feminism; at the cultural level the nostalgia and historicist pastiche of 'post-modernism' without the astringent purgative of modernism. We are entering the future, as some wag has commented, walking backwards.

Modernism remains an untried project. Its critical and emancipatory ideal and commitment to experiment with new forms and new mediums in order to create new publics and contemporary relevance remains a source of inspiration. In the post-modern era we will constantly return to its critical legacy to develop the programmatic base of a genuinely 'critical regionalism' such as Irish culture might aspire to . . . .

> Critical-affirmative action on everyday life and its institutions (education, design, environment, spectacle and mass media etc.); critical transformation of culture from within. Critical collaboration with institutions of mass and public media, design and education in order to raise consciousness (or critical unconsciousness) regarding urban experience: to win time and space in information, advertising, bill boards, light-

boards, subways, public monuments and buildings, television cable and public channels, etc. Address to passive viewer, alienated city dweller. Continuous influence of cultural studies enhanced by feminist critique of representation.

K. Wodiczko, 1978 [18]

18. Krzysztof Wodiczko, 'Strategies of Public Address: Which Media, Which Publics?', in Hal Foster (ed): *Discussions in Contemporary Culture*, Bay Press Seattle 1987.

Religion, Ireland: in Mutation

JOSEPH S. O'LEARY

Drive your cart and your plow over the bones of the dead
Blake

Since Ireland felt only faintly the impact of the scientific and philosophical Enlightenment, the defining event of *modernity*, and since her extraordinary contribution to the *modernist* revolution in literature – Yeats, Joyce, Beckett – was better understood abroad than at home, the notion of a *postmodern* Ireland can seem doubly misleading. The undermining and/or transformation of Irish Catholicism has mainly been the effect of the emergence of modern (Enlightenment) awareness in Irish society and in the Catholic Church worldwide since the sixties. If the modernization of Ireland was accompanied by an economic boom, the present suggestions of a postmodern mutation verify Frederic Jameson's diagnosis of postmodernism as 'the cultural logic of late capitalism'. The labyrin-thine specularity of a culture of the image can be studied in what has happened to the streets of Dublin in its millennium year, 1988. The city has lost its identity and is vainly trying to recapture it by a cult of images, images which serve as pawns in a consumerist economy. Dear dirty Dublin is being replaced by its own image. It is selling itself as a tourist attraction even to its own inhabitants. Brass plates of Mr Bloom gild the pavements; a sign of modernist consciousness? No, a sellable emblem of the city's pretentions to style and sophisti-cation, devoid of religious, political or ideological significance. Anna Livia bathes outside the GPO: a modernist mythic expression of the city's soul? No, it is an effort to associate mythic vitality with the banks and business of the city, an exercise in the engineering of imagination. Do yuppie pubs, new bookshops and pedestrianized zones betoken a general rise in cultural sophistication? No doubt, but they instill a new kind of civic pride, in which the citizen admires himself as consumer. This pride cements an emergent class consciousness, exclusive of the have-nots.

Postmodern: the name is a good one, like Enlightenment or Romanticism, suggestive, polyvalent, resistant to analysis yet bring-ing into clearer focus the obscure forces of the *Zeitgeist*. What was a malaise, prompting tragic apocalyptic talk in a bid for lucidity, has now become a comedy, as we realize that our trading in apocalypses was but another symptom of the postmodern lightness of being. But can the ascendancy of this notion be taken at face value? In its claim to provide a speculative definition of the age is it not as specious as the structuralist wave of twenty years ago? Has postmodernist thought, as represented by Jean-François Lyotard for example, really surpassed the Enlightenment and all the other critical movements of modernity? Is Marxism really finished, or has it found a new field of exercise in the analysis of post-modernist alienation? Has reason been atomized into the free play of local language games, or is it biding its time until we rediscover it?

For religious awareness, modernism rather than postmodernism still seems to me the most powerful innovatory instance. The textural change which all religious traditions are undergoing in the pluralistic milieu now defining their conditions of existence seems to be a modernist effect of transformation (analogous to cubism, atonality, relativity, the Mallarmean and Joycean revolutions of the word) rather than a postmodernist reduction of religious discourses to ironic citations and parodies of their tradition. The postmodernist aspects of contemporary religiosity – notably the replacement of religious substance by mediatic images, as in the multiplication of exotic Marian apparitions – seem to be a retreat from the task facing the Catholic Church after Vatican II, namely the advance from modernity to modernism. Postmodernist religion oils the wheels of Thatcherite capitalism, increasing the consumerist dynamics of religious behaviour and discouraging the growth of the masses to religious adulthood.

It took centuries to persuade the Catholic Church that it should embrace the *modern* world: unambiguous papal praise of democracy first came in 1943 and a limited recognition of religious freedom only with Vatican II. Why is it necessary that the Church now go on to espouse the *modernist* project and to bring its message in accord with the thought of people like Freud, Kafka, Heidegger, Wittgenstein and Beckett? The reason is that these shaping spirits of modernism represent the highest spiritual insights of the century and provide a *lingua franca* of spirituality which all, Catholic or Protestant, atheist or Buddhist, can fully understand. In fact we understand Kafka better than we understand the Gospels, since his world is ours, and carries with it none of the ancient cultural presuppositions which so often throw us in reading the Bible. The struggle of readers everywhere to become the spiritual contemporaries of the modernist masters is a vast ecumenical movement in which the classical religious traditions ought also to participate, in order to ensure their own adulthood, their liberation from a stifling archaism, and the credibility of their message. That Christians still feel threatened by modernist thought and art is an ecumenical scandal, dividing the spirit against itself.

Postmodernism as a recognizable style of art or thought is so heavily dependent on modernism that it is best classed as an epigonal footnote to it. The postmodernist epigone, condemned to citation and the *déjà vu*, thrives by making a virtue of this imposed weakness, revelling in the helplessness of a cultural latecomer. Theologians are very belatedly and clumsily acquiring a modernist sensibility, and as part of this the 'postmodern' note is sounded when they register the crisis of the legitimating narratives which have kept them in business since Augsburg and Trent and the pullulation of local theologies which retrospectively shows up the whole tradition as a constellation of localities, pluralistic in its very texture, despite the illusions of monolithic dogma. Those explicitly known as postmodern theologians are a rather brash group of Americans who attempt to re-read Christian tradition in light of the radical philosophies of Jacques Derrida, Jacques Lacan, and Michel Foucault. They can be faulted for a lack of engagement with the rich texture of that tradition, and for a hasty and superficial espousal of extreme Nietzschean postures. Yet these writers are far from exhausting the possibilities of such reflection and the truth they are aiming at in their sweeping negations may be brought into focus by a subtler approach dwelling more intimately in the great texts of Christian and Buddhist thought. In that ampler context, the drastic negations that lead to nihilism can be tempered into a Buddhist middle path, disengaged from fixated views, a wise realization of the conventionality and provisionality of all language, especially of religious language. That is only one of the possible paths: it represents a step back from the frivolity of the postmodern to the seriousness of the modernist enterprise.

Postmodern convictions are little more than ideological caricatures of lines of thinking already explored in the modernist masters. Thus the modernist suspicion of the identity of the self is hardened into a dogma in postmodernist discourse – to the effect that fixed identities, whether of the self or of God, of truth or of meaning, are shattered on the realization of how much we are creatures of the Heraclitean play of language which never allows our thought a secure foothold, as well as of the hidden violence of the systems of power shown up by Foucault and the fractured psychoanalytical structures postulated by Lacan. While some hail the postmodern flux as itself salvation and grace, it seems that the correct theological response is to attempt to do full justice to the modernist and postmodernist masters of suspicion while finally subordinating them to a hermeneutics which can retrieve the original power of the Christian revelation and continue its tradition with the required changes of key. Such a hermeneutics need not be limited by any apologetic or denominational foreclosure, but neither need it lose itself in the insouciant free play, the celebration of rootlessness, which so often seems to characterize the postmodern.

The religious culture of Ireland is one that has suffered greatly from fixities of identity, fixities which because they are false, and in conflict with the texture of reality, have produced a constant practice of self-deception and obscurantism. Rigid doctrinal and ethical views, denominational and national chauvinism, constricting definitions of social role and individual identity, reductive characterizations of alien groups and minorities: at last these pathogenic traits of Irish Catholicism are being subjected to sophisticated analysis by contemporary Irish thinkers. They can draw inspiration not only from the poets and novelists who have chronicled the cauterizing effect of such a culture and provided an antidote in their own unaided spiritual quest, but also from the Buddhist critique which sees all religious language as no more than a finger pointing at the moon; if the moon changes position what was an 'expedient means' becomes inexpedient, the icon becomes an idol. This general testing of the Irish Christian heritage is not merely destructive. It is a spiritual exercise in its own right.

What are delightfully known as '*à la carte* Catholics' usually practise a modern freedom of critical thought in their reception of church teachings, and many theologians would argue, though few bishops seem to agree, that they are perfectly within their rights in doing so, as long as their adult rationality does not become an irresponsible abandonment of the basic obedience of faith. But such Catholics could also be seen as a postmodern phenomenon, with the danger that all they retain of their religion are some reassuring images. In that case, postmodernism would once again show itself as a thwarting of modernism in the sense of advancement to a creative appropriation and transformation of the tradition. One floats passively into the postmodern lightening of one's religious identity, whereas a struggle of dissent, discernment and new vision is required for the modernist transformation. Just as a modernist artist sifts what is living from what is dead in the tradition and puts the former to new uses, so the modernist Christian plays off parts of the heritage against others and assumes no part of it without putting it through the crucible of contemporary adult spiritual awareness. The postmodern Christian juggles elements from tradition, often in a citational, ironic or eclectic mode. Where the modernist struggles for truth and vision, the postmodernist adopts a mere style and is 'just gaming'. Those who think of the postmodern condition as a happy one rejoice in invigorating dispersal, constant improvisation, decentralized vitality. But there's a tiredness about it too, a sense of the faded glow of the sixties – a libertarian sixties turned sour and decadent, not the liberationist sixties which remain as a prophetic challenge inaudible to postmodern ears. As postmodern inspiration plays itself out it takes on a pallid hue, and its weary sophistication recalls the sensibility of a Roderick Usher impotently registering from his armchair the slow crumbling of his house, the shrieks of madness from its crypts.

Alacartism at its best signifies the emergence within Catholicism of the Protestant principle, not only in its modern form (liberal Protestantism), but in a continuation of the modernist retrieval of Luther and of St. Paul partly achieved by Kierkegaard and the early Barth. It is from this marginal position rather than from one of angry alienation that the deconstruction of Irish Catholicism, its retrieval for the play of the Spirit, can best be carried out, but only if the marginalized groups are sufficiently free in their minds not to fall into a stereotyped and embittered anticlericalism. The best guarantee against this is theological education, a commodity still unavailable in most of Ireland's universities. Such education can give *à la carte* Catholics confidence that the stubborn dogmatism they are up against draws its vitality above all from a profound ignorance, and that their own search for essential Christianity is far more in accord with the message of Scripture and with the best contemporary theological reflection. Great is the power of the negative if it unfolds as a dialectic of reason, and of critical faith. But if criticism in turn becomes an emotive fixation it only adds to the prevailing paralysis. The Irish world of faith offers rich matter for interpretation, for a hermeneutics which will bring to bear on it all the most sophisticated techniques of critical inquiry, a hermeneutics which should be sympathetic enough to release those who conduct it from the sterility of mere carping. Of course the critique cannot be purely emotionless, but has to be guided by what Heidegger would call a fundamental mood or *Grundstimmung*. Hurt, anger, anguish, confusion, a general malaise, are to be found in plenty among Irish Catholics. The critical interpreter must fuse these emotions and raise them to a higher pitch, perhaps to the prophetic anger of a Luther, laced with pity and concern. Nor does the *Stimmung* of celebration of life carry less critical and liberative power.

Modernist sophistication has to be put at the service of an ethical and political imagination, in a spirit of constructive optimism. It is not modernity or modernism as such that can move Ireland forward, but a modern or modernist faith. The core of faith is a capacity to act from conviction. In that sense, it could be argued that the Japanese have much more faith than the Irish, although there is no word in their language for God, and their religions are a charming medley of aesthetic mood and custom. At least they don't wallow in lipservice to things they only partly or halfheartedly believe, and when a faith dies on them they let it die, and move on, making the changes necessary to their new situation. Since the values to which they subscribe are always close to the ground, tried and tested against their daily effect in improving the quality of life, these values have an energizing and regulating effect, building up an ordered and industrious society. Irish values are usually too abstract to inspire such steady, practical faith, and lend themselves to fanaticism, devotionalism and rhetoric. Perhaps we could learn something from the functional Japanese approach to religion, and find a way to give our religious heritage a life-enhancing place in our culture. This would mean admitting the provisionality of our dogmas, identifications, institutions, liturgies, and moral codes, all of which can function as 'skilful means' for guiding our lives and opening an awareness of the absolute only if we refuse to idolize them and immunize them against questioning. Certainly, it would be a big come-down for Irish religiosity to accept this fragile status. But not so big a come-down as its recent sectarian adventures in Northern Ireland have brought about. (Having said this, I should add that Japan is also the capital of postmodern empty-headedness, very evident in its current fads, and that the quiet Irish sense of concern for the neighbour and awareness of the presence of God gives a substance and reality to Irish life which is older and deeper than anything modern or postmodern.)

All religious traditions are relative. They indicate the absolute effectively, and can be bearers of a word from the Lord, only when they are conscious of how much their historical finitude and the very texture of their language testifies to their own relativity. The greatest error of religious thinkers has been authoritarianism, understandable in cultures governed by sacral figures such as kings and priests and subscribing to the absolute authority of sacred texts. The continuation of the religious quest demands now a demythologization of these traditions, a demythologization whose only limits are those prescribed by full exposure to truth. Irish Catholics, who have wasted so much energy on the fine print of ecclesiastical claims, should offer up their religion on the altar of truth and pray: 'Lord, take from us these hallowed constructs, and give back to us only what is true; take these identities, and give us back only some viable paths for continuing to seek you.' Even the monotheistic narration shared by Judaism, Christianity and Islam is perhaps only an expedient means, historically constituted, for narrating the absolute. The absolute is equally manifest in the quite different narratives of Eastern religion, and is most fully revealed in the mutual solicitation of East and West, the biblical word and the Buddhist silence. Christianity thus finds itself anew as one voice in the global polyphony of divine revelation, and is as impoverished when left to itself as an Isolde singing the *Liebestod* without the orchestra.

So far, I have been urging a Protestant-modernist transformation of Irish Catholicism. But there is also much to be said for homelier methods of reform. And there is much to be said against the unhomely methods of the Catholic Restoration. The younger Irish bishops include representatives of both policies. The reforming bishop is likely to work on the renewal of the parish structure and of the clergy, naturally, since he is the kingpin in both. This renewal comes late in the day and many opportunities have been lost. Nor can it fully meet the needs of Irish Catholicism today, since the greatest promise of renewal seems to lie with small groups working outside the parish structures. Such groups – born again Christians, charismatics, political action groups, co-counselling groups, bible discussion groups – are often looked on with suspicion by the clergy. The more disorderly and uncontrollable Christianity they herald is however a necessary supplement to the traditional structures, for though the parish and the clergy still have sufficient vitality to blossom anew, and though these structures remain necessary for the stable functioning of the Christian community, not all Catholics can find a meaningful religious identity in relation to these structures. Inter-denominational communities, or simple 'human communities' with a religious tinge, are also beginning to emerge here and there, and they promise to bring a clearer perspective and fresher air to the spiritual quest of the Irish people.

The restorationist movement is probably the most vital in Ireland in recent years, and is in line with the 'retrenchment' reflected in recent Vatican policies in the appointment of bishops, the disciplining of theologians, and the promotion of such movements as Opus Dei. What is most disturbing about this trend in the Irish context is its narrowly sectarian understanding of Catholicism and its imperviousness to the challenge to outgrow such sectarian identity which both the Gospel and the world present. If one can grant that anything savouring of denominationalism puts one directly in league with the hatred and terrorism of Northern Ireland, then it is disturbing to reflect that almost everything in Irish Catholicism seems to carry this denominationalist taint: the imposition of Catholic ethics in legislation and through Catholic control of hospitals and schools, the gut-level reaction against interdenominational schooling, the confinement of belief and devotion to a pre- or anti-ecumenical horizon, the uncritical identification of Catholic with Christian identity, the inability to expose the Church to the critique of the Gospel or the world, or to take seriously the voices of those who claim that they have been crushed by the Church. The Catholic restoration, in which Ireland is offered a place of pride, is a temptation that must be turned down. It is itself a quite postmodern phenomenon, in its excess of medium over message. Spectacular papal travels are emblematic of a multiplication of religious signifiers while the signifieds become increasingly elusive and exiguous. The narcissistic specularity of restorationist consciousness differs immensely from the unbroken faith that sustained the *ancien*

régime in the days before Vatican II. It elicits not faith but the
suspension of disbelief that allows one to enjoy a play. Its
figureheads seem to be enacting a historical drama. Vatican II gave
a small glimpse of what a non-sectarian Church, fully open to free
discussion and the search for truth, might look like; but Vatican II
seems to have failed, not only because of the weak, compromising
character of its documents, but because the *Zeitgeist* recently has
been so opposed to the kind of freedom that the Council fathers
timidly prophesied: freedom to reform social and institutional structures, to set the Church humbly at the service of humanity, to
change the world. Such grandiose political ambitions are seen as
typically unrealistic dreams of the sixties.

So the Church succumbs to postmodernism in both the positive
sense, clutching at the residue of the sixties freedom, now
privatized, and in the negative sense, wallowing in a cult of images.
It may be objected that Catholic values were never so serious and so
militant as in recent years. The Church is battening down its
hatches, cutting off lukewarm members, and rigging itself up as a
mighty ship of state capable of making its majestic moral presence
felt in all the troubled waters of the world. Old and young are fired
by new zeal, and even the children of the sixties find themselves
bending to the prevailing wind. Everywhere in the world bishops
are being appointed who are willing to be the architects of this
Church of the third millennium. Under their leadership the Church,
so the theory goes, is growing smaller, but stronger. Catholic funds
and institutions are coming back to the exclusive control of those
who alone have a right to them, namely, those Catholics who are
100% loyal to Rome.

Certainly, the restorationist movement is not entirely comic, not
entirely a matter of histrionics, opportunist role-playing, rhetorical
inflation. Many of its adherents are 'full of passionate intensity'.
History may be repeating itself as farce, but farce can thicken into
deepest tragedy. The grand opera of late nineteenth-century diplomacy produced the hecatombs of the Somme. The Catholic Church
too has its evil heritage, waiting to be reactivated. This ancient
history is of a piece with totalitarian tendencies in the Church today,
which affect not only the faithful but all States in which the Church
has influence. Of course, every historical institution has its shadow
side, and loyalty to an institution, as to a friend, implies the duty of
being aware of this shadow-side and keeping a critical eye on it.
What is peculiarly dangerous in the case of Catholicism is the creed
that the Church, since it is not a human institution at all but a divine
one, can do no wrong. The Catholic Church has long regarded
certain figures and texts as above suspicion, much as doctrinaire
Marxists used to hallow Marx or Lenin. The lesson we are having to
learn now is that even the pages of the New Testament, and much

more so those of Saints Athanasius, Augustine, Bernard of Clair-vaux, and Thomas Aquinas have to be read with suspicion. Dark currents of history flow to, through, and from these great spiritual monuments. A recognition of this fact does not preclude, but rather enables, a contact of faith with the sublime truths also contained therein. Deconstruction as moral discernment is a duty of adult Christians today. Of course in suspecting the classics it is our own deepest persuasions that we are putting in question *Nostra res agitur*. 'Simple faith' can no longer be used as an excuse for avoiding this awful examination of conscience, for such simple faith turns out on examination to be a quite contorted posture of biblical or born adherence to the letter of some recondite text, the letter that kills.

The major pastoral problem of the Irish Catholic Church is that very many people, including clergy, no longer know why they continue to be Catholics. The meaning of the Gospel has become veiled, or even when that is not the case, the link between the Gospel and the activities of the Church remain disquietingly obscure. The focal point of this religious unease is perhaps the celebration of the Eucharist. When a papal voice in the Phoenix Park thundered 'It is the Mass that matters' one could almost hear the echoes answer: 'It is the Mass that *is* the matter.' An endless song and dance is made about Mass attendance, the crude barome-ter of the nation's faith, and daily attendance is held up as the ideal for the truly religious. Why this obsession with quantity and this lack of concern about the meaning or meaninglessness of what goes on at the ceremony? As long as the priest goes on saying Mass and the people keep on coming, no questions need be posed about Christian identity or the meaning of Christian faith. The Mass is fundamen-tally reassuring. It also has the advantage of being automatic. There is no occasion for disruption, spurts or failures of creativity, or even real communication apart from the stylized sermon-slot. Renewal of the Mass demands a total renewal of Catholic life: better art and architecture, better theology, a greater capacity for emotional and spiritual expression. But above all what it demands is a learning attitude towards religion, including a willingness to expose and share one's doubt, anxiety and questioning. As long as we feel we have it all wrapped up, the Mass will continue to be a routine, stifl-ing the emergence of any word from the Lord.

But the Mass is only the main instance of the Irish ability to wallow in token religious gestures and in lipservice to what is no longer a matter of real conviction. The very depth of the crisis of faith, or of the oblivion of what faith means, forbids the kind of discussion which could get to the roots of the malaise and reveal us to ourselves in all our poverty. We fear such a revelation, for we imagine it would leave us with nothing. But if the word of the Gospel can be heard again, that return to nakedness might also be the discovery of fresh possibilities. Let psychoanalysis serve as an encouraging analogy: only by tracing the deep hurts underlying its present sclerosis can the Church hope to recover a viable *raison d'être*. It fears the pain of this probing, and prefers to hold on to its surface equilibrium rather than embark on a process so upsetting.

It is very difficult to undertake a serious quest for religious truth – which must also be a quest for human truth – in a culture where every religious possibility has been mapped out in advance in a conventional frame of reference. Those who find the parish churches deadening often have nowhere to turn. Hence the need of alternative movements running across denominational lines and remaining free of church control. Such movements should breathe the spirit of play and celebration, a mood which more than any other can solicit (cause to tremble) the heavy, dull routine of the institution. Alternative movements would not replace the main bodies of the Churches, but would play deconstructively around their margins, parasites or gadflies, making more imaginative use of the resources of tradition than can the archaic giants whose slumbers they incommode. The continuation of the tradition as a living thing demands this multiplication of voices, this decentralization. Such a freer approach to the religious debate is supposed to lead to 'religious indifferentism'. But there is a very salutary form of indifferentism which takes lightly the historic differences between the Christian denominations.

If the Irish Catholic Church could become a place of free exchange and communication, untold spiritual energies would be released. Free speech is the foremost clue to the solution of the malaise. The obstacles to it include the sense of inferiority induced in most Irish Catholics by the teaching of their Church, and by the powerlessness and passivity to which its structures condemn the laity and the lower clergy; the cowardice and prudent trimming which are part and parcel of clerical culture; the lack of a secure perspective and an articulate theological language in which to identify the problems – because of this lack people fear to open their mouths lest they reveal their own confusion, making fools of themselves, and disturbing the faithful. The attack on the media conducted by conservative Irish Catholics often springs from a fear of free discussion. A phobic attitude to the media often stems from a fear of being honest, and of having to answer awkward questions. Irish clerical conservativism conceives itself as a bulwark of reason and common sense against the emotivism of the Church's critics. In reality this is a deceptive self-image. Very often the rationality on which people pride themselves consists in a refusal of thinking and questioning outside certain tight limits. The underlying emotions, when they burst out, either in victory or in defence, are rather unattractive ones. Irish clergy often appeal to the people's will as the justification of their acts or lack of action. Thus the arguments for mixed schooling in Northern Ireland are rejected on the grounds that it is not what the people want. The people's devotions, which the clergy handle with kid gloves, when they do not go overboard in support of them, have increasingly taken a primitive hue, for as the Church turns its back on rational debate, hyper-emotional religiosity gushes in to fill the vacuum. It is clear that the people need to be educated on how to outgrow sectarianism, how to respect the rights of minorities, and how to find the meaning of the Gospel in a realistic and effective form.

The hope of Ireland is the honesty of its disaffected Catholics (or those clever enough to be able to stay on as *à la carte* Catholics). The straight talk and penetrating analysis that has been pouring from their lips in recent years has greatly helped to clarify our religious situation. What needs to be urged, however, is that this critical movement not consider itself to be cut off from the heritage of Gospel faith. It should confidently claim the Gospel for itself, even against the Church. If it does so, it may bring about a wider religious and human vision, which could once more make our country's voice one of the respected voices in the concert of civilization.

— PART IV —
INTERNATIONAL PERSPECTIVES —

The Debate on
European Cultural Identity*

THE CULTURAL STORM
ALBERTO MORAVIA
(*Trans*. Joseph Long)

The first metaphor which comes to mind when one thinks of Europe
and her history – which is nothing else than the history of the West
from its origins to the present day – is the image of a rich and
precious fabric showing two sides. On one side are the specific
feudal, monarchal and national characteristics and differences. On
the other, the cultural universalism of Europe. On the first side, a
multicoloured, patchwork cloth. On the other, a single colour,
vibrant and deep. And throughout the course of her history, Europe
has shown herself draped sometimes in one side, sometimes in the
other side of this thousand-year-old mantle. But such a metaphor
has the fault of being too calm and unconcerned, too elegant.
Above all, it does not indicate that the relationship between universalism and the specific differences has never been an easy or
continuous one, but on the contrary, a dialectical, even dramatic
one, with sudden and explosive interruptions, contrasts and
upheavals.

Perhaps a different metaphor will better help us understand what
one can only call the tragedy of the European spirit: a metaphor
drawn from the ever excessive climate of the tropics. In Africa, as
you know, there is a season of rains and a season of drought. Africa
lives out the drama of its existence between these two moments of
excess. If you would know what a storm really is, you must go to
Africa during the rainy season; if you would know what drought

*The following are extracts from the *Symposium International sur L'Identité
Culturelle Européenne* held in Paris, 1988. The contributions, from seventy-eight
leading European intellectuals, have been published in French by Albin Michel,
Paris, under the title *Europe sans Rivage*. We wish to thank the publishers Albin
Michel for permission to translate the extracts below and also the French Ministry
of Foreign Affairs who hosted the Symposium.

really is, you must likewise go to Africa on the eve of the rains, when the reservoirs are dry and the ground is cracked and split by the great thirst working within it.

The first sign of storm at daybreak is a gathering of black clouds, like a forehead puckered by evil thoughts. Then the lightning zigzags across this threatening curtain with ever more blinding flashes, soon followed by the growl and crash of thunder. Then comes a cold, raging wind which shakes every growing thing from the blade of grass to the baobab. And then, at last, the rain: the heavens literally open and torrents of water pour down upon the earth. They fall – and here reality and metaphor merge into one – without any account of where they fall, without a thought for frontiers, possessions or boundaries, and wherever they do fall, they slake the earth, impartially. And that African storm, dramatic and universal as it is, is European culture in its finest moments. The lands slaked and rendered fertile by the storm, divided as they are by boundaries, frontiers and possessions, are the specific national characteristics. The state of things today is this: the European spirit is not always there to be seen, and when it is, it is not calm and decorous like the cloak with its two sides. It is dramatic and explosive, like a hurricane. And the specific national characteristics and differences, like lands flooded by that beneficial wave, would languish without the storm, and finally die for lack of creative renewal.

But let us leave metaphors aside and declare bluntly that there was more European spirit, more European cultural universalism, two centuries ago than there is today. The European spirit was so teeming and creative then, that it transcended the narrow boundaries of Europe and spread further afield, beyond the Atlantic to America, and later beyond the Ural across all Russia. It is the European spirit that created what we call the super-powers: it can be seen not only in their constitutions, but also in every aspect of the daily life of those two countries.

The specific differences have had less positive a history. They were for a long while regarded as the glory of Europe, but their rapid degeneration shows that their glory, without the support of the European spirit, without European cultural universalism, can only reveal itself to be mediocre and empty. The Europe of nations provoked the First World War, which was the war of all nationalisms in arms against each other. Then, to free herself from nationalism decayed into fascism, Europe struggled against herself. But unable to win the battle alone, she had to appeal to the two super-powers, the United States and the Soviet Union. Such is the history of latter-day Europe and of her strange and despairing struggle against herself, from which she has emerged exhausted, but from which tomorrow there may emerge a new European spirit –

the beneficial storm which once again will render fertile her lands overcome by drought.

As a member of the European Parliament, I attended the session during which the President of the United States spoke to the people of Europe. At first sight, it was a depressing spectacle. Ronald Reagan was speaking, and whatever he said, one half of the Assembly would applaud unconditionally, and the other half, equally unconditionally, would show its disapproval. What I had before me was a thumbnail sketch of what Europe is today, divided as it is into nations in turn divided into so-called left and so-called right, that is, into parties of conservation and of revolution. As for the European spirit, it was most noticeable by its absence.

Then, upon reflection, I felt less pessimistic. Yes, indeed, Europe was a weak and divided continent, caught between two monolithic and over-armed super-powers. But within these two super-powers, there is no revolutionary party, there is only a conservative party. And one can understand why: what Europe gave to the two super-powers at the moment of her greatest expansion is still thriving and effective and should not at any price be changed.

It is precisely this monolithic character of the two super-powers that may tomorrow leave them once more in Europe's debt – when Europe finds the strength to forge a new spirit from her dramatic division, a new universal and creative response to the questions of the modern world. The world of tomorrow may well be neither American nor Soviet, but once more European. But such a wish, of course, concerns an invigorated European culture, which even in the case of ultimate defeat could never display a calm acceptance of inevitable fate, but must once again give dramatic proof of a spirit of liberty and creativity, intransigent and extreme.

A EUROPEAN CULTURAL 'IDENTITY'

EDGAR MORIN

(*Trans*. Phyllis Gaffney)

At the outset, let me make it clear that I am perfectly aware that the concept of identity is extremely complex, that the concept of culture is polysemic, and that Europe is a concept at the same time multi-faceted, fluid and diverse.

Obviously, given the shortage of time, I do not propose to deal with these problems, and I shall embark at once upon the general theme of our discussion: Europe seen from the outside. Seen from

America, for instance, Europe is a united entity – and therein lies the paradox – united precisely by those things that we perceive as differences. Indeed, from the American point of view, Europe is something small, extremely compartmentalised, where frontiers between nations are really frontiers between provinces and where unity is supplied by the cohabitation of the Dutch peasant woman in her clogs, the Basque beret, the Tyrolean yodel, the Venetian gondola, the flamenco, the corrida, and so forth.

Why do such diverse phenomena give us a feeling of unity? Well, doubtless not only because the common feature of this diversity lies in this extreme cultural compartmentalisation, but also because, embedded within each compartment, there are age-old or millenarian historical depths, expressed as much in agricultural traditions (themselves compartmentalised) as in the diversity of domestic architecture, romanesque art, and the gothic art of cathedrals. And so, we have already a negative common feature, if only in the fact (but this presents another problem) that these diverse cultures which are regional, and which can even be microscopic within a single region, are today threatened by a dominant homogenising trend: the common sense of threat is something which, paradoxically, should unite us in the defence of this diversity. The word 'culture', which I have just used, I take almost in the ethnographic sense of the term. But there is another level, another sense of the word 'culture', the sense which is clear to us when we say: Europe is a synthetic product, the synthesis of Judaism, Christianity, Greece and Rome. And, in fact, that second type of culture is not simply a culture of the clerical and intellectual classes, but an important culture, since it has given rise to phenomena which have revolutionised our communities – for example, scientific and technical development.

Now to conceive of Europe as a Judeo-Christian-Graeco-Roman synthesis may be only an approximation for the Middle Ages (a sort of cathedral whose centre of gravity is the Christian faith), but it captures the essence of the second Europe, modern Europe, which springs into being by shattering medieval cultures, which brings in its wake an explosion of ideas with the Renaissance. And the Judaic, Christian, Greek and Roman authorities become separated, estranged, autonomous, entering into a process of new interactions but, above all, of conflict.

God becomes problematical; likewise the world, the physical, natural universe: what is it? And then man himself will become problematical: what is his situation? His destiny? His place? And in this questioning process, rationalism attempts, as we know, to provide the answers. The idea of reason is to become the foundation for everything, all knowledge, even all behaviour. Humanism will found the dignity of man in himself, science will try to unveil the mysteries of the physical universe.

But these answers themselves will continue to provoke new questions, and in the midst of all these elements there is at work what I call 'dialogics', that is to say a combination of dialogue and antagonistic opposition at one and the same time. So that today, when one asks the question: 'What is the essence of European humanism?', one can find two types of pertinent answer. One has been given by Kolakoski. Kolakoski says: the essence of European humanism derives indubitably from the Judaeo-Christian tradition, since God created man in his own image and Jesus came to assume human flesh, form and suffering in order to save mankind. But this is countered by the answer given by another great European philosopher, Patochka. In his view, the essence of European humanism derives indubitably from 5th-century Athens. For that was the moment of history when society was founded upon itself, the moment when citizens were free, the moment when reason became autonomous; thus, European humanism was founded in the Greek city-state.

It is evident that, from the point of view I wish to put forward here, each of these two propositions is absolutely true and absolutely false. Because the founding of European humanism derives from the conflict and collaboration and invisible exchanges between the Judeo-Christian tradition on the one hand, and, on the other hand, the secular Greek tradition which evolved subsequently.

What is striking, if one is talking about conflicts – for European culture can be defined, not in terms of essence, but in terms of multiple conflicts – is the fact that these conflicts and exchanges occur in a common space. In spite of the wars between European countries, right up to the First World War, there is a trans-European zone. This is manifest because as soon as one centre flourishes, bringing innovation, such as the Renaissance in Florence, or humanism in the Netherlands, the trend spreads throughout Europe. When the Renaissance finally reached St Petersburg, an Italian city on ice, it arrived in the new capital of Russia at that very moment when the country was coming back to Europe with Peter the Great – because, in fact, Europe was coming back to Russia. Similarly, the humanism of the Enlightenment started off from one pole. Paris spread its wings across Europe, and, even more extraordinarily, it was from the tiny German town of Jena that the prodigious movement we call Romanticism set out to be diffused throughout the trans-European zone.

Of course, within these traditions, there are national cultures; one can say that France has a culture which tends to be rationalist in emphasis, that England has a culture which tends to value empiricism, Germany a culture which is more inclined to be idealist or metaphysical, and so on. Conflict develops at the heart of every national culture, and this is what makes it fruitful; and I believe a culture is never as great as when that conflict is crystallised in a single thinker, a single creator.

I am going to take three examples very quickly. What is Pascal's greatness? It is that the struggle between doubt and faith arose within him, and at the same time he resolved the conflict in the end by turning faith into a bet, into something risky and random. What is the great quality of German Romanticism? It is its involuted preoccupation with those mysterious Germanic origins which were never latinised, and at the same time its contrary preoccupation made it extrovert, and turned it towards the Mediterranean, towards the land where the orange blossoms, towards Greece which Hölderlin sublimely celebrated. And from the Russian perspective, what could be more powerful than that extraordinary conflict in the Dostoevsky who is revealed to us through *The Brothers Karamazov*, the hero Ivan Karamazov and of course the apologue of the Great Inquisitor?

What is of interest in European culture is that it accelerates the process whereby philosophers seek an absolute foundation for certainty, like Descartes with his 'cogito' or Hegel with his dialectic, and also that this foundation is continuously re-evaluated.

Such was the development that the 19th century believed it could find its foundation, no longer in the foundations of the past, but in the promise of the future, which was to justify the whole of human history, perhaps even the entire development of the world. Stepping-stones on this path were the discovery of historical evolution, and the belief that historical progress would bring the answer to the enigma of humanity, to the enigma of the world: all this to be based on evolutionism.

But in the course of our own century we have come to realise that this, too, is problematical. As Patochka has put it: 'Development is made problematical, and will always be so, because we live in a universe the fundamental meaning of whose evolution we cannot explain, and because we have learned that history features neither automated progress nor remote control by quasi-providential faiths.' We have entered the era of generalised and radicalised problematics, as we are beginning to understand that it is useless to seek a foundation for certainty. And hence we can understand, finally, that European identity resides in that characteristic, extremely intense, extremely rapid dialogical process.

But at the very moment when I try to define what constitutes this specific European-ness, it simply escapes me. Why? Because, of course, our fundamental achievements, the most particularly European products such as science, regionalism and humanism, have been scattered and dispersed throughout the world. Besides, the West, which in the 17th century was only a tiny fraction of Europe, has now expanded into the world, and Europe itself is no longer anything more than a small fraction of the West – the West, that is to say, which includes not only the United States, but even a Siberia which has become Westernised along with the Soviet Union, and even far-off Japan, a mixture of the Far East and the Far West.

We live indeed in a Euro-world, a world dominated by Europe – just as there used to be a Hellenistic world after Alexander's conquest – through which, in effect, all the contributions of European culture have been diffused. This means, in effect, that we are no longer the owners of what used to be, what used to constitute our cultural originality.

So, what is left to us? As I have said, there certainly remains, not the need to defend our cultural diversity artifically, by folklore or museum-lore, but the realisation that even without being the owners, we are the heirs, and must become the custodians, of what used to constitute our originality. In other words, the capacity to bring forward, in particular conditions and in a particular way, ideas with universal potential, while remaining rooted in our particular identity; the idea, precisely, that we can have a plural identity which is local, regional, ethnic, national, European, and I would add planetary, and truly human, without these identities contradicting one another. And furthermore, it is clear that our European as well as our planetary identity are tragically under-developed today.

What remains, I believe, is our ability to become the custodians of the art of posing problems, of that generalised problematics which has informed our culture. Patochka, once again said: 'the posing of problems is the essence of European culture'. But even if I avoid using an essentialist term, I believe that an absolutely motivating element is crucial, which is why we must preserve in our rationality not only critical reason, critical rationality, but also that self-critical rationality which can discern the limits of reason, and the elements in the universe which are incapable of being rationalised.

And we must somehow conceive that this dialogic process in which we confront ourselves is to be dominated, not by a new Hegelian-type unity which would synthesise it, but by a profound awareness for example, that in every faith, in every belief, there is in us an element of doubt and an element of uncertainty which cannot be eliminated, and that in every doubt there is an element of belief, an element of faith, of adhesion to values, which cannot be eliminated. We have to make choices, but we must be aware of this.

This constitutes, I believe, – and I shall end on this point – one of the conditions of a new renaissance, since the Renaissance was the period of the rise of the problematical view of the world while at the same time of an openness to the world. That was when we discovered that man is not at the centre of the universe, but an occupant of a third-class planet, in the third row of the orchestra, the centre of which turns out to be the sun; and at the same time we discovered an unknown world in America, and the civilisations and cultures of the American continent.

Now, today, I believe that the new renaissance means a new opening to the world, a world beside which Copernicus's planet is well and truly out of date, since from now on we dwell on a small planet belonging to a peripheral sun, a suburban sun, which is itself part of a peripheral galaxy of a universe which no longer has a centre.

We must open ourselves to the worlds of other cultures – the Asian cultures which we neglected, and even those ethnic cultures of the American and Amazonian Indians which we despised or destroyed. We can perhaps become the builders of a new renaissance, but it has not been decreed that destiny has chosen us to build that renaissance, it has not been decreed that the universe contains no other cradles for renaissances. It has been said often enough that we live in a universe which has become irreversibly multi-centric. But that is the challenge, and such is our wager.

TOWARDS A EUROPE OF CULTURE AND CONSCIENCE

EDGAR FAURE

(*Trans.* R. Kearney and P. Marsh)

Sometimes the word 'culture' is, quite wrongly, considered as reductive. We often think it is a question of an added or additional value, of which we can see aspects which are perfectly honourable, but which are at the same time somewhat home-spun or of secondary importance – associations for young musicians, films, cinema clubs. The reality of the situation is that the notion of culture must be taken in a much more powerful way. I once tried to express this by using a particular turn of phrase at a Brussels assembly of the European regions. I launched the idea of a 'consciously alert' Europe (*L'Europe conscientielle*), wishing to put the emphasis on 'conscious' so that this description should not be confused with the idea of 'conscientious' which has the more restricted sense of scrupulous or meticulous.

Having championed the idea of Europe since the end of the last war, I have been able to see quite clearly the two main lines which we have followed, and between which we have hesitated because of the demands of other priorities or time-scales. On the one hand an economically united Europe, and on the other a politically united Europe. Moreover, most of us have conceived of such a Europe in political terms. This was the case for those of us who went to a large meeting organised by Winston Churchill at the Albert Hall in 1946 when we expected him to make some announcement about Europe and England's participation within it. He made what was in fact a magnificently pro-European speech, but which finished with these words: 'We must create Europe, but you must start without us.' And this was indeed the case. Encouraged and disappointed at the same time, we undertook to create a Europe without England, and the first idea to present itself at that time was an economic idea, the idea of Europe as outlined in the Schuman plan – a Europe of coal and steel, an important entity but nevertheless quite clearly limited. And then, with one leap, we were launched into the idea of a great European political union.

In 1955 I was called upon to lead the French government, and it was at the Messina conference that the decision was taken to create the European Common Market. We took this decision in a very discreet way. Somebody said to me recently: 'Monsieur Faure, people don't really make enough of the essential role you played in Europe – you should be considered as one of the fathers of Europe.' As I am not without vanity, I was at first very pleased, but as a politician I must above all make concessions to efficiency, and quite often when one wants to make a brilliant success of something, one makes a mess of it. In the situation in which I found myself, with French opinion deeply divided – particularly because of the question of the army and the national flag – with members of the Gaullist party in my government who at the time were not very enthusiastic, had I said: 'Today sees the birth of Europe!' There wouldn't have been a birth, but there would have been a death – mine, the death of my ministry. I took steps to calm things down by saying: 'We must look into the question of customs, tariffs and permits!' The result was that the people who are attracted by great ideas took no interest in the Common Market; and the Common Market ended up by becoming a very considerable reality.

At the moment it is quite clear that the idea of an economically united Europe is being blocked and no advance can be made in this direction without certain political initiatives. We have taken political decisions like creating the European Parliament, which was a good decision. There is one decision which will be much more difficult to take, but nonetheless it is an essential one: to achieve a satisfactory monetary organisation, political decisions have to be made, and it is here that economic and political issues meet up; because if you create a common currency, you are obliged to have minimal coordination of budgetary policy. So at this juncture you cannot ascend to some higher level of economic policy without making certain political arrangements. We have two paths open to us – one of which is difficult because it does not at the moment offer a sufficient prospect of solving the problems of self interest; the other path, which is the political one, is partially blocked and made difficult by conflicts of sovereignty and the desire to hold on to power which are the hallmarks of national administrations.

It is at this point that the whole dimension of culture and conscience comes into play. Because if we succeed in creating a Europe which has both culture and conscience, difficulties which exist in other areas will be seen in a different way. Take, for example, economic problems. Sometimes there is resentment about the idea of Europe amongst the producers of milk products. A region like mine, la Franche-Comté, becomes aware of the fact that it is in competition with, say, Bavaria; but the competition doesn't simply come from Bavaria – there is also competition from Brittany; however nobody in France is asking for France to be divided into two so that Brittany and La Franche-Comté can be in different countries. On the contrary, people will more readily demand that Europe be changed when they see competition between certain regions which are of different nationality.

I would like to go further and emphasise the idea of a 'Europe of culture' in the fullest meaning of the term by returning to the idea of a 'consciously alert' Europe. We are going to have a unique area of activity in 1992. It is the only topic of conversation at the moment. What unique area of activity is this? The unique area of economic activity already exists. What does not exist is the harmonisation of VAT rates, and we must face this problem. People are saying: for the first time we will have an area of economic activity. It's not true. It exists. The only problem, the big problem, is to know how it can work within the different VAT rates. Which is another question, a political question, a question of sovereignty if you like. Well, we shall eventually succeed. But why not take into consideration the common European area of cultural activity? The calculation of VAT may very well be important for vested interests, but one does not live by VAT alone.

How can we further explore the implications of this Europe of culture and conscience? I tentatively mention some of the principal directions. The first concerns education. If we could bring the typologies of education and professional training closer together we might be able to give more credence to the real Europe. There is the Europe of intellectual production, of literature, the arts, cinema, media, television. Why not make our own European soap-operas instead of always importing them from America? And who knows maybe we might even concoct one less soap and less kitsch than most. We also have the old chestnuts of environmental pollution, the threat to the quality of life, the division of labour. I recall once, as Minister of Social Affairs, proposing a European project to eliminate, over a certain number of years, obligatory work in the automobile industry as well as other forms of alienating and dehumanizing labour, such as the three-shift formula or other health-risk schemes. And then there is the question of University education in Europe; the task of making generally acceptable the idea of professors, students and researchers journeying more freely through Europe. Would it not be desirable for a French student doing law, for example, to spend at least one of the four years of his education in Germany studying German Law? Such a notion is not yet feasible of course, for it requires that teachers and researchers can operate on a moveable basis without risk to their career prospects.

Finally, there is the whole international dimension of European culture. It is not a matter of mixing up ministries of Foreign Affairs but of creating a common state of mind with regard to international problems. One hears much talk of a Europe of defence (no easy matter); but why not talk of a Europe of disarmament? A Europe of peace capable of pronouncing on the crucial subjects hitherto confined to Misters Reagan and Gorbatchev? Is there not something surreal about an East-West dialogue from which Europe is absent, with its enormous weight of civilization, culture, soul? Europe could well be making its voice heard, saying: 'Look at what we, who have no ambition for hegemony, propose'.

There is also our relationship with the Third World. Would it not be possible to interest European youth in the ideal of a European conscience and consciousness by saying: 'Seek a politics of solidarity which gives European milk quotas to countries which are starving or suffer from protein deficiency conducive to serious illness. Just think that with one per cent of the France-Compté milk quota we could save 100,000 people a year'. And should we not be thinking about confronting the European epidemic of youth unemployment? In my own little domain as President of the Assembly of European Regions, we are launching a European youth travel project which is not a matter of tourism or student exchanges but of finding real jobs on a temporary basis for young people from the different countries of Europe. The project is based on the principle that if a youth can actually work in another country, he or she will acquire a consciousness which could not be gained from a quick hitchhike trip or visit to a university for a few weeks. I would like to see work schemes for European youths lasting for six months. And we will manage it by applying the same system that I applied to professional employment: we will find companies, industries, garages, boutiques and say to them: 'If you take on a young European we will facilitate your social security payments and you will have the benefit of a foreign language in the family'. So when we've settled a hundred Europeans in Besançon, we'll settle a hundred Besançonians in other European countries, enabling each to experience something of the life of another culture. And, of course, there is no reason this scheme couldn't be used to promote the European spirit by encouraging cooperative work and intellectual assistance in Third World countries to help combat the enormous poverty there.

The last point I would like to emphasize is the considerable role which the regions of Europe can play in the task of culture and conscience. For inter-regional collaboration is not hamstrung by problems of sovereignty and political protocol. I cannot overstate how struck I have been by the way in which regional meetings and assemblies have been able to incarnate the European spirit of the heroic period of Monnet and Schuman. It has been a truly great joy to witness.

EUROPE SEEN FROM ELSEWHERE

WIM WENDERS

(*Trans.* Richard Kearney)

'European cultural identity' . . . I am still trying to understand what each of these words means, and what they mean together. In spite of all the philosophical and historical accounts I've been hearing or reading about in recent days, I am still struggling with these three words, trying to form an image or emotion around them.

A path for my reflections was indicated by the title 'Europe seen from elsewhere'. *Seen*, *see*, that interested me. Seeing is my profession: I make films. I decided to try to see Europe, rather than analyse it.

'Europe seen from elsewhere' . . . I said to myself: it is because you have lived and worked in the United States that you've been given the task of looking from 'elsewhere'. And not without reason, I must admit. After all, wasn't it when I was abroad, away, in the States, that I first defined myself as a European. 'I am a European film-maker', I would say. Once I had so defined myself, once I had accepted that I was not and never would be an 'American film-maker', once I was therefore ready to return home, because of and for the sake of these definitions, I found myself saying: I am going back to Europe. I didn't say, to Germany. I didn't say, to France. I said, to Europe. Was it the distance that accounted for this new definition of my origins? Was it perhaps because, seen from the United States, all European countries appear small or shrunken? I do not think so. It was not a matter of distance or of geographical size. When I was over there in America there was something fundamental I so badly, so urgently needed that it wasn't enough to say: I am going back to Germany or I am going back to France. Europe alone was where I felt destined for; it alone corresponded to what I needed and desired.

Why did I never feel this need before, when I still lived in Europe. Why did Europe only become visible from afar, and not from within? Sometimes, you have to lose something in order to appreciate it. But what was it I had lost in going to America? Was it, in brief, an identity? Which? Why? Was it because I couldn't become American, or was it rather because I could and did?

Let me go back a moment and try to grasp, by association, the terms I am dealing with. Identity – what helps overcome the fear of nothingness. Lack of identity – that, in my view, means anguish. Loss of identity – despair, death. Identity would be for me a weapon of protection. Earth under one's feet, security, force, pride. And then the combination of the two words – cultural identity – what does that mean for me? An identity with a culture, through a culture, in a culture, by a culture. And 'culture', what does that mean – if not food for the soul? It is something that helps you survive, physically and morally. I think I did suffer a loss of identity in America; my soul wasn't sufficiently nourished. I think that was my malady over there.

It seems to me now that my German identity wasn't enough to protect me. It wasn't able to resist the American temptation; but fortunately I had another protective skin which did resist. Under my German coat I discovered a European coat of armour. One isn't nourished well in the United States. But that is another subject: American culture, American identity, the terrible feeling of inferiority towards the Europeans which goes hand in hand with a terrible feeling of superiority. I am the last to accuse them; and I am not going to go on about American imperialism. On the contrary, I pity the Americans because they are missing something. They are all alone with their problem of nationality, nationalism, superiority and inferiority, while we in Europe are well used to these problems. We have suffered from them; and we have made others suffer from them. Especially us, the Germans. But we in Europe – at least, that's my experience – had some protection; we all lived in the same house together. Our national identities lived and still live under the one roof which protected them all: Europe.

I spoke earlier of a European profession. The European art and language *par excellence* is cinema. There has been no better expression of European identity in this century than European cinema. Better than all the other arts in their national expressions. Let me cite here the great European artists Eisenstein, Dreyer, Lang, Renoir, Rossellini, Bunuel, Truffaut, Tarkovski, as well as all those still working, such as Fellini, Antonioni, Godard, Bergman, Angelopoulos. Where does the list stop? European cinema is alone in a position to give some moral dignity to the cacophony of televisual communications by satellite and cable which is inundating us more and more. This inflation of images threatens to bring about the same loss of identity caused by American images and television. This is why we must protect European cinema, European images, our common art and language.

I don't care about defining this art. I don't care about defining a European cultural identity. The important thing is that it exists. It has often been described as undiscoverable but evident. I pray it will remain undiscovered so as to remain evident. I hope we will all remain French, German, English, Irish, Portuguese, Greeks and Swedes – provided we share this evidence which is European identity. And provided we preserve the privilege of living under the same roof of this citadel called Europe.

DIALOGUE WITH THE 'OTHER' EUROPE

JULIA KRISTEVA

(*Trans* R. Kearney)

The cultural unity of Europe that we are in the process of seeking and saluting, has an ethical and spiritual foundation. And whatever differences of tradition exist, there are also convergences to be identified. A spiritual unity – I retain the image of that Europe extending from the Atlantic to the Urals which is particularly important to me: in part because it determined my destiny, but more especially because I understand it in the sense of de Gaulle – a sense which is interesting at a pragmatic level and which transcends all partisan divisions. The phrase 'from the Atlantic to the Urals' refers to the 'place' of Europe. As an image it was invoked in the name of both spiritual preoccupations and of political and economic conditions which would correspond to such a spiritual reality. I would like here to make some practical suggestions for the future.

Eastern Europe, it has been said, is like the pain of an amputated limb. My own experience, however, as someone from the East and also as a teacher, has shown me that it is also a reservoir of enthusiasm. I'm thinking particularly of the hunger for culture, and especially Western culture, which the young generations there experience. And it seems to me that this cultural hunger today is taking the role of faith and replacing that weariness with culture and civilization which is often felt here in the West in the guise of a cultural crisis.

My attitude towards this 'adjoining Europe' (*Europe mitoyenne*) is neither one of absolute pain nor of paradoxical optimism; it is an attitude which might be formulated in this question: are we ready to respond to the desire in these young generations for Western culture in contrast to the prevailing disillusionment and crisis of faith?

In this perspective, I would like to make some practical proposals. I have the impression that the policy of awarding grants to applicants from Eastern Europe in recent years – whether it be at national or European level – is essentially geared towards the technical sciences. Such an attitude fits in with the technological unification of Europe – something very useful but, I fear, too conducive to uniformity. And I wonder if a policy rethink which laid more emphasis on the *human sciences* might not be more interesting from the point of view of our present debate – for it would be in a position to respect the symbolic particularities and differences while cultivating that European spirit which resides in the humanities themselves.

It seems to me important, therefore, that we emphasize the human sciences while also declaring an increased interest in the reception of grant-assisted foreigners. Often these people who are over-supervised in their own countries – it is one of the effects of totalitarianism – find themselves without any supervision here, in a state of solitude and disorientation which impedes rather than assists contact with Western culture. I would recommend therefore that 'European antennae' be set up not only in the *cités universitaires* but in the different universities so as to cater for the leisure activities of these foreigners and ensure their links with native families. This is a problem not yet touched on: if the *family* is a place of national closure maybe we could also try to make it a place of international openness.

One hears much recently about European countries wishing to preserve and expand their languages (English, German, Spanish, French). Contacts with Eastern Europe, while based upon the acquisition of a Western language, should be primarily a dialogue of ideas over and beyond languages. I know that many of the young researchers come here to France to learn the new history, the new critique, the new anthropology – all the methodologies which have been recently developed in the West – while remaining anxious to preserve their national identity. And here we touch on a concern which is also felt today in a culture like France: how to be French *and* European, French *and* international . . . .

How are we to reconcile the concern for national culture with this openness towards an advanced and cosmopolitan Europeanism? I think we should develop more our departments of Slavonic Studies and Slavonic Civilization (for the Slavs are the preponderant grouping in Eastern European countries) as well as others, of course. Polish history, Yugoslav folklore, or Rumanian sociology could all be studied in a new way, bringing the most up-to-date methodologies in the West (which have provoked such interest in young researchers from the East) to bear on the local corpus of material.

A final word on Gorbatchev's celebrated 'perestroika'. According to the most generous hypothesis, it is as yet no more than an intention. But would it be so absurd to grasp this opportunity to try to relaunch the projects of establishing French, Italian, Spanish (etc.) centres of culture in Eastern Europe – projects which have encountered great difficulty to date? And why not centres of European culture in Moscow, Sofia or Warsaw? I was speaking yesterday with the Soviet delegate to this conference, Velikhovski, and he seemed to think that given the present climate in Moscow it might not be at all impossible. Let us take up the Gorbatchev challenge. He wants to be European? Well, let's start with a European centre in Moscow.

I would like to conclude with a wish – still very much utopian. I imagine a future conference where European intellectuals in Eastern Europe (and not simply exiles) will attempt to realize in their own country the link between national concern and the European project that they would have amplified and fortified here in our universities and in our international forums.

A CASE FOR EUROPEAN CULTURAL TELEVISION

GEORGES DUBY

(*Trans.* Johnnie Gratton)

Channel Seven (in French *La SEPT*, standing for *Société d'Édition de Programmes de Télévision*) is a public company, supported by public funds, set up two years ago to help produce television programmes of a cultural nature. Culture, as you know, is an ambiguous word. Let's say that our main concern is one of quality.

No genre or subject-matter is ruled out in advance, we simply apply high standards across the board. We are looking for works of beauty, we want attractive programmes, so that culture will no longer be synonymous with boredom in the mind of the general public. We want a culture accessible to all audiences, not an elitist ghetto. Our wish, then, is to respond to a wide range of audiences.

We are therefore endeavouring to make better use of television. We must get away from apathy and adopt a more active, thoughtful approach. Firmly committed to being cultural, Channel Seven has insisted from the outset, and just as firmly, on being European. Its active function is to feed the French direct broadcast satellite, due to be launched shortly. In fact the best of the channels beamed via this satellite has already been allocated by a decision of government to the public service bodies grouped under the aegis of Channel Seven. As a result, the programmes Channel Seven has been producing and compiling over the last two years, will be transmitted all over Europe.

From the very beginning we have asserted our commitment to Europe and taken care to adjust the company's structures accordingly. Thus we wanted the programming committee to include not only technical experts and persons of culture but a panel of broadcasting professionals, both French and European who would work together in their own right on planning and decision-making. For the time being there are four European members, appointed by production companies which are equally concerned with quality and high standards, in other words with culture: RAI from Italy, the German channel ZDF, Britain's Channel 4, and French-speaking Swiss Television. Indeed two of these top professionals, representing all that is boldest in creative broadcasting across Europe, were entrusted with conceiving Channel Seven's very first appearance on the screen, a two-day package shown by the French station FR3.

This was our way of demonstrating our open-door policy towards Europe, for we have no intention of staying locked inside the French hexagon. On top of this, a number of co-production agreements were signed in 1987, and these are weaving a network of closer and closer relations around Channel Seven, from Austria to Portugal, and as far afield as Iceland. Some of these agreements call for close collaboration and will involve not only exchanges of programmes but a sharing of ideas about the policies we must carry out. Recently a further step has been taken with an agreement between the French and German Ministers for Culture and Communication to set up a process giving German public companies the right to gradually become shareholders in Channel Seven and, rather less gradually, to take seats on its administrative council. We hope that other countries too, such as Italy, Switzerland, Belgium, Spain and Portugal, will follow suit. Let's get together, let's co-operate. So much is at stake it will be worth the effort.

What we are talking about, in fact, is nothing less than an effort to strengthen the European ideal. For it may well be that primarily, by exploiting its cultural resources, Europe can become more fully conscious of its unity and affirm both its identity and its strength in the face of global competition. Over in the East they are waiting for us, beckoning, and we are responding. Links are being forged. We already have a link-up with the German Democratic Republic, and we have made a start with Hungary and Poland. Through culture, through our sense of jointly inheriting the same knowledge, the same set of values and beliefs, I am convirced there exists a real opportunity to close the gap which divide⌐ Europe. The time has come to grasp that opportunity. If the European ideal is to become a reality, it will be to some extent as a result of good television, by which I mean television stubbornly committed to openness and quality. It seems to me that there are three ways of moving towards this goal.

The first job of a European cultural television network is to look after its common heritage, to put its treasures on display. For example, what the BBC began to do when it presented the complete dramatic works of Shakespeare, other nations must also undertake to do. And let's not forget that this heritage of ours also includes the output from television over the last thirty years. Numerous master-pieces lie dormant in the archives, where they are slowly deteriorating. It is up to us to exhume and restore them. Indeed, Channel Seven has already begun the work of salvaging valuable French works.

Another task facing us is to stimulate creativity by commissioning work. How can we drag creativity out of the doldrums? Well, for one thing, by giving a free hand to acknowledged masters of the art of film, the likes of Fellini and Wim Wenders; but also by offering younger up-and-coming talents the chance to prove themselves. We must encourage writers and artists who still shun television to work directly for the medium. We must be more imaginative and experimental in the way we relate to cinema, in the way we make use of it. I also think it crucial that we should support the idea of setting up workshops for European scriptwriters. Our plan is to bring about a television service nourished by genuine creative writers to breathe new life into the very language of television.

Our third and final mission is to bring the various cultural regions of Europe into closer contact with one another, to break down the walls which still partition Europe, to restore each of these regions to its rightful place in a cultural spectrum at long last assured of its own vitality. Here too there is no lack of demand, as was made quite evident just last June with the success in France of Channel Seven's second day on FR3, entirely devoted to Berlin on the occasion of its 750th anniversary as a capital city. That a broadcasting event such as this should so instantly have earned double the normal expression of satisfaction among its audience leaves us in no doubt. Right across Europe people would like to get to know their neighbours better. They want to know what unites them but also what distinguishes them in this diverse cultural space we call Europe.

Such diversity, of course, is likely to be our main source of problems. The most obvious stems from the multiplicity of languages, though equally tough obstacles arise at a more basic level. From one area to another we think, behave and live differently. Then there is the simple fact that we don't all take our meals at the same time, or that in Holland, Poland, Finland and Spain children don't all go to school at the same time. Technology and dialogue, however, promise gradually to resolve such practical problems. By means of satellites we can now take advantage of sophisticated procedures to translate pre-recorded programmes and fit them into a variety of schedules. What matters is the will to work in unison to open doors, break down barriers and keep exchanging information.

I like to think of European cultural television as a fertile crossroads for all kinds of initiative and talent. Our aim is to foster better mutual understanding in order to reinforce a deep sense of community. While at the same time preserving and strengthening the identity of cultural zones which don't necessarily coincide with state frontiers. I am sure all Europeans look forward to this. It will of course take time, but I am convinced that in the end, if we persevere, if we pool our efforts, our hopes will not have been in vain.

Notes on the Postmodern Debate

JEAN-FRANÇOIS LYOTARD

(*Trans.* Thomas Docherty)

Preview for a New Stage*

The thought and action of the 19th and 20th centuries are governed by the idea of the emancipation of humanity. This idea fashions itself at the end of the 18th century in the philosophy of the Enlightenment and in the French Revolution. Progress in science, technology, arts and political liberty would free humanity entirely from ignorance, poverty, barbarism, despotism, and will not only produce happy people but also (notably thanks to the Academy) will provide enlightened citizens who are masters of their fate.

All the political currents of the last two centuries, with the exception of traditional reaction and Nazism, spring from this source. Between political liberalism, economic liberalism, Marxism, anarchism, 3rd Republican radicalism, socialism, the divergences, even the strong divergences, count for little beside the unanimity which reigns regarding goals to be attained. For all, the promise of liberty is the horizon of progress and its legitimation. All these lead to – or believe that they lead to – a humanity which is transparent to itself, to a world citizenship.

These ideals are in decline in the general opinion of those countries known as 'developed'. The political class continues to talk in the rhetoric of emancipation, but it doesn't manage to heal the wounds which have been made in the 'modern' ideal during some two hundred years of history. It is not the lack of progress, but on the contrary the developments in technoscience, arts, economics and politics which have made possible total wars, totalitarianisms, the widening gap between the wealthy North and the poor South, unemployment and the 'new poverty', a general deculturation with the crisis in the academies, that's to say in the transmission of knowledge, and the isolation of the artistic avant-gardes (and today for a time their disavowal).

*Originally published as 'Billet pour un nouveau décor' in *Le Postmoderne expliqué aux enfants* (Galilée, Paris, 1985). Another English version has been published in *Copyright*, No. 1, 1987.

You can put names to all these wounds. They are strewn across the field of our unconscious like so many secret hindrances to the peaceful perpetuation of the 'modern project'. Under the pretext of safeguarding the latter, men and women of my generation in Germany have, for forty years, imposed a silence on their children about the 'Nazi interlude'. This interdiction opposed to remembrance has the value of a symbol for the entire West. Can there be progress without remembrance? Remembrance leads, by painful elaboration, to the articulation of the grief of attachments, of affections of all kinds, loves and fears, which are associated with these names. I admired the fact that the federal authority had sunk into the utopian lawn of the Mall in Washington the sombre trench lit by candles which is called the 'Monument for the Dead in Vietnam'. For the instant, we are only at a vague 'fin de siècle' melancholy, which is apparently inexplicable.

This decline of the 'modern project' is not, however, a decadence. It is accompanied by the apparently exponential development of technoscience. Now, there is not, and never will be any more, any loss or regression in knowledge or know-how, except in the destruction of humanity. This is an original situation in history. It translates an ancient truth which explodes on us today with a particular evidence. Never has scientific or technical discovery been subordinated to the demands issuing from human needs. It has always been moved by a dynamic which is independent of that which men have been able to judge desirable, profitable, comfortable. The desire for knowledge and know-how is incommensurable with the demand for benefit that one may hope for from their aggrandisement. Humanity has always found itself belated with respect to the capacities for understanding (the 'ideas'), and for acting (the 'means'), which result from inventions, discoveries, research and chance.

Today three facts are remarkable: the fusion of techniques and sciences in the enormous technoscientific apparatus; the revision in all the sciences, not only of hypotheses, or even of 'paradigms', but of ways of reasoning, of logics considered as 'natural' and imprescriptibles: paradoxes abound in the theories governing maths, physics, astrophysics, biology; finally a qualitative transformation brought about by new technologies: the machines of the last generation accomplish operations of memory, consultation, calculation, grammar, rhetoric and poetry, reasoning and judgment (expertise). They are extensions of language, that's to say, of thought, still summary but called upon to refine themselves in the next decades when their software will be in proportion to the complexity of the logics used in the most advanced research.

It has become evident, after the fact, that the work accomplished by the artistic avant-garde during more than a century inscribes itself in a parallel process of complexification. This has to do with sensibility (visual, auditory, motor, linguistic), and not with knowledge or know-how. But the philosophical import or, if you will, the powers of reflexion which these works bring in their wake, is no less in matters of receptivity and 'taste' than is the change brought about in technoscience in matters of intelligence and method.

What is sketched out thus as a horizon for your century is an increase in complexity of most domains, including 'lifestyles', everyday life. And a decisive task is thereby circumscribed: to make humanity able to adapt itself to great complexity in the ways of feeling, of understanding and of doing which are in excess of what it needs. It implies at least the resistance to simplicity, to simplifying slogans, to demands for clarity and facility, to desires for the restoration of sure values. It appears already that simplification is barbarous, reactionary. The 'political class' will have to take this exigency into account, as it must already be doing, if it does not want to become obsolete, or to drag humanity down with it in its demise.

A new stage is slowly putting itself in place. To sketch in its cruder details: the cosmos is the dropout of an explosion; the debris is still spreading itself in the aftermath of this inaugural push; the stars transmute the elements by their burning; their days are numbered; as are those of the sun; the chance that the synthesis of the first algae took place in the Earth's water was pretty low; the Human is even less probable; its cortex is the most complex material organisation that we know; the machines which it engenders are an extension of it; the network that they will form will be like a second cortex, more complex; it will have to solve the problem of the evacuation of humanity, before the death of the sun; the sorting out of those who can leave from those doomed to the implosion has already begun, in terms of 'under-development'.

Final achievement of humanity's narcissism: it is in the service of complexification. This decor is inscribed in the unconscious of youth from now on. In yours.

Svelte Appendix to the Postmodern Question*

Here are some remarks without theoretical pretention and in no particular order.

One hears it said everywhere that the great problem of society today is that of the State. This is a mistake, and a serious one. The

---

*Originally published as 'Appendice Svelte à la questian postmoderne' in *Tombeau de L'intellectuel*, Galilée, Paris, 1984. 'Sveltesse' is difficult to translate. It means a kind of slimness or slenderness, but carries connotations of a 'litheness' or 'malleability' (trans.). An alternative and abbreviated version of this paper was published in *Cultural Critique*, Vol. 5 (1987), trans. Massumi under the title 'Rules and Paradoxes and Svelte Appendix'.

problem which outweighs every other, including that of the contemporary State, is the problem of capital.

Capitalism is one of the names of modernity. It presupposes the compression of the infinite into an instance already described by Descartes (and maybe by Augustine, the first modern), which is that of the will. Literary and artistic romanticism thought it was struggling against this realist, bourgeois and shopkeeper's interpretation of the will as infinite enrichment. But capitalism knew it had to subordinate the definite desire for knowledge which motivates the sciences, and to submit the realisation of that desire to the criteria of technicity which is capitalism's own; the rule of performativity which exacts the endless optimisation of the expenditure/revenue input/output relation. And romanticism was thrown back, still kicking, into the culture of nostalgia (Baudelaire: 'the world will end'; the commentaries of Benjamin) whereas capitalism was becoming, has become, a figure which is not 'economic', not 'sociological', but metaphysical. The infinite is posed in capitalism as that which has not yet been determined, as that which the will must indefinitely master and appropriate to itself. It bears the names of chaos, energy, and it gives rise to research and development. It must be conquered, or be made the means to an end, and that end is the glory of the will. A glory itself infinite. In this sense, the real romanticism is capital.

What strikes one on returning to Europe from the United States is the weakening of the will, at least as taken in these terms. The 'socialist' countries also suffer from this anaemia. Will as infinite power and as the infinite of 'realisation' cannot allow itself to be instanced on one State, which exploits it for its own survival, as if the State was an end in itself. The will needs only a minimum of institutionalisation to take wing. Capitalism does not like order, it's the State that likes it. Capitalism does not have as its end a technical, social or political work which would be made according to rules, its aesthetic is not that of the beautiful but of the sublime, its poetic that of genius, creativity in capitalism is not bent to rules, it invents rules.

Everything that Benjamin describes as 'loss of aura', aesthetics of 'shock', destruction of taste and of experience, is the effect of this will which has little regard for rules. Traditions, statutes, objects and sites charged with the individual and collective past, received legitimacies, images of the world and of humanity coming from classicism, even when they are conserved, are conserved as means to the end, which is the glorification of will.

Marx saw all this very clearly, notably in the *Manifesto*. He tried to show where the figure of capital fell apart. He thought it not as a figure, but as a thermodynamic system. And he showed that (1) it could not control its hot springs, labour-power; (2) it could not control the gap between this supply and its cold springs (feeding through production-value); (3) it would extinguish its hot springs.

Yet capitalism *is* rather a figure. As system, the hot springs are not labour-power, but energy in general, physical energy (the system is not sealed). As figure, its force comes from the Idea of infinity. It can present itself in the experience of people as a desire for money, for power, for novelty. And you may find all that very ugly, very upsetting. But these desires are a translation into anthropological terms of something which is ontologically the 'instantiation' of the infinite upon the will.

This 'instantiation' does not organise itself according to social classes. These are not the pertinent ontological categories. There is no one class which incarnates and monopolises the infinity of will. When I say 'capitalism', that does not mean either the owners or the managers of capital funds. There are thousands of examples which show their resistance to the will, even when that will is a technological one. The same goes for the workers. It's a transcendental illusion to confuse that which is of the order of ideas of reason (ontology) with that which is of the order of concepts of understanding (sociology). This illusion has produced all States, and most notably the bureaucratic States.

When the German philosophers today, or the Americans, speak of the neo-irrationalism of French thought, when Habermas gives lessons in progressivism to Derrida and to Foucault in the name of the project of modernity, they are making a serious mistake about what is at issue in modernity. It was not, and it is not (for modernity is not finished), simply the Enlightenment, what was and is at issue is the introduction of the will into reason. Kant spoke of a thrust in reason to take it beyond experience, and he understood philosophy anthropologically as a *Drang*, as an impulse to fight, or to generate disputes (*Streiten*).

And let's ask ourselves a little about the ambiguity of the aesthetics of a Diderot split between the neoclassicism of his theory of 'relations' and the postmodernism of his writing in the *Salons*, in *Jacques*, and in the *Neveu de Rameau*. The Schlegels didn't go wrong here. They knew that the problem was not just that of consensus (of Habermasian *Diskurs*), but that of the unpresentable, of the unexpected power of the Idea, and of the event as presentation of a sentence that was unknown and unacceptable, but which became accepted through being tried out. The Enlightenment was complicit with preromanticism.

What is decisive in what's been called the postindustrial (Touraine, Bell), is that the infinity of will invests language itself. The great affair for around twenty years, expressed in the flattest terms of political economy and of historical periodisation, is the transformation of language into a productive commodity; sentences considered as messages, to be encoded, decoded, transmitted and arranged (in bundles), reproduced, conserved, kept available (memories), combined and concluded (calculations), opposed (games, conflicts, cybernetics); and the establishment of a unit of measurement, which is also a unit of cost, of information. The effects of the penetration of capitalism into language have only just begun. Under the guise of market-expansion and of a new industrial strategy, the coming century is marked by the investment of the desire for the infinite, according to the criteria of the greatest performativity, in the affairs of language.

Language is the entire social bond (money is but one aspect of language, the accountable aspect, payment and credit, in any case play of differences, of places, of times). It is therefore the living works of the social itself which will find themselves destabilised by this investment. One would be mistaken to fear an alienation from this. That is a concept which comes from christian theology and also from a philosophy of nature. But god and nature must succumb as figures of the infinite. We are not alienated by the telephone, nor by television as means (media). Nor will we be alienated by language machines. The only danger is that the will will abandon them to States whose only care is to survive, that's to say make themselves credible. But it's no alienation to have the human give way to a complex aleatory assembly of (innumerable) operators transforming messages (Stourdzé). Messages are themselves only metastable states of information, subject to catastrophes.

With the idea of postmodernity, I situate myself in this context. And in this context, I say that our role as thinkers is to deepen awareness of what is at issue in language, to criticise banal ideas of information, to reveal an irremediable opacity in the heart of language itself. Language is not an 'instrument of communication', it's a highly complex archipelago made from domains of sentences belonging to regimes so diverse that one can't translate a sentence from one regime (a descriptive for example) into a sentence in another (an evaluative, a prescriptive, say). Thom writes in this sense: 'An order contains no information'. All the researches of the avant-gardes in science, literature and the arts during the past century have gone in this direction, laying bare the incommensurability of regimes of phrases with each other.

The criterion of performativity, from this point of view, appears as a serious invalidation of the possibilities of language. Freud, Duchamp, Bohr, Gerturde Stein, but also before them Rabelais and Sterne are postmodern insofar as they put the stress on paradoxes, which always testify to the incommensurability I'm speaking of. And they thereby find themselves nearest to the capacity and method of ordinary language.

What you call French philosophy of the last years, if it has been postmodern in any way, has been so by dint of its reflections on the deconstruction of writing (Derrida), on the disorder of discourse (Foucault), on epistemological paradox (Serres), on alterity (Levinas), on the effecting of meaning by the nomadic encounter (Deleuze); thus has it put the accent on incommensurabilities.

When one reads Adorno now, especially in texts such as *Aesthetic Theory, Negative Dialectic, Minima Moralia*, with these proper names in one's head, one is alive to what there is of anticipation of the postmodern in his thought, even though it remains most often reticent, or refused.

What moves him to this refusal is the political question. For if my hasty and crude description of the postmodern here is correct, what then of justice? Does what I have to say lead to recommending the politics of neo-liberalism? I don't think so at all. Neo-liberalism is itself a red-herring here. The reality is concentration in industrial, social and financial empires, served by States and the political classes. But it begins to appear that, on the one hand, these monopolitical monsters do not work for every eventuality and that they may be blockages of the will (which we call barbarism); on the other hand, work in the nineteenth-century sense is that which should be abolished, and by means other than unemployment. Stendhal, at the beginning of the nineteenth century, said it already: the ideal is no longer that of the physical force of ancient man, it is that of suppleness, speed, a capacity for metamorphosis (you go dancing at night, and at dawn the following morning you go into battle). Svelteness, alertness, a zen and italianate term. It's a quality of language *par excellence*, because language needs very little energy to create something new (Einstein in Zurich). Language machines are not expensive. That already throws the economists into despair; they will not absorb, they say, the huge overcapitalisation from which we suffer now that growth is at an end. That's probably so. We must therefore reconcile the infinity of will with svelteness: much less 'working', much more learning, knowing, inventing, circulating. Justice in politics comes from a push in this direction. (We must one day come to an international accord on the concerted reduction of time spent working without a diminution in purchasing power.)

Passages to Postmodernism

THOMAS DOCHERTY

epigraph: 'a place takes place by itself . . . ' J. F. Lyotard

Thirty or so years ago, intellectuals found themeselves in the midst of 'The Structuralist Controversy', for which the institution of the Academy was somewhat unprepared. To announce then that one was or was not a structuralist was a call-to-arms, and not just the statement of a critical position. Today, arms have been taken up, but the controversy has shifted somewhat: we are in the midst of the 'Postmodern Debate'. In this vitriolic controversy, when the reputations of intellectuals are being polemically shot down, perhaps it is better to adopt an attitude of a lithe malleability, a 'shiftiness' which will enable the suave negotiation of the troubled field of postmodernism: 'whatever you say say nothing', as Heaney once suggested.[1] In this shifty article, I 'slip' – from the translations of Lyotard above – 'into something more comfortable', an elaboration in my own voice of the terms of the debate; this postmodernism does say something. The twists and turns of the argument will themselves partly illustrate what I shall refer to as a 'postmodern disposition'. The postmodernist has no single identifiable position; postmodernism demands a lissome 'sveltesse', the ability to more or less elegantly 'dis-position' oneself or to adopt a flexibility in thought and practice. That seductive disposition, I shall argue, is both politically and ethically valuable.

Much of what passes for debate on postmodernism is not debate at all; too often, the opposing camps have different views of what it actually is that they are arguing about. For instance, one way of understanding postmodernism has been to think of it as the cumulative effects of culture, the arts and social life in the West since 1945. This view sees postmodernism as an aftermath of the Modernist cultural experiments of 1870-1939. In this version, postmodernism marks a defined cultural/historical period. As a corollary of this view (held in the main by Marxists), postmodernism comes to mean an art which is characterised by a seeming exhaustion of ideas and by the more or less cynical recycling of older ideas in the eclectic,

---

1. Seamus Heaney, *North* (Faber and Faber, 1975), 57.

pointless form of parody – or worse, pastiche.[2] Those who adopt this view of postmodernism tend, unsurprisingly, to think of it as a somewhat reactionary neo-conservative force, deploying a cultural and aesthetic repertoire but to no real ends, with no desire for progress towards enlightenment or emancipation of humanity, and with no theoretical concern for social justice. In short, having no guiding principle except a kind of repackaging of the past, postmodernism is deemed to have no principles at all – except the late-capitalist principle of persuading consumers to buy the same old artistic commodities, repackaged, time and again. Postmodernism is the banner under which parade those cynical and irrational intellectuals who have (at best) removed themselves from the social domain and from their social and political responsibilities, and (at worst) have given up all their radical credentials, succumbing finally to the advance of Capitalism.[3]

This is, however, an extremely weak understanding of the term. It simplifies to the point of falsification all the complexities of postmodernism, preferring to take an easy path of understanding it as just 'recent/contemporary culture'. Clearly, however, the very term 'postmodernism' proposes a difficulty for understanding. If to be 'modern' is, in a specific commonly understood sense to be 'up to the minute' or 'contemporary', then how is it possible to be 'post-modern'? A certain untimeliness or even unpreparedness is inscribed in the very term itself; and this should be addressed if we are to get anywhere in elaborating the terms of a possible debate or *différend*.[4]

One of the figures who has made a significant contribution to the understanding of the term at this level has been Jean-François Lyotard. For Lyotard, 'postmodernism' implies a practice which is

2. See Fredric Jameson, 'Postmodernism, Or the Cultural Logic of Late Capitalism', *New Left Review*, 146 (1984), 53-92. This has something in common with one architectural understanding of the term; for recently, architectural theorists such as Paolo Portoghesi and Charles Jencks gave up on a specific version of 'progress' in architecture, and began to assert 'the presence of the past'.

3. See, for example, Terry Eagleton, 'Capitalism, Modernism and Postmodernism', *New Left Review*, 152 (1985), 60-73.

4. 'As opposed to a litigation, a différend would be a case of conflict between two parties (at least) where, for lack of a rule of judgement which would be applicable to both argumentations, an equitable decision could not be made. That one is legitimate does not imply that the other is not. If, however, one were to apply the same rule of judgement to both of them in order to decide their différend as if it were a litigation, one would do one of them a wrong (at least, and both of them if neither admitted this rule). A damage results from an injury done to the rules of a genre of discourse, and can be healed according to those rules. A wrong results from the fact that the rules of the genre of discourse according to which one judges are not those of the genre or genres of discourse which are thus judged.' (Jean-François Lyotard, *Le Différend*, (éditions de minuit, Paris, 1983), 9.

radically experimental, in the sense that it is never guided by pre-established rules or already known or established dogma. The rules determining the postmodern work of art are, in fact, among the very things which the elaboration of the work will have revealed once it is in place:

> A postmodern artist or writer is in the position of a philosopher; the text he writes, the work he produces are not in principle governed by preestablished rules, and they cannot be judged according to a determining judgment, by applying familiar categories to the text or to the work. Those rules and categories are what the work of art itself is looking for. The artist and the writer, then, are working without rules in order to formulate the rules of what *will have been done*. Hence the fact that work and text have the characters of an *event*; hence also, they always come too late for their author, or, what amounts to the same thing, their being put into work, their realization (*mise en oeuvre*) always begins too soon. *Post modern* would have to be understood according to the paradox of the future (*post*) anterior (*modo*).[5]

Three crucial points follow. Firstly, the postmodernist in her experimentation transgresses or crosses the borders which have been already established and taken for granted in her field of activity. Secondly, this produces not a work so much as an 'event', a happening which cannot be easily identified as an artistic product or object, something for which we have no known categories of understanding. Thirdly, postmodernism becomes, paradoxically, the very condition of the possibility of the Modern. A work is postmodern before it is Modern; to become Modern, it has to have formalised the rules governing the experimental (postmodern) work, and to have articulated itself according to those rules, guided by the prior example of the successful postmodern event. The Modern is, as it were, a kind of fossilisation of the energetic impetus towards radical experimentalism which pervades the postmodern; it takes an inexplicable event and places it in categories which make that event comprehensible, which make it, in short, recognisable as a 'work of art' or a 'philosophy'. Accordingly, Lyotard argues that the 'post' in postmodernism should not be understood as a simple temporal indicator of belatedness, but rather that it be understood by analogy with the prefix 'ana-', as in analysis, anamnesis (remembrance), anagogy, anamorphosis and so on.[6] This has the virtue of addressing

---

5. Lyotard, *The Postmodern Condition* (trans. Geoff Bennington and Brian Massumi; Manchester University Press, Manchester, 1984), 81.
6. Lyotard, 'Note sur les sens de "post-", in *Le Postmoderne expliqué aux enfants* (editions Galilée, Paris, 1986), 126.

the postmodern work's typical anachronicity, the sense it gives of being out of its proper moment, a temporal dislocation such as we have it in some postmodern architecture, painting or music.[7]

In this characterisation of postmodernism in the aesthetic field, one finds a recurring trait of 'experimental energetics'. Indeed, the effect of the postmodern is above all to reactivate and redistribute the energy which lies potentially in all orders of stability. Postmodernism generates instabilities, and hence provides the mechanics for a radical critique of the existing organisations of energy, that existing social enertia known as the 'Modern' social formation itself. Here lies Lyotard's debt to Nietzsche; for it was Nietzsche, among all the philosophers, who saw that the energies of art could provide a radical critique of the stable, monumental and totalising order of philosophy itself. He sought a mode of thinking which was beyond the borders of philosophy, outside the parameters set by the established philosophical discourse. David Carroll writes:

> For Nietzsche, 'art' (a category including literature; the poetic, the tragic, the fictive) is *the* 'countermovement' to religion, morality, and philosophy, and, as such, has a privileged affirmative and disruptive force. But the danger of privileging any term (and this is especially true of art), is that it will begin to take on the very characteristics it is supposed to counter. The use of art 'against' theory (philosophy and religion in Nietzsche's case) can very easily end up being a mystification of art . . . . The problem can be formulated . . . in the following way: can the aesthetic be used to point to the limitations of the theoretical, the speculative, the moral-religious, without becoming a replacement for them and a transcendent order in itself?[8]

For Nietzsche, it is where art escapes understanding that criticism becomes possible. A work of art can only be 'understood' if its kinetic energy is dissipated and controlled; the philosophy and logic according to which a society operates, by offering certain recognisable 'templates' according to which art can be classified, work to harness the disruptive energetic force of art. As a result, the work becomes an illustration of the philosophy and a validation of the society's norms; all the radical critical potential of the work is thus dissipated, reduced to inertia.

---

7. Consider as random examples Portoghesi's Casa Baldi, the paintings of Carlo Maria Mariani, Messiaen's *Quattuor pour la fin du temps*. For a fuller articulation of this entire argument, see my *After Theory: Postmodernism/Postmarxism* (1989).

8. David Carroll, *Paraesthetics* (Methuen, 1987), 3.

The analogy in Lyotard is simple: a postmodern 'event' is a radical energetic series of impulses; it becomes *Modern* when it is 'understood', that is, when it is assimilated to the norms or conventions of a given social formation, when it is claimed by that social formation's ideology as somehow representative of the society or of its moment in the history of the society. For the possibility of critique, to escape such a totalising ideology (be it fascist or Marxist: in any case, 'modernist'), it is imperative that the postmodern disruptive energetics of art or of the aesthetic as such be released. This, of course, has the corollary effect of producing an art which is radically incomprehensible. But for Lyotard, this is no great problem. The postmodernist, he avers, pays no heed to the requirements of her audience; she works without rules and without the determining principles of a given ideological reception of the work, in order to break new grounds, to transgress boundaries. Postmodernism, through its radical aesthetics, eradicates the notion of a fixed boundary or border. Such fixity or definition is the result of a harnessing of energy or of the arrest of history itself; it is exactly what happens when the postmodern event (history) becomes reduced to the Modern work (the art-object); all the potential for change, even for new thinking, is removed.

This makes it sound as if the Dionysian release of energy is an end in itself. But this experimental energetics, especially when it is accompanied by a tendency to elitist obscurantism or to the irrational, is a primary breeding ground for fascism. The opponents of postmodernism take this as grounds enough for its repudiation. Habermas and others in the Marxist tradition point out that the kind of 'svelte' pragmatism advanced by postmodernism leaves one with no theoretical grounds on which to make choices concerning the *direction* of this energy.[9] But Lyotard indicates that this is precisely the point at which philosophical and political critique become available. The question of *justice* intrudes on the play of energy, and it is here that one must be most 'svelte', most lithe and flexible; for one must judge one's course of action, one's practice, without fixed criteria, without stable or given grounds upon which to make the judgement. If one had such grounds (be they the grounds of the commonplaces of a society, or the grounds of a critical philosophy such as Marxism), then, in fact, one makes no judgement at all. The very terms and outcome of the judgement are determined, predetermined by the rules of the game; one remains in Modernism without the possibility of that postmodern transgression of categories or borders, a transgression called 'thinking'. One can

---

9. For an elaboration of the terms of this debate, especially as it affects the différend between Habermas and Lyotard, see Richard Rorty, 'Habermas and Lyotard on Postmodernity', *Praxis International*, 4 (1984), 32-44; see also the articles and discussion between Lyotard and Rorty in *Critique*, 41 (1985).

thus have no established rules for judging, no system of thought no matter how seemingly natural or logical. One must be like a philosopher or artist; that is, one must, if one is to think at all, judge 'experimentally', without criteria. It is here, in the passages between theories that thought becomes possible; thought, as an event or as a historical actuality, is possible only when it is not always already spoken for: that is, only when it is not the effect of a system of thinking or of a theoretical dogma or prescription. Here, Lyotard effects a svelte passage from Nietzsche to Kant.

Kant distinguished what he called 'reflective judgement' from 'determinant judgement'. The latter, determinant judgement, is appropriate to what we now think of as the modern scientific order. In this, concepts are produced and the scientist must find a number of specific cases which will be subsumed under that concept, thus validating it; this is called 'proof'. According to this, 'understanding possesses a rule of explanation and is trying to select references to which it can be applied'. Reflective judgement, on the contrary, is 'the synthesis we are able to make of random data without the help of preestablished rules'.[10] Determinant judgement is 'modern'; reflective judgement is 'postmodern', in short. Further, despite the prevalence and normativity of modern, scientific, determinant judgement in a contemporary world which is obsessed with the criteria of performativity and efficiency, there remain other kinds of discourse, notably, the aesthetic or matters of taste, in which determinant judgements cede place to the reflective.

But why should postmodern judgement be preferred to the modern modes? The answer is simple: it is only the postmodern judgement which has the character of a genuinely historical event; modern judgements are like works of art – and in political matters, they thus represent a prime example of the aestheticisation of politics against which Benjamin warned philosophy.[11] The totalising tendency and claims upon normativity which modern determinant judgement have preclude the possibility of historical change: every situation in which a judgement is required is already spoken for. For example, given a specific problem in maths, the mathematician proceeds to a solution by following the rules of the game, that is, by making the specific problem conform to an already-known mathematical procedure; the system of maths itself does the 'thinking', and the results are predetermined by the system. A similar determinant judgement dominating the political life would be dangerously totalitarian; hence Lyotard's preference for reflective judgement in these matters.

10. Lyotard, *Peregrinations* (Columbia University Press, New York, 1988, 21; 8.
11. See Walter Benjamin, 'The Work of Art in the Age of Mechanical Reproduction', in *Illuminations* (trans. Harry Zohn; ed. Hannah Arendt; Fontana/Collins, 1968).

In reflective judgement which is appropriate to aesthetic matters, one thinks without boundaries: that is, without categories. Politics can learn from aesthetics in this. Lyotard writes of a kind of puritanical *askesis* in Cézanne who would stare endlessly at the Montagne Sainte Victoire, waiting for unexpected colour to reveal itself: 'No longer is the mastery of forms the first task of a work like Cézanne's; on the contrary, the goal is to become dependent on the 'matter' hidden in the 'data'.[12] Lyotard would like to assert a profound congruity between this aesthetic *askesis* and a political self-discipline which makes the political Subject able to witness and partake in the unfolding of a real historical event. But this is impossible, and at best there is an analogy between the two. Both politics and art belong to Kantian reflective judgement – that is, there are no predetermining rules guaranteeing the evaluation of their events. The result of this is that 'There are no more criteria [of judgement] in politics than in aesthetics'.[13] One must always be, as it were, in passages between political states or events; nor can one have a knowledge of exactly where those passages are, much less a knowledge of what a model for the organisation of a just social formation would look like. As Lyotard writes:

> The stakes in poliltics are definitely not to know something but to change something, and the stakes of art are to make something that has been given to one's sensibility and is transferable to others. I am merely arguing that both art and politics are excepted, although in different ways, from the hegemony of the genre of discourse called cognitive.[14]

It is as if knowledge itself 'forms an earth' for the dissipation of energy which is thought; like Baudrillard, Lyotard sees this movement towards inertia as a problem which has reverberations in politics.[15] Politics does not depend upon knowledge, but rather upon change, mutability: sveltness. In claiming that one 'knows' the truth of a given political state of affairs, one is ascribing to oneself a stable, quasi-transcendent position, divorced from the flow of history, from which politics can be judged according to the predetermining rules which ground or underpin that stable position. This is the aestheticisation of politics, its desecularisation. To save the possibility of politics, indeed of genuine thinking (reflective judgement), the subject of action must become genuinely historical, must give up the privilege of claiming knowledge, of having a stable

12. Lyotard, *Peregrinations*, 20.
13. Idem, 20-21.
14. Idem, 21.
15. See Jean Baudrillard, *In the Shadow of the Silent Majorities* (trans. Paul Foss, Paul Patton and John Johnson; Semiotext(e), New York, 1983), passim.

ground on which to found that knowledge. In other words, she has no 'position', but rather a 'dis-position': she stands in a place whose borders are circumscribed by the shifting 'locality' which she is negotiating at any given moment.

Reflective judgement, then, is profoundly localised, and makes no explicit claims upon universality. In aesthetics or taste, 'The unanimity concerning what is beautiful has no chance of being actualized'.[16] There is only a series of locally diverse judgements, with no possibility of consensus. In politics too, the strategy which postmodernism advances is one which gives up on the idea of consensus. The establishment of consensus depends upon a kind of imperialism, under which diverging and discordant acts of reflective judgement are themselves judged according to an imposed overarching determinant judgement; again, the possibility of a postmodern justice is eradicated under the aestheticisation/'modernisation' of the political. There can be no consensus without a corollary imperialism. In the face of this, postmodernism proposes an elaboration and complexification of dissensus, dissent, irreconcilable *différends*. An exponential production of and assertion of difference becomes the riposte to demands for 'identity' or any form of totalitarian 'unity'. The passage to thought, and to ethical and political justice, is thereby opened up.

Two differing 'passages' to thought: 'The idea that thinking is able to build a system of total knowledge . . . constitutes *par excellence* the sin, the arrogance of the mind';[17] opposition to a dominant ideology is always accommodated by that ideology, whose borders must be questioned otherwise.

---

16. Lyotard, *Peregrinations*, 38.
17. Idem, 6-7.

CONTRIBUTORS

RICHARD KEARNEY From Cork. Ph.D. Studied at University College Dublin, McGill University, Montreal, Canada and The University of Paris. Lecturer in Philosophy in University College, Dublin. Co-editor of *The Crane Bag: Journal of Irish Studies*. Author and editor of several books on philosophy and literature including *La Poetique du Possible* (Beauchesne, 1984), *Dialogues with Contemporary Continental Thinkers* (Manchester University Press, 1984), *The Irish Mind: Exploring Intellectual Traditions* (Wolfhound Press 1985), *Transitions: Narratives in Modern Irish Culture* (Wolfhound Press 1987 and MUP 1988) and *The Wake of Imagination* (Hutchinson 1988).

T. J. BARRINGTON From Dublin. Educated at University College Dublin. Honorary LLD (NUI 1986). Civil Servant in Departments of Finance and Local Government (now Environment) 1941-60. First Director, Institute of Public Administration 1960-77. First Editor, *Administration* (1953-63). Publications include *From Big Government to Local Government* (1975), *Discovering Kerry* (1976), *The Irish Administrative System* (1980).

JOHN HUME From Derry. Leader of Northern Ireland's SDLP. Member of European Parliament since 1979 where he is a member of the Bureau of the Socialist Group and serves on Regional Policy and Planning Committee. Presented a Report to the European Parliament in 1987 on the Regional Problems of Ireland. Socialist Co-Chairman of European Parliament Intergroup on Minority Languages and Cultures. Member of Westminster Parliament for Foyle since 1983. Member of New Ireland Forum 1983-1984. Served as Minister for Commerce in Northern Ireland's Power-Sharing Executive in 1974. Founder member SDLP 1970 having been elected to Stormont Parliament as MP for Foyle in 1969.

MICHAEL D. HIGGINS From Galway. TD (Member of Dáil Éireann – the Irish Parliament). Educated at the National University of Ireland, Indiana University and Manchester University. Statutory lecturer in Political Science and Sociology, University College Galway and Visiting Professor at Southern Illinois University. Founder Chairman of the Labour Party from 1977 to 1987 and currently its spokesman on foreign affairs, educator and the Irish language. Mayor of Galway 1982. Member of the Irish Senate 1973-77, 1982-87. He is author of the Labour Party's policy document on regional development and has published numerous articles in books and journals.

PAUL BEW From Belfast. Born 1950. Studied Modern History at Cambridge (1968-71) and took his Ph.D. there in 1974. He is Reader in Political Science of Queen's University, Belfast, and the author of *Land and the National Question in Ireland* (1978), *Parnell* (1980), *Conflict and Conciliation in Irish Nationalism* (1987), and co-author of *The State in Northern Ireland 1921-72* (1979), *Sean Lemass and the Making of Modern Ireland* (1982), and *The British State and the Ulster Crisis* (1985).

HENRY PATTERSON Senior Lecturer in Politics at University of Ulster. Author of *The State in Northern Ireland* (1979), *Class Conflict and Sectarianism* (1980), *Sean Lemass and the Making of Modern Ireland* (1982), *The British State and the Ulster Crisis* (1985).

EITHNE MURPHY From Cork. B.Comm., M.Econ.Sc. degrees. Educated at University College Dublin and she has also studied at the Kiel Institute of World Economics and presently works as an International Economist for the Rural Economy Research Centre of TEAGASC. Her principal research interests are in the area of international trade and economic integration.

ROSEMARIE ROWLEY From Dublin. M.A. Educated at Trinity College Dublin. She has taught in Birmingham; worked with the BBC and in the Irish Film Industry. She has co-ordinated various community writing groups and developed Green politics in Ireland. Joint Co-ordinator Green Alliance 1984-86; European Representative 1985-86. Publications include *The Broken Pledge* (Martello 1985); *The Sea of Affliction* (Rowan Tree Press 1987).

DESMOND FENNELL Born in Belfast, grew up in Dublin. MA degree. Educated at University College, Dublin and Bonn University. Teaches English at Rathmines College of Commerce. Recent books: *Beyond Nationalism* (Ward River, 1985), *Nice People and Rednecks* (Gill and MacMillan, 1986), *A Connacht Journey* (Gill and MacMillan, 1987).

ALAN MATTHEWS From Dublin. M.S. Educated at Trinity College Dublin and Cornell University. Now a Lecturer in Economics and Fellow of Trinity College, Dublin. Has published extensively on international trade and development matters. Previous publications include a book entitled *The Common Agricultural Policy and the Less Developed Countries*.

FRANK BARRY From Dublin. Ph.D. Educated at University College Dublin, University of Essex and Queen's University, Ontario. Currently lecturing in Political Economy at UCD, he has been Visiting Research Fellow at the University of Stockholm and Visiting Professor at the University of California. Writes on economic theory and policy, Irish society, and Central America.

IVOR BROWNE From Dublin. FRCPI, M.Sc. (Harv), DPM FRC (Psych). Educated Blackrock College, the College of Surgeons, Dublin and Harvard University. He is Professor of Psychiatry at University College Dublin and Chief Psychiatrist, Eastern Health Board. Established the Foundation for Human Development and has published extensively. His *Journey to Ithaca*, co-authored with Kevin Clear is a major forthcoming book.

PAUL HEWSON (Bono) From Dublin. Educated at Mount Temple School. Lead singer of international rock group U2. LPs include *Boy* (1980), *October* (1981), *War* (1983), *Joshua Tree* (1987), *Rattle and Hum* (1988).

PAUL DURCAN Born Dublin 1944 of Co. Mayo parents. Poet. Most recent books include *Jesus and Angela* (1988),*Going Home to Russia* (1987), *The Berlin Wall Café* (1985) and *The Selected Paul Durcan* (1982). He has undertaken reading tours throughout Europe, the USSR, the USA and Canada. Member of Aosdána.

NEIL JORDAN From Sligo. Received BA from University College Dublin. Author of *Night in Tunisia, Dream of a Beast* and *The Past*. As director and scriptwriter his film credits to date include: *Angel, Company of Wolves, Mona Lisa* and *High Spirits*.

ROBERT BALLAGH From Dublin. Studied Architecture at the College of Technology, Bolton Street. Worked as an engineering draughtsman and freelance designer. In 1969 held his first exhibition in Dublin. Since then he has painted on a full-time basis. Commissioned work includes portraits, stage design, murals, film titles, posters, stamps and bookcover design. Currently Treasurer of the International Association of Art (UNESCO Affiliate). Member of Aosdána (a self-governing trust of distinguished Irish artists) and fellow of the World Academy of Art and Science.

LUKE GIBBONS From Roscommon. Educated in UCG and Trinity College Dublin. Lecturer in Communications at the National Institute for Higher Education Dublin. Has published articles on Irish culture, the media and Irish society. He is co-author of *Cinema and Ireland* (Routledge, 1988) and is an editor of the forthcoming Field Day *Anthology of Irish Literature*.

DESMOND BELL From Derry. Educated at Foyle College, Derry and The University of Warwick. Taught at Magee College, Derry and Ruskin College, Oxford, before taking up his current post as lecturer in Communications at NIHE Glasnevin. He will shortly hold the Chair as Professor of Media Studies at The University of Ulster, Coleraine. Published widely on the political economy of the Media. Forthcoming publication *Acts of Union: Youth, Culture and Sectarianism in Northern Ireland* (MacMillan). Directed and produced a documentary for Channel 4: *We'll Fight & No Surrender: Ulster Loyalism & the Protestant Sense of History*.

JOSEPH O'LEARY From Cork. Ph.D. Educated at St Patrick's College, Maynooth, and in Rome and Paris. Irish theologian, philosopher, Catholic priest. Has lectured in Theology at the University of Notre Dame. Currently doing research at the Nagoya Institute in Japan. Author of *Questioning Back* (1985) and co-editor of *Heidegger & La Question de Dieu* (Paris 1981).

THOMAS DOCHERTY Teaches Theory and English in University College Dublin. Author of *Reading (Absent) Character* (1983), *John Donne, Undone* (1986), *On Modern Authority* (1987), *After Theory: Postmodernism/Postmarxism* (1989), and of numerous articles on theory. At present, he is working on *Critical Philosophy*, a book exploring the relations between criticism and philosophy in postmodernity.

JEAN-FRANÇOIS LYOTARD Professor of Philosophy at the University of Paris, Vincennes and at Irvine University, USA. Author of numerous works including *Discours, Figures* (Paris 1971), *Économie Libidinale* (Paris 1974), *Le Différend* (Paris 1983) and *The Postmodern Condition* (Manchester University Press 1984).

WIM WENDERS German film-maker. His films include *Paris-Texas*; *The American Friend* and *Wings of Desire*.

EDGAR FAURE Former French Prime Minister, former President of the Council of Europe and President of the Regional Council of La Franche-Comté.

EDGAR MORIN French sociologist and author of *L'An Zéro de l'Allemagne* (Paris 1946); *La Nature de la Nature* (Paris 1981); *Science avec Conscience* (Paris 1982); *La Vie de la Vie* (Paris 1985) and *Penser l'Europe* (Paris 1987).

JULIA KRISTEVA Bulgarian linguist and philosopher; Professor of Linguistics at the University of Paris (VII). Author of *Desire in Language* (Basil Blackwell 1981); *Le Soleil Noir* (Paris 1986) and former co-editor of the Paris journal *Tel Quel*.

GEORGES DUBY Member of L'Académie Française, historian, Professor at the College de France; President of La Société d'Édition de Programmes de Télévision (SEPT).